* * *

"This groundbreaking and comprehensive resource is the *Our Bodies, Ourselves* for trans and gender-expansive folks who bind. Frances combines their expertise honed through 10+ years of working with clients, personal narratives, and peer-reviewed research to offer an accessible, compassionate, and affirming roadmap for healthy binding and holistic wellness. Readers will come away with a new understanding of their body and how to structure a sustainable binding practice that is right for them."

—*Dr. Sarah Peitzmeier*

* * *

"This is a practical, comprehensive, inclusive, empowering, and extremely helpful book. Highly recommended."

—*Yenn Purkis, autistic and non-binary author and advocate*

* * *

"Read this book if you are binding or thinking about binding. It is clear, friendly, and anatomically detailed. It gives you a thorough understanding of the impact of unhealthy binding across your whole body and how you can instead easily take care of your body and bind safely. It's a book you'll come back to again and again, and then pass on to your friends."

—*Ed Whelan, author of* Gender Confirmation Surgery

* * *

"The ultimate guide for trans masculine and non-binary folks exploring the art of binding—it's like a friendly chat with your favourite binding buddy. This book is your go-to for clear and concise tips on feeling fabulous in your own skin or becoming the ultimate ally on this journey. I wish I had this gem during my binding days—it's like the superhero sidekick I never knew I needed! Trust me, it would have saved me from those bruises and rib issues. Get ready to make binding a breeze with this must-have manual."

—*Fox Fisher, trans author and a*

* * *

T0321423

of related interest

Gender Confirmation Surgery
A Guide for Trans and Non-Binary People
Edward Whelan
Illustrated by Nicholai Melamed
ISBN 978 1 83997 096 2
eISBN 978 1 83997 097 9

Trans Survival Workbook
Owl and Fox Fisher
ISBN 978 1 78775 629 8
eISBN 978 1 78775 630 4

The Trans Guide to Mental Health and Well-Being
Katy Lees
ISBN 978 1 78775 526 0
eISBN 978 1 78775 527 7

HEALTHY CHEST BINDING FOR TRANS AND NON-BINARY PEOPLE

A Practical Guide

Frances Reed, LMT
Illustrated by Ocean Grove

Jessica Kingsley Publishers
London and Philadelphia

First published in Great Britain in 2024 by Jessica Kingsley Publishers
An imprint of Hodder & Stoughton Ltd
An Hachette Company

1

A CIP catalogue record for this title is available from the British Library and the
Library of Congress

ISBN 978 1 78775 948 0
eISBN 978 1 78775 949 7

Printed and bound in the United States by Integrated Books International

Jessica Kingsley Publishers' policy is to use papers that are natural, renewable
and recyclable products and made from wood grown in sustainable forests. The
logging and manufacturing processes are expected to conform to the environmental
regulations of the country of origin.

Jessica Kingsley Publishers
Carmelite House
50 Victoria Embankment
London EC4Y 0DZ

www.jkp.com

To my beloved trans and gender non-conforming clients, thank you for sharing your stories and allowing me to treat your bodies. I hope that I have honored your vulnerability with this book.

And to Wes... So much of this book began with your rib cage. My deepest gratitude for your trust, friendship, and encouragement.

Acknowledgments

I won the lottery when I found Ocean Grove to illustrate this book. I knew from the beginning that I wanted readers to see their gender non-conforming bodies reflected honestly. Deepest gratitude, this book wouldn't be what it is without your time and talent. Thank you also to the JKP editorial team whose patience and persistence ensured this book came to fruition.

I'm humbled by the vulnerability of the people whose personal stories of joy and pain added invaluable narrative to these pages. I'm grateful to the colleagues who shared their time and expertise, especially Hannah Schoonover for their knowledge of hypermobility joint disorders; Emmett Patterson for reading the manuscript with a harm reduction lens; Tina Celenza-Remillard for sharing insights on transition-related care; Amanda Long and Carolee Youngblood for editing very rough drafts; Gabrielle Zwi for research, editing, and support; and the QQ for being my sounding board and cheering section. Heartfelt thanks to friends and family for encouraging me not to give up, hosting me in your homes for writing retreats, volunteering to be test subjects, and celebrating each small victory.

To Beth Wheeler, you helped me overcome every wave of imposter syndrome and attack of writer's block, and never let me lose sight of the invaluable resource I was creating. To my wife, Jessica VonDyke, thank you for riding the first-time author roller coaster with me. Somehow you managed to keep your sanity and consistently remind me of mine.

Contents

Preface

In my early thirties, I suffered a binding injury that would end up defining my career. At that time in my life, I hadn't figured out how to name my gender identity, but I knew that I was uncomfortable in my skin. Nature cursed me with a large chest, and no matter what I changed about my gender expression, the world saw breasts and made up its mind that I was a woman. The more I experimented with genderqueer expression, the more apparent it became that I was unseen by the world. And then a friend of a friend offered me one of their old binders.

It was stained from the previous owner's sweat and frayed where it had been cut shorter, but when I put that ratty thing on for the first time, I felt positively euphoric. I was suddenly aware of the dysphoria that I couldn't even name until I felt it abate. That was over a decade ago, and I have not forgotten that feeling.

Elements of my gender were being successfully expressed in the world and I could finally explore who I wanted to be. I was no longer leading with my breasts. They were no longer defining me before I had a chance to. People still read me as a woman, but I felt a shift in their perceptions. I sensed strangers noticing my gender expansiveness, and I was nothing short of high on the affirmation.

I was a massage therapist doing physically demanding work with my upper body for long hours. My career was just getting off the ground and

I was pushing my body too hard. A day at work was like doing eight hours of resistance-band training on arms, back, and pecs. I believed binding was having no impact. I didn't consider that my muscles were working much harder against the power-mesh fabric of my binder.

I had no way of knowing it, but my second-hand binders were almost certainly too small for me. They didn't have tags, so I didn't know the brand or size. Even if I'd known the brand name, their website didn't mention any advice, especially for assigned female at birth (AFAB) bodies, about when and where to bind. Why? Because their products were designed for and marketed to cis men for gynecomastia (derogatorily called "man boobs"). But, even in the queer and trans community, I didn't hear anyone talking about binding health. It genuinely never occurred to me that wearing my binder when doing strenuous physical work was a bad idea.

I wanted to wear this life-changing, but overly constrictive, binder all the time. It replaced my bra. I didn't know it was harming me. If I'd had a resource spelling out the risks and best practices, it could have changed everything that came next in my life.

I'd been working in my binder at a stressful pace for about six months and suddenly a pain wrenched the right side of my chest. Certain movements sent a lightning bolt of pain so intense I would cry out uncontrollably and gasp for breath. Turning my head, lifting my shoulder, and projecting my voice all triggered the pain. Laughing and crying hurt. It was exhausting to be in constant pain. I stopped doing activities I loved.

It wasn't long until my right shoulder joined in on the pain. With reaching or pushing, the inflamed tissue burned inside the joint. Every night I built an elaborate pillow fort to prop up my arm, and the smallest shifts woke me up in sudden pain. My wife had to help me get dressed because I couldn't lift my arm over my head. Ibuprofen didn't touch it; muscle relaxers didn't change it; and cannabis couldn't dull it. The pain was ever-present—as was my binder.

It seems outrageous to say now, but, at the time, I didn't connect my pain to binding. I assumed that I'd hurt myself working, but I couldn't lose my income so I kept pushing through it. I dissociated and used the muscles and joints of my upper body in strenuous repetitive ways on a daily basis. I made a fool's gamble and lost. Eventually, I ended up unable to work for five months.

On my way to meet friends one day (wearing my binder, of course), the center of my chest started to ache intensely, and it was frighteningly hard to breathe. I thought I might be having a heart attack and ripped off my shirt and binder at a stop light. Within a few minutes of removing the binder, the ache became more manageable, and it finally hit me: binding was the root of all of my upper body pain.

Though binding was an integral part of how I coped with my dysphoria, I had to prioritize my physical health; I'd let it go on too long. I was too injured to bind for short periods—even when it mattered most. Whenever I put on my binder, the crushing ache in my chest became intolerable almost immediately. As if losing the ability to bind wasn't bad enough, I couldn't wear a sports bra or even a regular bra without pain. The only way that I could function was with my DDD chest hanging free. These appendages were bigger and more obvious as womanly breasts than ever before, and I was plagued by seeing my reflection.

After binding but before the injury, my self-confidence was at an all-time high. Now, not only was the glorious affirmation gone, but it was replaced by excruciating pain and poor self-image. The trifecta of symptoms—chest ache, shoulder inflammation, and a stabbing pain—persisted and eventually I was desperately doing anything to make it all go away.

I spent a few thousand dollars trying everything: doctor, acupuncturist, chiropractor, energy healer, massage therapist, and physical therapist. I endured transphobic appointments twice in hopes of getting relief. Each practitioner had a theory, but none knew anything about binding or how it impacted the body. Ultimately, combining the wisdom of a chiropractor, a fellow massage therapist, and my own insight, we teased apart the three injuries. The stabbing pain came from the partial dislocation of my third rib that was affecting how I moved my shoulder. I'd activated an old rotator cuff injury and had tendonitis and impingement in my shoulder, which explained the joint pain. And by not listening to my body's pleas for rest, I developed inflammation in the ribs called costochondritis.

Once the rib got adjusted, I was slowly able to heal the three injuries and regain the strength I had lost. When I could finally tolerate wearing an undergarment again, it had to be a positively horrendous bra that I hated. It took almost a year but the costochondritis healed enough for me to switch to a sports bra. I accepted that I would never be able to bind again.

In 2015, I heard about a new, safer binder called gc2b. I purchased one immediately. The euphoria returned the minute I put it on. I'd been frozen in place on my gender journey. Now I finally resumed becoming my truth in the world. Although I was tempted, I never wore a binder while giving a massage again.

* * *

My self-esteem, my physical health, my finances, my social life, and my gender identity were all impacted by a binding injury. I almost had to choose between doing what I loved and being fully who I am. No one should be in that position or in that much pain, so I've used my training as a massage therapist to study how binders impact the body and specialize in the treatment of people experiencing binding pain. This book is a combination of a decade of observation, dozens of informal case studies, years of continuing education, and personal experience of binding.

Since 2012, I've treated transmasculine clients who were binding and studied their cases. As word got out that I treated binding pain, more clients showed up on my table in need of help. I've consulted with colleagues on exercises to treat hyper-stretched and hyper-contracted muscles. I studied trigger point release to help alleviate referred pain and structural integration to free the rib cage and shoulder blades from collapsed posture. To spread this information, I started teaching workshops at conferences and college campuses. I went on podcasts and launched a website, www.healthybinding.com, to centralize information. I took each of these steps guided by the goal of creating tools for the transmasculine community to benefit from these techniques.

Cautionary tales are important because they remind us to be responsible. But trouble lies in purely focusing on the injury. My story proves that there are some risks involved, yes. But throughout this book, I will teach you what not to do, how to find a binder option that suits your needs, and how to get the most out of self-care, and then binding is a perfectly healthy choice.

INTRODUCTION

As complex beings, staying "healthy" is an interplay between our physical, emotional, and intellectual needs. Everything we do or wear leaves an impact on our body which can make our bodies healthier, less healthy, or a little of both. We modern humans voluntarily subject ourselves to high heels, sun exposure, smartphone overuse, over-exercising, long commuting, and a host of other activities that satisfy our needs in one area and can cause complications to our health in others. Binding, as well as all of the activities mentioned above, can cause chronic pain and permanent alignment issues or skin maladies if it is done without proper fit, movement, and/or self-care.

As you read this book, I encourage you to keep in mind that regardless of who, how, or where we each live, we are choosing daily stressors that impact our bodies. This book is intended to guide people through binding correctly and addressing physical side effects if they occur. If you experience low back pain from high heels or neck pain from your smartphone, there are similar resources for mitigating these discomforts. The solution is not to stop using binders, heels, or smartphones, it's to learn to properly care for your body so that you can use them comfortably and safely. When anyone gets a blister from their shoes, a migraine from their phone, or rib tenderness from their binder, they must be empowered with the knowledge of how to care for themself and recuperate back to a healthy state, regardless of whether the discomfort is related to their gender.

Maybe you are considering binding and need to know what it's all about. Or maybe you have been binding for years and need strategies to live a more free and fulfilling life in a binder. This book is for you, I am so glad that you are here. Let this be your guide to making binding a liberating and healthy part of your life.

In order to write this book, I have drawn on a decade of experience observing and treating binding pain, my own lived experience with binding, and the limited research on binding health. I have several goals in sharing this information. First, I want you to know what's going on inside your body under a binder because I believe understanding our bodies makes it easier to take care of them. Chapter 1 broadly covers the effect of a binder on your upper body and discusses important concepts of self-care. Second, I want you to know your binding options. Chapter 2 gives you a sense of the variety of features and styles that exist for safe binding (hint: there are way more than you think) and breaks down all of the high-risk forms of binding that must be avoided. This is where you will find a lot of cautionary tales about binding injuries, but these are totally avoidable as long as you know how to bind safely. Third, I want you to know how to care for your body and your binder so that you are at a low risk of binding discomfort. There's a lot to know about the day-to-day practice of binding. Chapter 3 shares tips on big questions like "how long can I bind" and tips for getting your binder on and off. The majority of questions that I receive are about specific activities and whether it is safe to bind while doing them. In Chapter 4, I draw on my observations of anatomy and of real people who bind to make educated recommendations about binding in a variety of activities. And fourth, if a problem does occur, knowledge is power. Chapter 5 is about medical conditions and is the densest and longest chapter of the book. I recommend using it as a reference section. It covers: heat-related conditions, something everyone who binds should review so you know the signs and symptoms; the intersection of binding and eight chronic health conditions; and, in the final section, basic symptoms, prevention, and treatment for a list of conditions that relate to binding. If you are experiencing uncomfortable symptoms, this is a great place to look before asking Dr. Google. I hope that you will never experience a complication of binding that requires you get medical attention but if you do, Chapter 6 is a guide to navigating discussions with health providers of many kinds about the practice of binding.

In Part 2, the focus turns to empowering you to care for your own body. Chapter 7 teaches you the tools and techniques you'll need for the exercises that follow. In Chapter 8, I return to a discussion of anatomy with a detailed breakdown of the impact that binding and dysphoria have on 18 specific structures or functions of the body. After each section, there are recommended exercises connected to that part of your body and you will find a symptom index at the end of the book to help you narrow down which exercises to try for the problems that you are experiencing.

I've offered self-care classes for 10 years, teaching exercises and self-massage to prevent, manage, and self-treat pain resulting from binding. In Part 2, you will find 23 fully illustrated exercises which have helped hundreds of my workshop participants improve their day-to-day experience of binding. Bodies have different needs and capabilities so I've done my best to offer tips and variations to help you make the exercises work for your body. It is my hope that you will develop a routine of exercises that you find helpful and do them regularly to keep your body resilient to the stress of binding. And, when a new symptom arises, it is my hope that you will pull this book back down off the shelf and try new exercises to alleviate the discomfort.

If you're not already familiar with the practice of binding, I'm glad you're here too.

Binding is the practice of wearing a garment or specialized body-safe tape to compress the chest tissue in order to achieve a flatter chest contour. The majority of people who bind their chests are assigned female at birth (AFAB) and want to achieve the outward appearance of a more masculine or genderless gender expression. People bind for other reasons too: cosplay, LARP, drag, acting, and other performance arts as well as cisgender men who have gynecomastia. In all cases, the goal is the same: change the silhouette to reduce the appearance of breasts.

If you are the parent or partner of someone who wants to bind or you are a practitioner with clients/patients who bind, my hope is that this book brings you ease by giving you the information to better support the people in your life.

Your concern and desire to learn more has the power to make a profound difference for someone who won't get this access to this book. First, give them your enthusiastic support for their desire to bind and tell them you want to help. Many people who bind won't tell a parent or doctor that they are experiencing pain in a binder because they fear being forced to stop binding. Instead of perpetuating that harm, be the one to share the resources with them. You can help them realize how many options for binding they have and be the one to share simple exercises with them to resolve aches and pains. You can deliver the message that they don't need to endure pain to feel like themselves.

If you are a friend, teacher, or colleague reading this in order to support someone in your life who binds, thank you for being here!

Support and celebrate the array of our gender expressions. We need you to look out for us and share your concern if we are struggling physically or emotionally with binding. We need you to normalize binding and be an ambassador when others are judging or misrepresenting binding. You are our voices when we can't speak up and this book better equips you for that.

WE'RE NOT SO DIFFERENT AFTER ALL

Take 30 seconds to scan your own body—recognize where there are aches and pains in your body, notice whether you take full or shallow deep breaths, and review the health of your skin and how much time you devote to protecting it. In the margins of this page, write down three things that you choose to do that cause discomfort or increase future risk of harm.

Do you wear tummy-tucking underwear so you look great in that favorite outfit even though you won't take a deep-enough breath all evening?

Do you wear sunscreen even though it makes your skin break out? Or do you avoid it?

Do you skip taking a stretch break from your computer because you have to meet your deadline?

What other choices do you make for your own body that have an upside and a downside?

When you feel the urge to judge transgender or gender non-conforming (TGNC) people's choice to bind, return to this list and ask yourself how you would feel if someone judged you for and sought to prevent you from making those choices for yourself. Choose empathy; it is one of the greatest forces in the universe.

* * *

A note about language: I use the term TGNC, which stands for transgender and gender non-conforming, to refer to the gloriously broad spectrum of non-cisgender identities and presentations. Not everyone who identifies as transgender is gender non-conforming and not everyone who is gender non-conforming identifies as transgender but people who bind their chests largely fall into those two categories. I also use the term transmasculine to refer to people who were AFAB yet their gender identity moves in a direction away from traditional femininity. Language is imperfect and ever evolving, and the intention with these terms is to include the vast majority of people who bind for gender identity reasons. If these terms do not resonate with you, I understand and I am hopeful that you can insert an identity word that feels right and still be empowered by the knowledge offered here.

PART 1

BEST PRACTICES FOR HEALTHY BINDING

CHAPTER 1
BINDING AND THE BODY

I vividly remember trying on, and then buying, my first binder. I'd read so many guides and tips and warnings about what to look for or what to avoid, and I had built it up in my head until it was something almost terrifying. And then all of a sudden it was just me, in a cramped fitting room in the back of a store, pulling a thick tube of white elastic fabric down over my head. I squeezed and pulled and shifted around and it was bizarre how freeing something so constricting could feel.

Wearing a binder allowed me to move through the world without feeling self-conscious. I began to "become me again"—to borrow the words my family used. Binding became something that I did when I wanted people to see *me*, not my chest. I had "top surgery" three years ago and no longer had a need for my binders. It's funny, but as uncomfortable as they may have been at times, I kind of miss them.

– R, 43, Vermont, USA

What Is Binding?

A binder is something that is worn on the upper body to create a flatter physical contour by reducing the visibility of chest tissue. Binders can be garments, worn like undershirts, or specialized body-safe tape worn on, but never around, the chest. In the past decade, companies with commitments to transgender health have emerged to offer a variety of new styles and innovations making binding more comfortable and more supportive of overall health than ever before.

Garment binders   **Tape binding**

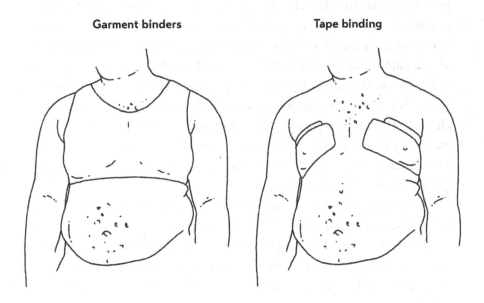

Though these innovations in binding are new, chest binding is not a new thing. For centuries, gender non-conforming people have used available materials to reduce the appearance of their chest tissue in order to be perceived by society in a manner aligned with their true gender identity. The practice of binding today is primarily associated with people who are TGNC and who bind for the purpose of more authentic gender expression. In the conservative backlash against transgender people, binding is accused of being mutilation and part of the "trans agenda," but the practice of binding chest tissue has been used by cis women throughout history when fashion trends favored flatter chests, to allow women to enter the workforce with less sexualization of their bodies, or for cis female athletes to get enough breast support to compete against small-breasted peers. Binding is not an agenda and it is not an inherently unhealthy practice; it is a tool used by many people who have a reason—physical, social, or emotional—to reduce the appearance of tissue on their chests.

Why Bind?

Binding the chest is a life-saving and quality-of-life-enhancing strategy that can safely allow assigned-female-at-birth TGNC people to fully express their identity. Many, but not all, TGNC people experience dysphoria or distress related to the mismatch between our gender identity and the sex we were assigned at birth. Dysphoria can be triggered by physical, social, emotional, and cultural factors and is different for everyone. It can manifest as anxiety, depression, rage, or fear and ranges from mild to severe. For many young people, dysphoric distress arrives in tandem with chest development in puberty. The presence of unwanted chest tissue is extremely isolating and often results in severe depression and crippling social anxiety. Tragically, TGNC people who die by suicide are often struggling with dysphoria in some form.

Depending on where a TGNC person lives, we may be in danger of being assaulted if our trans identity is exposed. Trans men who have chest tissue but are otherwise perceived as cis men in their daily lives may depend on their binder to conceal their trans identity and afford them more safety in their school, workplace, or community. Yet again, binders are life-saving.

As I mentioned above, not every TGNC person experiences dysphoria so binding is not always a tool for managing mental health challenges, but it still may provide safety or allow a person to wear the style of clothing that allows them to engage with the world as their most confident and authentic self. It may allow a person to participate in activities or enter social spaces that feel off limits to them when their body is visibly feminine. In professional settings, especially for people who do physical labor, it can be essential to being treated equally and maintaining job security. So, even when the misalignment between body and gender identity is not causing depression or anxiety, binders are allowing TGNC people to work, study, play, and love because of the confidence that binding gives them.

Binding does more than just keep trans people alive and safe; it creates gender euphoria, the experience of joy and contentment from the experience of feeling aligned with one's true gender identity. Throughout this book, you will have the opportunity to read people's stories of how wearing a binder filled them with joy, hope, self-confidence, and opportunity.

Healthy binding is a simple, affordable, safe, and non-permanent way for TGNC individuals to receive relief from dysphoria, increase social engagement, and experience euphoria from being perceived accurately by others. Unfortunately, TGNC folks who cannot access safe binding methods will resort to unsafe methods (detailed in Chapter 2), which cause the most severe pain and injury. When TGNC people are able to access correctly sized, commercially made binders, their mental health improves and their social isolation decreases.

Unapologetic Euphoria

When I pulled the binder snuggly onto myself for the first time and looked in the mirror, I saw with bewilderment someone who looked how I'd always felt. Suddenly, the person my family loved was someone I could see with my eyes. I felt ready to take on the world. I felt confident, beautiful, and unapologetically right in my body.

– G, 35, Maryland, USA

How Does Dysphoria Impact the Body?

Before we can discuss the ways that binding adds stress to the muscles and bones of the upper body, we must discuss the most common ways that dysphoria shapes and strains the body. It's common, even among cis women, to feel betrayed at the start of puberty when permission to be a "tomboy" is suddenly revoked due to the changes in your chest. It's confusing that running shirtless in the sprinkler was fine until there were budding breasts that must be hidden. For people assigned female at birth (AFAB) whose true gender deviates from the norms of femininity, the beginning of puberty is often a traumatic and confusing time when we begin to notice how we are different from our peers.

The message is: your body (which feels out of control in puberty anyway) gets the final say on how you get treated in the world and if you can't accept it, then you are wrong. When humans feel like something is wrong with us, we often try to hide, get smaller, or be invisible. If what's wrong is mounds of tissue growing on your chest, you hide them. Without being conscious of it, TGNC preteens start curving their shoulders, collapsing their torsos, and dropping their heads. While this posture often starts for TGNC people in puberty, others do not encounter dysphoria about their chests until they are older but the physical pattern that develops is the same.

I refer to this position throughout this book as the dysphoria hunch. The bowing of the shoulders changes the position of the shoulder blades and causes the upper back and neck to strain. Collapsing the torso tilts the rib cage forward and collapses the space which is used by the lungs when taking a full breath. The curve in the back and slump of the rib cage make it impossible for the head to be fully upright on the spine which results in the effective weight of the head increasing and the cervical muscles becoming fatigued by holding it up (see the box on page 282 to learn just how heavy the head can get!). This is called Forward Head Posture (FHP) and is discussed extensively in Part 2 in sections about breathing constriction, chest pain, headaches, jaw pain, back pain, limited shoulder range of motion, and more. Though this book is not about the social and emotional impact of dysphoria, I must mention that the impact of these postural changes creates a vicious cycle where people's body self-consciousness collapses their posture and their mind concludes from the new posture that they are not as confident as their "normal" peers. As this gets repeated, TGNC people withdraw and their opportunities diminish.

Before a binder is ever put on, a TGNC person has probably already begun to experience a lot of symptoms of upper body pain. Migraines, shallow breathing, or jaw pain may be chronic conditions before the binding is even a consideration. When a binder gets added to dysphoria hunch posture, all of the postural elements are exacerbated—pulling the shoulders down and forward, curving the upper back, straining the neck, and crowding the lungs. Without the posture to hide the chest, a person wearing a binder might not be as vulnerable to much of the chronic pain which results from the intensifying of the dysphoria hunch. I often wonder if I would have developed a more confident adult posture if I had been able to control the appearance of chest tissue in my tender tween years.

Thrilling Euphoria

I put on my first binder about 10 years ago, but the memory is still vivid. I wrestled it on right out of the packaging, threw a T-shirt over it, and looked in the mirror. My first, absolutely thrilled thought was: Holy shit, I look so much flatter!

With a binder, I was misgendered far less often in public. It helped me eventually come out at work, and I started to actually enjoy shopping for clothes.

— *L, 34, Washington, DC, USA*

How Do Binders Impact the Body?

To answer that question, we need to examine two things: displacement and compression.

Force of compression on the rib cage

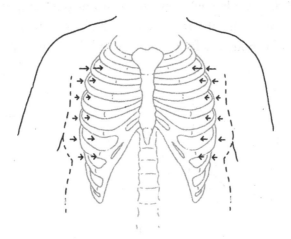

All garment binders (which excludes kinetic tape binding) rely on compression because their job is to hold chest tissue tightly against the body. In the process, the binder exerts a force on the ribs and shoulder blades that has an immobilizing effect which reduces the range of motion that a muscle, tendon, cartilage, or joint has. Everything in the body is

25

connected so when one structure cannot move as intended, other parts must work harder and/or be pulled into unnatural positions in the body. The results of these changes include overexertion, pain, weakness, trigger points, fatigue, numbness, and inflexibility. Luckily, postural changes and imbalances between muscles in the body can be changed with targeted movements to release and strengthen muscles so that they are strong enough to function properly even with the added force of compression.

This illustration shows the direction of force that the compressive fabric exerts on the rib cage. This pressure exists in virtually all binding garments but to varying degrees. Some binders rely entirely on compression fabrics, sometimes called power mesh, to squish fat, muscle, and mammary tissue against the rib cage, while others combine lighter compression fabric with non-elastic panels which will be discussed later when we talk about displacement. The strength of this compression varies from company to company, and the higher the elastane content, the stronger the inward force it exerts. When binders are constructed of this high-intensity compression fabric on both the frontside and backside (panels A and C in the diagram below), it creates a 360-degree compression. The more surface area of the rib cage covered by high-compression fabric, the fewer options the body has for movement and the more opportunity for injury to occur.

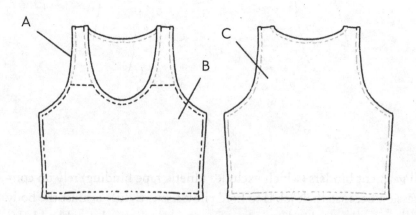

Not all binders that use compressive fabric as their primary force use the same strength of fabric on both panels A and C. In fact, the trend in binding is moving away from 360-degree compression, and most companies now make panel C out of a fabric with more stretch similar to the elasticity of bathing suit fabric. Since less surface area of the rib cage is compressed by the fabric, these binders generally cause less weakness, fatigue, overcompensation, and strain. However, binders with 360-degree compression are not inherently unsafe. If that is the binder that works best for a person's body, they must simply be more diligent with movement exercises to keep the structures mobile and strong under the binder.

It's important to make the distinction between 360-degree compression and wrap binding methods which are unsafe ways to bind and are responsible for the most severe binding injuries. Wrap binders are fabric, tape, or elastic wrapped around the chest and secured in place. They are often homemade or repurposed garments intended for other uses (like neoprene belts). Binding should never be done with a wrap binder of any kind because the compression exerted on the rib cage can easily become far more force than the body is capable of withstanding. Serious injury can occur at that point. Read much more about the types of wrap binding on page 45.

Let's examine the impact compression has on breathing since most people who bind experience this effect. Chapter 8 explains how many more of the body's functions and structures are impacted. In order to breathe properly, the individual ribs move outward and upward to allow the lungs to expand. The force of the binder compresses the rib cage and prevents the fullness of the rib movement. In 360-degree compression, ribs have resistance to expansion on both the front and back of the rib cage, effectively giving them nowhere to go. Over time, the body thickens the connective tissue between muscles, and the ribs can become so mired in restrictive tissue that even when the binder is off, they remain too constricted for the person to get a full breath.

The ribs are not the only bones whose movement is restricted by compression. The shoulder blades allow the diverse movements of the human shoulder by gliding over the surface of the rib cage on the backside of the body. In order for the binder to effectively compress the tissue on the front of the chest, it must simultaneously inhibit the free movement of the shoulder blades. Over time, the same connective tissue that immobilizes the ribs adheres these flat bones to the muscles underneath which limits range of motion, reduces upper body flexibility, and weakens neck and back muscles.

Not all binders apply the same force to the shoulder blades. Among safe binding methods, 360-degree compression limits the movement of shoulder blades the most and, without proper care, can result in injuries to the rotator cuff, atrophy in some of the 17 muscles attached to the shoulder blade, and reduced flexibility in the shoulder joints. Binders in which panel C is made of a lighter elastic fabric allow the shoulder blades to move more freely and with minimal resistance. Typically, people wearing these types of binders experience fewer problems related to shoulder blade immobility. Doing regular exercises to move and strengthen these muscles is important, especially if a person is not very active in other movement-intensive activities or does repetitive arm movements.

Similar to compression on the rib cage, wrap binding methods are never safe for shoulder blades. The kind of pressure exerted by wrapping something around the upper rib cage can cause nearly complete immobilization of the shoulder blades, making it difficult to move the arms at all. A wrap binder worn for any length of time will cause bruising, at minimum, and rib dislocation or rotator cuff damage in more severe cases.

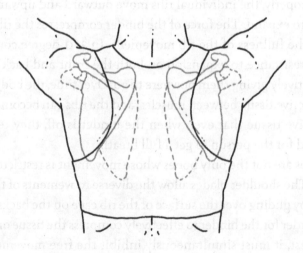

The racerback design offered by some binder companies covers the least surface area of the shoulder blade and allows for the most unencumbered movement because compression fabric only covers some of the muscles which control the movement of the shoulder blade. The image of the racerback tank above shows the path of movement of the shoulder blades. The degree of compression is still an important factor in racerback binders because if panel C is made of highly compressive fabric, it may still provide more resistance than a tank binder with panel C made of low-compression fabric.

Now, let's discuss displacement. Some binders utilize a non-elastic front panel, marked B in the diagram, to flatten the chest tissue directly into the ribs. To flatten something, you must displace its mass, right? So, the question with binding is: where does the chest tissue go?

Chest tissue is a mixture of glands, fat, and connective tissue which makes it dense. To create the desired flattened contour, a binder compresses this dense tissue inward toward the rib cage, applying force into the center of the chest at the sternum as shown in the diagram below. This inward force causes

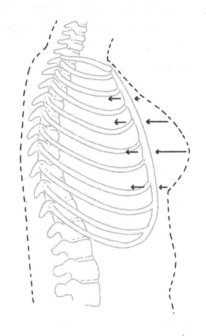

Pressure to sternum and upper rib cage

the upper rib cage to curve into a slightly bowed shape, exaggerating the bowing that is often present from dysphoria. The depression of the rib cage is usually indiscernible to the eye but to the ribs, sternum, cartilage, and muscles, even a small shift can cause strain.

Thinking of cardiopulmonary resuscitation (CPR) can help illustrate how the displacement of the chest tissue occurs. Cartilage, a tissue more elastic than bone and more rigid than muscle, allows the sternum and upper ribs to absorb force and depress inward, as is done with CPR chest compressions. Then, when the pressure is released, the bones can spring back up. When a binder forces dense rounded tissue to flatten into the body in the center of the chest, it causes a *slight* version of CPR compression. The surface of the body looks flat because the chest tissue can hide in that slightly concave depression.

In order to provide enough inward force, a binder is constructed differently than a bra. In a binder, the garment is designed with a panel down the front that will deliver enough pressure that the tissue will be adequately pressed inward with a flat appearance. By contrast, a sports bra is constructed to leave a cup-shaped space in the garment so chest tissue is not compressed inward with the same force and, while a sports bra does compress chest tissue, the person's profile retains a rounded contour.

Panels of a binder

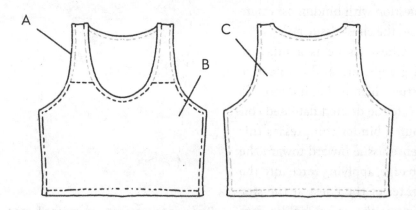

Displacement into the center of the chest is most pronounced in binders where panel B in the diagram is made of a non-elastic fabric, like canvas, which exerts a consistent pressure across all of the tissue. Binders that do not contain panel B but where panels A and C are made of highly elastic fabric, like power mesh, can also cause a concave upper chest from displacement. The most dangerous factor when considering displacement from binding is size. A binder that is intended to compress a smaller chest will exert more force on larger chest tissue into the sternum. That increased intensity can result in a compression of the sternum which is beyond the tolerance of the body, even with good self-care. I have seen clients with permanent, visible concave depressions in the center of their chest from this long-term wear of a binder that is too small. These clients ultimately struggled with disappointment after top surgery because they were not able to achieve their desired chest appearance with the sternum sunk so far into the body.

Bodies have no wasted space, so when this concave area is created for the chest tissue to hide in, the space that's reserved for lung expansion is encroached upon. This concavity requires the ribs and sternum to depress for hours without springing back up (instead of seconds like when performing CPR). The rounding of the chest will pull the body into a slight hunch, bringing the head forward and the shoulders inward, and rounding the thoracic spine. From the outside, these changes aren't usually visible to the untrained eye but, to the tissues, these are massive changes. The sustained pressures and postural changes can cause inflammation in the muscles and cartilage, and pain in the shoulders, neck, and upper back, as well as crowding of the upper gastrointestinal tract. The exercises in this book can offset the effect of this sustained pressure by releasing constriction in the muscles and can build strength to support healthy posture.

Wearing a correctly sized binder is not inherently dangerous for an otherwise healthy person provided they are attentive to the needs of their body. Chronic pain develops when the body does not receive relief in the form of tissue release (exercises) and rest (time out of a binder). A connective tissue called fascia, which is discussed at length in Part 2, will thicken and get sticky in response to this unnatural alignment. Unfortunately, the thickened fascia prevents the ribs and sternum from springing back and forces the shoulders, neck, and spine to become locked in a curved posture. Exercises in Part 2 use self myofascial release (SMR) techniques that allow you to relieve the effects of the inward force and enable the sternum and rib cage to spring back to their natural shape more easily when you remove your binder.

If you are feeling daunted by hearing the impact that a binder is having on your anatomy, I understand. Let me reassure you that this kind of immobilizing is not unique to binding. My job as a massage therapist requires me to look closely at the strains and stresses that our everyday lives put on our bodies. Take it from me, we are *all* putting our anatomy through hell. If you are reading this because you are worried about whether binding can be safe, I encourage you to keep your perspective on the countless ways we constrain our bodies and never stop to consider it. Consider the sustained posture of looking down at our cell phones: it creates a curve in our upper rib cage and immobilizes the muscles that support our neck. And bucket seats in cars leave the spine and pelvis locked in unnatural alignment, causing pain and postural problems. We wear shoes that immobilize bones in our feet, and we overuse our mouse and keyboard until the muscles and tendons in the forearms are adhered together. Even something as innocent as sleeping on certain pillows can create a strain that results in neck pain. Binders are just one more thing that we utilize in our daily lives that have unintended consequences for our anatomy. We don't need to stop binding (or using cell phones, keyboards, cars, or pillows); we need to start paying attention and tending to our bodies so they can bounce back.

Euphoria Even in Dark Times

I was hypomanic when I bought my first binder. It was a cheap model, black and shiny, and it zipped up the front. I put it on immediately, donned multiple shirts to see what worked best, and was so elated with the way a particular button-down sat atop it that I had to go and jog through the neighborhood blasting Death Grips through my headphones. I felt unstoppable, as though I could punch through the hood of a car.

The hypomania peaked, retreated, and left me depressed. But the binder remained, and the spark of hope that came with it kept me going during the dark months that followed.

– *M, 38, Massachusetts, USA*

Pay Attention to Your Body

"Listen to your body" is usually the first piece of advice on every list of tips for healthy binding. It is great advice but what does it really mean?

For many people "listen to your body" is easier said than done, but it is an invaluable skill so let's begin by exploring what it means and how to learn to do it.

Sensation is the one and only language that the body has to communicate. When muscles strain under tension and need relief, they send electrical signals to the brain where they're translated to sensations your conscious brain can understand. Some of the body's most common ways to communicate distress related to binding are: sharp pain, dizziness, rapid breathing, increased body temperature, tingling, pulsing, and numbness.

When these sensations are present, the tissues are alerting you to an unsustainable situation. The tissues may need immediate attention (e.g., removing or loosening your binder), or once your binder is off, they may be saying that they need to be restored with self-treatment like exercises, stretches, and massage to relax the excessive tension, trigger points, and stiff fascia.

Wearing the wrong binder will hurt, and your body will let you know via tenderness, irritation, and soreness. It's important to pay attention to new, unfamiliar soreness in your ribs or spine, red marks where the binder chafed, painful skin irritation, and difficulty breathing. These are the signals your body is sending to tell you that that binder is probably not the right fit.

I'm forever grateful to the brave workshop participant who raised their hand, and asked, "Everything says 'listen to your body' but what does that even mean?" Heads all over the room began nodding in agreement. It's excellent advice, but only if it makes intuitive sense to you. You may be a highly analytical person or neurodivergent or the phrase may just seem confusing, vague, and frustrating. Try substituting the word "sense," meaning to identify sensory information. The advice then changes from "listen to your body to tell you if the binder is too tight" to "sense your body's reaction to know if the binder is too tight."

Sometimes, the problem with receiving signals about sensations in the body is that you don't have much practice doing it. Our culture encourages us to ignore our bodily needs and keep going at all costs. Before I address how tuning out your body's signal relates to binding, I want to acknowledge that without adequate compensation, affordable healthcare, free childcare, or equitable sick-leave policies, most of us are forced to tune out discomfort for basic survival. However, when you don't feel and decipher the sensations, you're essentially putting your fingers in your ears and singing "la la la" in the conversation between your brain and your body. Do that long enough and the nervous system will stop bothering to send messages unless they are severe, like a broken bone. If this describes you, no judgment—binding is a great reason to start cultivating this skill.

TRAUMA

Dissociation is a natural, protective response to trauma. It takes many forms but often causes a person to feel detached from their body's sensory information which can make perceiving sensations feel as impossible as trying to taste the color blue. If you have a history of trauma, it may be best for you to explore bodily sensations initially with a therapist who can support you if you become overwhelmed or triggered.

The cultural conditioning to ignore our body's communication isn't the only silencer. If you have experienced trauma, lack of connection to part or all of your body may be another barrier to "listening" or noticing sensations. The trauma of dysphoria leads many gender-expansive people to ignore or dissociate from parts or all of their body to protect the psyche. Dysphoria is real. I've experienced it, and I see you. And I want to help you discern more of the important sensation messages that your body is sending you so that you can be safe while binding.

If you are someone with chronic pain, you may have yet another factor impacting your ability to track sensations related to binding. With chronic pain conditions, defined as pain which lasts more than three months, the nervous system changes as a result of the constant need to alert the brain to pain and discomfort. In some cases, people develop hypersensitivity to stimulation, making it hard to discern what is and what is not related to binding. It's like trying to hear someone at a loud concert when you're standing next to the speaker. In other cases, chronic pain causes the nervous system to deprioritize alerting the brain to less urgent pain and discomfort. In this case, it's like putting off calling the electrician about a broken light until after you call the plumber about the water flooding your kitchen from a broken pipe. If you are living with chronic pain, recognizing sensations related to binding is yet another uncomfortable thing to pay attention to, and that can be exhausting. You probably have your own strategies for discerning the body's pain sensations but fine-tuning those skills and taking care to notice changes immediately following binding can help you to pinpoint the most helpful information.

When dysphoria, pain, and dissociation are strong, my clients and I do this work in baby steps. I have them start by noticing familiar sensations in parts of the body unrelated to the parts that are emotionally or physically painful, like warmth on your cheeks or cold air in your nostrils. Slowly beginning to notice less triggering sensations will signal to your brain that you are willing and able to listen. Then, gradually, you can pick up sensations in your body connected to movement like vibration and stretching muscle. Eventually, the body and brain start exchanging information about sensation in the chest, torso, lungs, or shoulders. If you've been dissociated from your body, this will take intention and practice, but improving your body awareness skills will give you an essential tool for managing and preventing chronic physical pain. Because let's face it, none of us need that pain *on top of* painful dysphoria, trauma, or a chronic condition.

The following activity is an opportunity, regardless of whether you feel a lot of sensory information or very little, to practice and grow the skills. The goal is to gently foster a better information exchange between the brain and the body. With practice and intention, anyone can increase their access to these sensory messages from the body, or in other words, *listen*.

GROWING YOUR BODY AWARENESS

If you wish you were more connected to sensations happening in your body, this activity can help you understand and respond to your body's sensory language.

Find a place where you won't be interrupted and will be able to move your body.

It's best to choose a time when your dysphoria is not particularly intense. If, at any time, you become overwhelmed, panicked, or feel unsafe, **stop**. Distract yourself with another activity until you feel calm.*

Read this list of sensation words, stopping to consider what your experience would be like if you felt each sensation. Note sensations that you feel often and others that are unfamiliar.

SENSATION WORDS

Achy	Constricted	Itchy	Prickly	Stuck
Blocked	Contracted	Knotted	Relaxed	Sweaty
Breathless	Dense	Light	Releasing	Tender
Bruised	Expansive	Loose	Sensitive	Tense
Burny	Floaty	Nauseous	Shaky	Throbbing
Buzzy	Fluttery	Numb	Sharp	Tight
Calm	Frozen	Open	Shivering	Tingly
Clenched	Heavy	Popping	Sore	Trembling
Clicking	Hollow	Pounding	Spacious	Twitching
Cold	Hot	Pressure	Stretchy	Warm

Sensations may also register as sounds, colors, or images. That's just as valuable in the conversation as sensation *words*. The important part is to notice them.

Sensations are never good or bad, they are simply what is happening in your body.

1. Get comfortable and still. Feel the air on your skin and the ground under you.

- Are there pleasurable or unpleasurable sensations that you notice anywhere in your body?
- Simply observe them.

2. Move your head in five slow circles.**
   - Notice if there is any change in your neck, shoulders, or face.
   - What words, sounds, colors, or images describe what you are experiencing?

3. Form tight fists and hold them for 10 seconds.
   - Is there a difference between when you clench your hands and when you release them?
   - What words, sounds, colors, or images describe what you are experiencing?

4. Lightly stroke your face for 10 seconds.
   - Notice the sensations on your skin. Notice sensations in other parts of your body. Fingertips? Spine? Belly? Other places?
   - What words, sounds, colors, or images describe what you are experiencing?

5. Do a forward fold and hang limply for 10 seconds.**
   - Notice the sensations in your head, your arms, your back, and the backs of your legs.
   - What words, sounds, colors, or images describe what you are experiencing?

6. Move your body in a way that feels good. Dance, yoga pose, singing, etc.
   - Notice sensations throughout your body.
   - What words, sounds, colors, or images describe what you are experiencing?

7. Get still and in a restful position.
   - Slowly take 5 deep breaths.
   - Notice sensations happening as you do this.
   - If you aren't ready to think about chest and torso sensations, that's OK! Notice sensations of your limbs as they relax or the texture of fabrics touching your skin.
   - What words, sounds, colors, or images describe what you are experiencing?

The more that you listen to your body, the more information it will give you. This may feel unrelated to binding but I assure you that practicing this awareness of your sensation will increase the information you receive from your body about what needs attention before an injury or long-term pain develops.

*If it feels like getting in touch with your bodily sensations will trigger a trauma response, seek out a therapist to help you as you explore the sensations of the body.
**Do not do any of these movements if you have injuries or conditions for which the movement is not recommended.

Attend to Your Body's Pain and Discomfort

In most communities you won't find a bodyworker or physical therapist who is an expert in binding health (though I'm working hard to change that) and the vast majority of doctors are wholly unfamiliar with the practice. Many providers are closed-minded about binding which can make seeking care both invalidating and pointless. Many gender-expansive folks have simply had so many bad experiences in healthcare that they won't bother trying. On top of all of that, the cost of seeing a physical therapist or massage therapist can be prohibitive. This is why the queer and transgender communities have a rich history of taking it upon ourselves to create resources that provide us with information about our own bodies and empower us to address our own pain. It is in that spirit that I have written this book. I want you to be able to heal yourself whenever possible.

Part 2 of this book is entirely devoted to self-treatment. It lays out in detail 23 exercises that you can do on your own to prevent or address binding pain and discomfort. If you are binding in a healthy way, which is covered in the next five chapters, then pain, discomfort, and breathing restriction that arises from binding will most likely be treatable on your own.

Self-treating relies on self-motivation and self-assessment. When you notice discomfort, don't ignore it. Check the symptom index (page 311) and try those exercises. Being your own practitioner means being the voice in your head reminding you about the importance of self-care. It also means reminding yourself that it's not a quick fix and to be consistent with the exercises to receive results. Sometimes you will find that the exercises help, but when you stop doing them, the pain returns. In these cases, you will need to do the exercises regularly in order to bind pain-free.

Not ending up in pain in the first place is always preferable. You can prevent problems from developing by doing exercises as part of your daily routine. I encourage you to think of it as a fair exchange: you put in a little additional time and energy, and you get to bind without pain, discomfort, or shortness of breath. I think that it's a fair deal.

Being physically active is critical to physical, social, and mental well-being. If you bind, it's crucial to be thoughtful about how and when you bind for physically demanding activities. Evaluate your activities and review the information in Chapter 4 about physical activities. Make the healthiest possible choices for working out, playing sports, and working in physically demanding jobs. It's up to you to take care of your health, even when it's hard. I think back to my own story and how much physical pain, mental distress, and financial hardship I could have prevented with smarter choices about doing physical labor in a binder. Learn from my mistakes. We'll cover some guidelines in Chapter 3, but looser binders and alternative binding methods for certain activities should be part of your overall binding strategy.

CHAPTER 2

METHODS OF BINDING

When I started binding, there were only a handful of options and it was an investment and a luxury to own one. I was a poor, young adult with minimal resources—an Underworks binder was out of the question. So, the first time I bound, I did so with an ace wrap; my friend and I were in the restroom constantly pulling it up, taping it in place, rewrapping it—looser, then tighter. As exhilarating as it was to see my chest magically disappear, it was clear I needed a ["real" binder]. My self-assigned big brother gifted me a half-sized one [and] I struggled into it. [I] felt as though I'd never take it off. I gasped for air as I felt my chest compressed. When I finally found a shirt that covered it well, my breathing turned to excitement as I realized I could be comfortable just being me.

– K, 32, Amsterdam, Netherlands

Buy a Reputable Binder

Is wearing a binder safe? Bottom line: yes, as long as it is well made by a reputable company and correctly sized.

The safest option for binding is to purchase commercially made products and with so many options, there is no reason not to. Even when cost is a barrier, excellent options are available for less than $30 and through binder donation programs if that is still out of reach. Do-it-yourself (DIY) binding is just not worth it. Later in this chapter, we'll discuss the specific risks of DIY binding and how it poses the greatest danger to your health. These risky methods are tempting when options are limited, but life-long pain and serious injury are not worth it.

Tank style binder: safe   **Tape binding: safe**   **Wrap binding: dangerous**

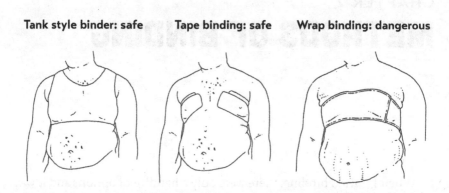

Reputable binder companies want you to bind without pain. In most cases, the owners and/or designers have lived experience of binding and dysphoria and are passionate about helping transgender and non-binary people achieve a gender-affirming silhouette. The binder manufacturers I mention in this book and on www.healthybinding.com have tested and refined their designs to ensure they are safe. They invest time in making accurate size guides to make it easy for customers to choose the right binder for their body. Read more about these owners and designers in the "By Trans, For Trans" sections throughout this chapter and read company profiles on www.healthybinding.com.

Cheap knockoffs are all over the internet, but remember, you get what you pay for. The reputable companies in this book do size testing and refine their designs with customer feedback. They are invested in and accountable to the transgender community. Many of them are transparent about where they source their materials, where they manufacture their garments, and what their labor practices are. Binders purchased online from unknown companies are notoriously uncomfortable with exposed seams and scratchy fabrics that irritate the skin. They generally don't offer size charts and when they do, many people find that they are inaccurate.

With $30 reputable binders available, don't waste money and risk problems by buying one for $15–20.

Commercially made binders can, however, be unsafe when incorrectly sized. The majority of injuries I see in my bodywork practice come from wearing binders that are too small. Some clients have told me that they thought that they were supposed to wear the smallest one that they could get their body into; others just assume the smaller the binder, the flatter the contour (which is not true). Still more people buy a smaller size, believing that the risk is inflated and that injuries "won't happen to them." That's a dangerous calculation that often leads to chronic pain. Some people make that calculation and become so injured in small binders that they are forced to quit binding altogether. For many people who don't follow size guidelines, especially those with larger chests, the irony is that they would achieve a flatter chest contour with the correct size since the chest tissue must have enough room to displace under the compression. After you read about all of the styles and features of binders available, you'll find this chapter covers more about correct sizing and measurements. For both safety and getting your desired results, the right size binder is key.

High-Risk Binding

Let's get the "don't's" out of the way first, so we can focus the rest of our time on the vast array of "do's" in healthy binding.

I get how people arrive at high-risk binding. You want your chest to be flat, so you tightly wrap something around your rib cage to flatten it out. In reality, homemade binding solutions can have serious consequences. In fact, the vast majority of serious binding injuries that I have come across in my career have been from people using DIY wrap binding methods.

While I discuss these methods as "risky" or "higher risk," I'm doing so without judgment. Binding is often about survival, and purchasing a binder isn't always an option due to access to internet purchasing, personal finances, or out-ness. If you are binding "under the radar" with DIY wrap bindings because you are hiding your binding from your family out of fear and feel you cannot own a commercially made binder, consider the risks carefully and read the rest of the chapter to learn about safer alternatives. If financial barriers are behind your choice to DIY bind, binder donation programs and other forms of financial support are available (see page 77 for some donation resources and visit www.healthybinding.com for an updated list of programs). If you are a family member reading this book to determine whether to support your loved one's desire to bind, please read about these risks thoughtfully. Most people who resort to these unsafe binding methods do so because they are prohibited from accessing a safe commercially made binder.

ARE "RISKY BINDERS" EVEN STILL A THING?

Sadly, yes.

In 2017, researchers from Johns Hopkins School of Public Health and Boston University's Schools of Medicine and Public Health, found that almost a third of the 1,800 transmasculine participants in their study used the highest risk binding methods.

- 298 people (16.5%) used elastic bandages.
- 118 people (6.6%) used neoprene sports wrap.
- 78 people (4.3%) used duct tape or plastic wrap.
- 55 people (3.1%) used binders they made themselves.

Increased attention to binding health in the media and more affordable binders on the market may have shifted these statistics since 2017 but the problem has not gone away. In my anecdotal research, it is young people in unsupportive homes who are most often resorting to these methods and, sadly, have the least support if they become injured.

Source: Peitzmeier et al. (2017)[1]

1   Peitzmeier, S., Gardner, I., Weinand, J., Corbet, A., and Acevedo, K. (2017) 'Health impact of chest binding among transgender adults: a community-engaged, cross-sectional study.' *Culture, Health & Sexuality 19*, 1, 64–75.

Wrap Binding Methods

A wrap binder is any material that wraps all the way around the torso and secures in place to compress the chest tissue. Many, but not all, wrap binders are homemade. This binding method exerts unyielding equal pressure on the front, sides, and back of the body. This force on the full circumference of the chest concentrates an unsafe amount of constriction on a single section of the ribs and lungs. Medical complications associated with wrap binding can be mild (skin discoloration and skin abrasions) but are more often moderate (bruised ribs and hyperventilation) or severe (dislocated or cracked ribs and loss of consciousness).

Wrap binders are any material wrapped around the chest and secured in place

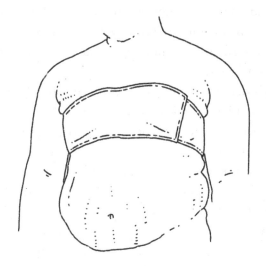

Wrap binding methods vary and will be described at length later, but they all rely on pressure exerted all the way around the rib cage like a belt cinching around the chest. Let's learn from history, shall we? Tightly laced corsets of the 19th century created the desired hourglass shape using a wrap method, and this practice deformed rib bones, atrophied abdominal muscles, and inflamed cartilage. While binding is a different practice than extreme corseting of the 1800s, those dangerous results can be cautionary tales for today's unsafe binding methods. Using tape or any other strong fibered material to bind is similar to wearing a corset over a six-inch section of the rib cage. It is not uncommon for people who bind with tape or elastic to develop a "waist-like" indentation under their armpits where the ribs have shifted under the pressure of the wrap binding. One guy used a wrap binder daily when he was in high school and his rib cage was so distorted by the binding that the circumference compressed from 32 to 30 inches. When I met him in his mid-twenties, his rib cage had still not regained those inches and he experienced chronic back pain.

The kind of strain exerted on the rib cage by wrap binding methods can cause rib fractures and dislocations. These injuries cause severe pain with movement and require lengthy recovery periods. I hear from folks in transmasc support groups who are suffering with extreme dysphoria because a binding injury is requiring them to recover without binding. They don't want to leave the house and some have lost their jobs because they don't feel safe or comfortable at work. I urge you to pause and consider the serious risks of wrap binding because it could lead to a scenario where you cannot bind at all.

The body's defense mechanism to prevent breaking or displacing ribs is cartilage: a hard, slightly flexible tissue that attaches the ribs to the sternum. To cope with the force on the ribs, the cartilage will bow slightly to absorb the pressure. While this prevents the displacement or fracture of bone, the strain on the cartilage can result in costochondritis, the painful inflammation in the center of the chest which was the third in my personal trio of injuries. This condition makes breathing and upper body movement painful. Even a mild case can prevent a person from binding for months or, in some cases, permanently. Take, for example, my client who developed costochondritis as a teenager and in his late twenties still suffers chronic flare-ups. (Read more about costochondritis in Chapter 5.)

With commercially made binders more available and financially accessible, fewer people are resorting to unsafe DIY wrap methods. Unfortunately, the misconception persists that occasional binding with these risky methods is OK, but these wrap binders do not need to be worn long to do damage. Wrap binding just once for cosplay, drag performances, or because you forgot your binder can result in acute or long-lasting injury to the rib cage.

The following section reviews the risks associated with the most common materials used as wrap bindings:

- Elastic bandages (e.g., ACE bandages, Tensor bandages)
- Elastic knit with closure
- Adjustable wrap binders (e.g., neoprene sport wraps, back braces)
- Utility tape (e.g., duct or packing tape)
- Plastic food wrap (e.g., Saran wrap)
- Medical tape

While most wrap binders are homemade, some companies sell binders that wrap, like a wide belt, around the rib cage. These are technically "commercially made," but pose a danger and must be avoided. Custom-designed binders for people with disabilities and pain disorders are the exception to this rule. These binders are made of less compressive fabrics and provide access to binding when tank styles are prohibitive.

ELASTIC BANDAGES

Think about a rubber band. When stretched, it loads potential energy and strains to pull back to its original shape. When you stretch and loop it repeatedly around your finger, it strains against the surface. Even if it's not super tight, the rubber band will squish tissue, reddening the tip of your increasingly throbbing finger, filling it with blood that isn't able to flow easily back into the hand, up the arm, and back to the heart.

Now, imagine that instead of your finger, it's your entire rib cage enveloped in elastic. The same principles of physics and anatomy apply as the elastic strains to return to a resting state. The body's fluids, muscles, tendons, and skin beneath the band get crushed against the rib cage, decreasing or cutting off the flow of fluids in two crucial systems: the circulatory (blood) and the lymphatic. Blood carries oxygen; lymph removes cellular waste; and both are crucial components of the immune system. Inhibiting their natural flow with tight elastic binding will eventually cause tissue damage. Lack of oxygen, increased cellular waste, and the inability to fight infection can cause acute and long-term damage to the affected tissue.

Elastic bandages (e.g., ACE, Tensor) are a combination of cloth and elastic used to immobilize injured joints. To best support the joint during movement, elastic bandages are specifically designed to get tighter as you move. This is excellent for supporting an unstable joint but extremely dangerous for a healthy rib cage. The pressure from the elastic gets increasingly tighter as you move your torso, causing the bandage to dig into the rib cage and highly constrict a few vulnerable ribs. When you do everyday movements under this pressure, there is a high chance of dislocated and cracked ribs. For example, a client ran to catch a bus while binding in an elastic bandage. The combination of the increasingly tightening band and increasingly heavier breathing cracked two of his ribs. The recovery lasted months, during which he could not wear his binder because of the pain.

When the elastic is cinched tight against a small section of the rib cage, the compression decreases the available space for lung expansion. While all binding methods will apply force on the chest wall and squeeze the lungs, commercially available binders distribute this pressure throughout the rib cage more safely. In a proper binder, my client would have had a hard time catching his breath and been pretty sore the following day, but he would have avoided cracked ribs and months of heightened dysphoria.

Mountaintop Euphoria
Traditional binders never allowed me to really feel free in my skin but with TransTape I feel like a whole new person. I was introduced to what seemed like an entirely new world and for the first time I felt confident and like I recognized the person looking back in the mirror. I became so comfortable with myself that I went on a two-month-long soul-searching trip to Montana with only my dog. We got to go hiking and camping in the Rockies and feeling the sun on my bare skin on top of mountains was one of the most affirming and magical moments of my entire life. And I wouldn't have had any of that without chest binding.

– J, 27, New York, USA

ELASTIC KNIT

On YouTube you can find how-to videos about making your own binder using wide elastic knit from a craft store and hooks or clasps. The problem is that any binder made with a single band of elastic will exert equal pressure around the rib cage, compressing a few of your ribs like a belt. Thankfully, elastic knit fabric doesn't tighten as you move, like elastic bandages, but it still creates problematic 360-degree compression. I talked to someone who followed the directions on YouTube to make this kind of wrap binder but without being skilled in garment construction he made it too tight. He recounted crying at school in pain and making up an excuse to go home. Though a DIY elastic binder might seem like an affordable and accessible option, the materials will cost almost as much as an affordable binder from a reputable company with the expertise to get it right. So channel your funds to a trans-affirming company and put your craftiness to use making other fabulous garments or accessories to express your gender.

ADJUSTABLE WRAPS

I see neoprene wraps and back braces suggested in transmasc groups as good DIY options. These products are designed to do a different job and won't provide the results for you that a proper binder will provide. Additionally, both will increase the likelihood of skin irritations. Back braces are not meant to be worn directly against the skin and neoprene sports wraps are designed to increase the amount that you sweat which invites heat rash as well as bacterial and fungal infections of the skin.

The biggest concern is not the skin, though. These one-size-fits-most products have Velcro closures that allow for a large range for tightening so the compression can fluctuate from wear to wear. This makes them especially risky on days when your dysphoria is at its worst. The part of you that is suffering can easily override your better judgment and you end up cinching the wrap painfully tight around your chest.

In this case, your ribs are in danger of dislocating or cracking as discussed earlier, but your breath capacity can become so limited under the constriction that you can hyperventilate, trigger a panic or asthma attack, or pass out from lack of oxygen. Take the case of a college student I met online who went to class wrapped as tightly as he could on a vicious dysphoria day. His breathing was so shallow that he couldn't catch his breath going up flights of stairs and, eventually, passed out. He was lucky not to be injured in the incident, but he wasn't spared major pain. The times he subjected his rib cage to that much stress meant that he experienced chronic pain for years, even after he stopped wrapping. Take it from him, it's too easy to give in to the temptation to over-tighten a wrap on dysphoric days so it's best to stick with binders that are designed to keep the amount of pressure in a safe range.

PERILOUS PERFORMANCE

Drag kings, actors, and cosplayers are vulnerable to risky binding because often they are not as aware of the risks and the options as gender-expansive people. I usually hear some variation of "a few hours won't hurt, I don't bind every day." This is simply not true.

A tight wrap binder only needs a cough or a sudden twist to crack a rib. And it does not take long for the plastic and adhesives on your skin to cause rashes, blisters, and skin tearing. Considering the activity levels of performance, the risks of rib, skin, and hyperventilation are highest for you.

Make the investment in one properly sized binder for your occasional use. Your body and your fans will thank you.

UTILITY TAPES (E.G., DUCT, PACKING, ETC.)
(This does not refer to kinetic tape, e.g., TransTape.)

You are not made of PVC, plastic, or wiring. Your body is not a busted bumper in need of an extra-strength DIY fix of duct tape. You deserve a softer, more giving touch. The most dangerous tapes used to bind are those made for utilitarian, mechanical purposes. Something designed to bond metal sheeting is not safe for a living organism, but there's more to it than that. The damage is not limited to the skin; it can also interfere with critical bodily functions. The types of harm break down into four categories: skin damage, movement constraint, circulatory restriction, and temperature dysregulation.

Skin Damage

Utility tape is made with adhesives that are not formulated for the skin; the adhesive is toxic to skin when there is sustained contact. A cosplayer I met used duct tape because they didn't think that it would hurt for just a few hours, and their skin erupted in painful blisters that immediately put an end to their Con fun and left them changing bandages for days. Skin will have severe reactions to the adhesive and bond so strongly that when the tape is removed, layers of skin will come with it, leaving raw, painful skin abrasions which are highly vulnerable to infection. Repeatedly removing the tape and abrading the skin can lead to scarring and/or hyperpigmentation.

Constraint of Movement

Since the job of utility tape is to bond inanimate objects to one another so that they don't move, it is designed to have no elasticity. Our bodies are designed to move, so when non-elastic tape is applied to the chest, we've got a problem. The restriction distorts the body's shape and the strain causes misalignment of the rib cage, shoulder blades, collarbones, and sternum. Immobilizing just a few of the 12 pairs of ribs puts them at a much higher risk of bruising, displacement, dislocation, and cracking. In my anecdotal research for this book, the most severe rib fractures occurred with the use of utility tape.

A tape wrap exerts a significant amount of compression onto a few ribs which stops those ribs from moving as you breathe, twist, lift, and reach. This limitation on breathing is illustrated by one of the most life-threatening cases that I have heard in my career. An eleven-year-old non-binary kid desperate with dysphoria used duct tape to tightly wrap their chest. Within minutes they were lightheaded with purple discoloration in their face and then they collapsed before they were able to remove it. Thankfully, someone was nearby to quickly cut them out of the binder, otherwise things could have ended tragically.

Restriction of Blood and Lymph Flow

When utility tape is bonded with the skin for hours, it acts like a dam preventing the tiny vessels under the skin from passing fluids which, in turn, prevents the delivery of vital resources to other parts of your body. This can cause fluid build-up and can trigger the body's inflammatory response, causing painful swelling.

Temperature Regulation

Since utility tape is non-porous and non-breathable, it prevents sweat from evaporating from the skin's surface, allowing sweat to collect under the tape which increases the likelihood of irritation and infection. Sweat evaporation is the body's mechanism for cooling. Preventing the body from properly regulating temperature increases your risk of overheating, heat exhaustion, and heat stroke.

PLASTIC WRAP (E.G., SARAN WRAP)

Leave the plastic wrap for leftovers. Though it does not have irritating adhesive, it still exerts 360-degree pressure around a small section of ribs and inhibits proper movement of the skin, muscles, bones, and cartilage of the torso and traps bacteria-breeding sweat. And if worn for sustained periods, plastic wrap does the same restriction number on your blood and lymph flow that utility tape does.

I know that plastic wrap is used by drag performers and cosplayers who say to me, "I just wear it for a few hours." This is a dangerous myth. A client of mine bound in plastic wrap for a hot, sweaty drag king show and developed a nasty rash that lasted for almost a week. With so many better options, it's simply not worth it—leave it in the kitchen where it belongs.

Euphoria for the Future

I remember when I first became aware of what a binder was and what it could be used for, I could not buy mine fast enough. The second I put mine on for the first time, I felt a rush I can't describe. It's like a real, full-on physical sensation flooded through my body and filled me with a sense of hope, I guess, as corny as that sounds. Like it was the first real glimpse of the person I could become, *would* become. It instantly relieved me of so much internal pain and angst. I felt like the heaviness of the weight bearing down on my chest just lifted and dissipated almost. I felt like I finally found my confidence when I started binding. It finally allowed me to see myself in a body that looked more like the one in my mind and it was super empowering and liberating.

– *G, 52, Washington, DC, USA*

MEDICAL TAPE (PAPER, CLOTH, OR SPORTS TAPE)

(This does not refer to kinetic tape, e.g., TransTape.)

Medical tape is cloth or paper tape most often used in healthcare settings and not a safe material to use for binding. Although tested and safe for use on the body, adhesives in medical tape still irritate many people's skin if worn too long. As with utility tapes, the cinching of a specific section of the rib cage can cause dangerous outcomes: damaged ribs, limited breathing, distortion of the rib cage, and chronic pain. The exception is kinetic tape. Primarily used in physical therapy, kinetic tape has been developed to adhere safely to the skin for days with limited skin irritation and unimpeded lymph flow. This tape can be safely used to bind and offers an exciting no-compression binding alternative. Kinetic tape binding is *not* a wrap method. Kinetic tape is never applied *around* the rib cage (for more about the use of kinetic tape for binding see page 65).

Post-Surgical Binders

Post-surgical binders are made to be worn after top surgery—and that's it. They are extremely tight to prevent post-surgical swelling and strain on the incisions which can be caused by movement. They are safe during recovery because it's a limited time of limited activity. Everyday wear impairs breathing, compresses and sometimes displaces ribs, and irritates the skin—all compelling reasons to never use them as a substitute for a commercially made binder. Many of your friends may be getting top surgery and have surgical binders to pass along. Be smart and turn it down. And, to help keep your community safe, encourage friends to throw away their post-op binders after recovery so that they don't put another person at risk.

Layering Binders

While it may be tempting to layer compression garments to achieve a flatter appearance, a single binder is already as much compression as is recommended. Layering binders with additional binders or sports bras exerts more compression than your body is designed to safely absorb. Many clients that I see with long-term chronic pain have bound with two or three binders for long periods of time. The majority of them have large chests, and as a large-chested human myself, I understand. Still, I urge you to resist the urge. Instead, wear a single binder and wear dark colors, heavy fabrics, and boxier shirts that hide tissue pushed to the armpit, and cultivate a style that flatters a barrel-chested physique.

I hear the myth online that layering a sports bra and a binder is OK. To the contrary, it's worse than layering two binders because the sports bra gathers the chest tissue to the center of the chest (hello uni-boob), and then, by compressing the entire mass of chest tissue inward, the binder depresses the sternum with greater force. This sets a person up for costo-chondritis, painful inflammation of cartilage along the sternum.

The risk of negative health outcomes from binding increases when you double or triple up binding methods. Bruised ribs and bruised chest tissue may sound less serious than some of the other injuries but they can be plenty disruptive to your life. A person came to one of my classes looking for relief from rib, back, neck, and chest tissue pain after having worn three binders for only two days. The intense pain was preventing him from taking anything more than a shallow breath. Unfortunately, there were no exercises to relieve the bruised tissue—only rest and anti-inflammatory medications could help. We kept in touch and eventually, the bruising healed and he could focus on exercises to relieve the muscles along his spine that were strained by the binding. He avoided lasting injury but if he'd made a daily habit of triple binding, he probably would not have been so lucky.

It can be hard to hear so much about what not to do. As I finish writing this section, I even feel the doomsday energy taking me over. But the risks are far from the whole story. We must learn about them to keep ourselves safe, but then we need to move on to the exciting prospect of finding the right binder to support us on our journeys toward feeling fully ourselves in the world.

Euphoria in a Button-down

I was a "late bloomer," as some may say. I fought hard to accept myself for years, but I turned 33 before I was finally able to put it into words: I'm a man. I was, unfortunately, well-endowed in the chest and, while it made my "woman" costume very convincing, it made reality less visible to the outside world. Wearing a pronoun pin didn't stop people from seeing a woman. I could have worn a sign and I felt no one would ever see Me.

When I put on my first binder, it was like a magic trick: under a slightly loose button-up, it really made me *look...* right. Who knew that flattening your chest could make button-ups usable?! The first picture of me in one is all smiles, with my eyes downward. I could see my feet. While standing. Without having to use my hands to press in and without having to lean forward. I realized then how impactful it was to have grown these body parts.

I looked in mirrors and photos and I saw myself: the man that's been wearing those costumes for all those years. Finally, I could see him. Finally, the world might see him, too.

– M, 37, North Carolina, USA

Healthy Binder Choices

It shouldn't physically hurt to express your gender. You deserve a binder that is comfortable and provides satisfaction with your chest appearance. For that you need to know your needs and your options. Whether this is your first binder or you have been binding for years, I bet you don't know all the available features of binders. This section focuses on choosing the binder, or binders, that meet(s) your needs. Knowing the differences may be the key to staying engaged in activities that matter to you.

Assessing Your Binder Needs

Choosing a binder today is nothing like it was just 10 years ago; there are many excellent options of commercially made binders, and new innovations are happening all the time! Most of the people I talk to are unaware of the range of options and have no idea if they are wearing the binder best suited to their body, lifestyle, and priorities.

In order to make the best binder choice, you need two to know two things:

- What your unique needs are
- What features and styles are available.

Before reading any further, take inventory of your personal priorities. Knowing this information will help you narrow the field of options and make it easier to compare binder options in the next section. Taking time to do this now can prevent decision fatigue as well as spending time and money on the wrong garment.

WHAT ARE MY PRIORITIES?

Rank the importance of the following 10 factors in your binder selection:

- ☐ Accommodating a large chest
- ☐ Affordability
- ☐ Breathability of the fabric
- ☐ Colors and patterns
- ☐ Compressing your belly as well as your chest
- ☐ Custom designs to accommodate body type/disability/pain condition
- ☐ Easy entry/exit (Velcro, hooks, zipper)
- ☐ Ethical business practices
- ☐ Matching skin color
- ☐ Waterproof
- ☐ Working out and/or playing sports

Think about the last time you shopped for shoes. You knew what kind of shoe you were looking for, right? You knew what activities you planned to do in the shoe: work out, dress up, get down, or go to the beach. You knew your size and likely had some clue about your foot width and arch height. Style definitely matters so you probably had a specific look in mind. And, whether we are disciplined enough to stick to it or not, we know our price range. (Ahem, I might have a bit of a shoe-buying problem.)

Why should finding the right binder(s) be any different? Until about a decade ago, binder shopping was like going to a shoe store with a single sneaker that came in either black or white, high-top or low-top. How limiting! (I could never abide by such limited options.)

Choosing the right binder can feel overwhelming, but since you're likely to spend a *lot* of time in it, it's worth the time to find a good match. And while there's no giant emporium of binders to shop in, there are options and there's no excuse not to investigate them all. You can assemble a binder collection as tailored to your life and your style as your shoe collection.

Features and Styles

Consult the brand comparison chart at www.healthybinding.com for up-to-date information about which brands offer which of the following features.

TYPE OF COMPRESSION

There are three basic ways of achieving compression in a binder:

- **Full-elastic compression:** A garment that uses strong elastic fabric to squeeze the chest tissue into a flatter profile. Panels A and C are made of equally strong elastic fabric and panel B is not present.
- **Non-elastic compression panel:** A garment that uses a combination of an elastic fabric and a non-stretchable fabric panel across the chest section to flatten the tissue by pressing it against the rib cage behind the panel. Panels A and C are made of elastic fabric which varies in strength and panel B is made of a non-elastic fabric such as canvas.

- **Less restrictive rear panel:** A garment where panel C is made of a less restrictive fabric which allows for more "give" in the front of your rib cage regardless of the type of compression (elastic or non-elastic) used on the front.
- **Kinetic tape (no compression):** A non-garment form of binding that uses body-safe tape applied over the chest tissue and never around the torso to displace the tissue into the armpits to create a flatter profile.

By Trans, For Trans: Amor Binders

Andy (owner and designer) had a vision to be the change they wanted to see, by designing chest binders that would be inclusive, accessible, comfortable, gender-affirming, and fun. Driven by a dream to turn dysphoria into euphoria, in 2018 the label Amor Binders was born.

– Amor Binders

GARMENT STYLE

In response to the vast diversity in the trans and non-binary community, binding companies are constantly innovating to create access for more bodies. Here's what's currently available as of publication. Check www.healthybinding.com for up-to-date information.

- **Half-length tank binders** are shaped like a form-fitting crop-top tank and cover the torso roughly from the shoulders to just below the chest tissue.
- **Full-length tank binders** are shaped like a form-fitting tank top, covering the torso roughly from shoulders to navel. This style provides some abdominal/belly compression.
- **Over-the-hip tanks** are shaped like a form-fitting tank top, covering the full torso. This style provides more abdominal/belly compression and is long enough to be tucked into pants. These may be called "full length" in some brands.
- **Racerback tank binders** are like a form-fitting tank top with a Y-shaped back panel cut so the shoulder blades are uncovered, for greater shoulder range of motion.

- **Strapless binders** are shaped like a form-fitting tube top, leaving the shoulders entirely uncovered. This style provides an alternative for people who cannot wear binders with shoulder straps for health or body-type reasons. (Strapless styles are technically wrap binders, so for safety purposes, they must be made of a less compressive fabric. Heavily compressive strapless binders should be avoided.)

- **Thin-strap binders** are shaped like a form-fitting tank top with thinner shoulder straps than average tank-style binders. Compression is generally light to moderate in this style.

- **Femme-styled binders** are binders that cater to femme-identified people who bind (yes, that is absolutely a thing!): this can be a combination of thin straps, necklines, and fabrics, or from Shapeshifters, a binder dress which combines a tank on top with a flared skirt.

- **V-neck binders** are shaped like a tank top with a V-shaped neckline. This neckline is less visible under shirts, especially button-downs.

- **High-compression sports bras** are form-fitting sports bras without cups, padding, or curved seams. These are cut to allow more room for chest tissue than binders but discourage chest tissue from having the rounded profile common in regular sports bras.

- **Mesh-back binders** have a back panel made of a highly breathable mesh fabric designed to allow more air to reach the skin for more sweat evaporation.

- **Water-safe binding methods** are made of fabric or kinetic tape that can withstand the extra wear and tear associated with getting wet. Read the fine print about whether it is safe for chlorinated and saltwater and follow the care instructions so that the elastic doesn't break down too quickly.

- **Binding swimsuits** are tank-style swim tops, rashguard-style swim tops, and one-piece gender-neutral swimsuits which are designed specifically for use as a swimsuit and suitable for all wet uses.

- **Custom-designed binders** are made to a variety of specifications, including shape, degree of compression, strap style, type and location of closures, fabric choices, and more.

By Trans, For Trans: Origami Customs

As a non-binary person, I saw the need for customized gender gear in my community. I didn't feel comfortable buying factory-made garments, so in 2014, I decided to expand my line of swimwear and underthings to include gender-affirming gear, like binders.

– Rae Hill of Origami Customs

METHOD OF ENTRY

Getting in and out of binders is challenging and can present additional challenges for people with range-of-motion or strength limitations. Fortunately, there are multiple styles to accommodate body types:

- **Pullovers** are designed without any clasps, zippers, or Velcro to be pulled over the head or stepped into.
- **Side-closure binders** enable a quick release to take "binder breaks" during the day and are recommended for people who bind for more than eight hours, bind in hot conditions, or have frequent asthma or panic attacks.
  - **Hook and eye clasps** open on the side for easier entry and close under the armpit with a row of clasps like the ones used in traditional rear-clasp bras.
  - **Velcro** opens on the side for easier entry and closes using a strip of Velcro under the armpit. The Velcro section is limited and does not allow for overwrapping the chest.
  - **Zipper** that opens under the armpit.
- **Front closure binders** with a zipper, Velcro, or clasps open in the center of the chest for easier entry and quick release. They are recommended for people who find it difficult to reach the underarm closures because of ability or body type.
- **Custom-designed binders** allow the wearer to specify the location and type of closure. The custom approach is especially good for people with mobility and range-of-motion limitations, stroke survivors, and those with arthritic conditions.
- **Kinetic tape binding** doesn't have a closure because it is applied directly to the skin. Kinetic tape method is excellent for anyone

wanting a no-compression method, especially musicians needing full breath capacity for performance and athletes engaged in cardio activities. To apply tape, you'll need full range of motion in your upper body or assistance for optimal results.

By Trans, For Trans: Shapeshifters

[When] I came out in 2012, the available binder options were either Underworks or sketchy overseas sources labeled For Lesbians. The color options were black, dirty white, or ugly beige, and the size options were S, M, L, or XL. I was between sizes and I knew how to sew spandex, so I made my own. And then it didn't quite work, so I made three more... By the time I started the official store in 2014, people all over the gender spectrum were hungry for binders that both fit them and looked good.

– Eli, co-owner of Shapeshifters

COLOR

How open each person chooses to be about their trans or non-binary identity is a personal decision. Some people want to show off their binder, and others bind for discretion. The industry is creatively offering options for people to either minimize or maximize the visibility of their binder. If style is what you want, you don't have to sacrifice your personal style to find a binder that meets your needs. To keep your binder hidden, several brands are committed to an ever-increasing spectrum of skin colors.

Color and Pattern Selections

- **Black and/or white.**
- **Skin-tone options** have grades of skin tones (between four and seven shades, depending on the company). If you're looking to minimize visibility of binders through or peeking out of clothes or want to wear a binder in shirtless situations, this is a great choice.
- **Solid-colored fabrics** in colors such as gray, red, purple, and green. If you'd like your binder to be visible (or semi-visible), a part of your attire, and/or need a color match so the binder blends in with formal outfits, this is your go-to.

- **Patterned fabrics** add flair and range from Pride designs to mer-person scales to superhero themes. A great way to celebrate your personality through your binder.
- **Designed-to-order fabric** is made on demand with a person's custom design. Special event? Cosplay? The sky's the limit!

By Trans, For Trans: B.UR.SLF Binders

Elliott (co-owner and designer) is trans masculine and a cosplayer. He realized that a comfortable breathable chest binder would be a benefit to the LGBTQIA+ community *and* the cosplay community of chest binder wearers... [They tested] the idea out with a group of trans masculine boys from local medical adolescent gender-confirmation programs. The panel gave great feedback, we found a manufacturer, scaled-up, started a website and went to market. We have a great group of followers who really understand and appreciate the benefit points and style of the B.UR.SLF Breathable Binders.

– B.UR.SLF Binders

MORE FEATURES

Innovations are born out of the personal experience of designers and the company's response to needs arising in the community. They will continue to create new solutions as the industry grows, but for now, here's what's out there:

- **Sensory-friendly binders** are designed without bulky internal seams, scratchy labels, rough fabric, or tight elastic. This creates greater access for people with sensory processing disorder, autism, or sensitive skin.
- **Breathable mesh binders** use a thin elastic mesh where other binders have spandex panels and are designed to be more breathable and allow for more sweat evaporation. This is beneficial for people in warm climates or who work outside or in hot settings, such as restaurants or landscaping.
- **Binders with silicone tape** use a rubbery edge on the bottom hem to prevent the bottom edge of the binder from rolling up which can

be uncomfortable. Also, when compressive fabric rolls up around the bottom of the rib cage, it intensifies pressure and increases the chance of rib displacement. This is especially problematic for people with belly rolls.

- **Differently sized arm openings** in binders can reduce irritation and bulging in the armpit.
  - **Larger armholes** can be a good option for people with large chests or upper arms for whom binders either chafe the skin or don't leave enough room for displaced tissue. Since chest tissue is displaced in different ways based on chest size, density, and personal preference, this feature doesn't solve bulging problems for everyone.
  - **Smaller armholes** are offered in sports bras with armholes cut close to the arms in the front to avoid side bulge or "side-boob."
- **High-neckline sports bras** avoid the appearance of cleavage.
- **Low-pressure shoulder straps** reduce pressure on neck and shoulder muscles with low-elasticity fabric on the shoulder straps. Individuals with migraines, temporomandibular joint disorder (TMJD), and chronic headaches should wear binders with this type of shoulder strap. Most, but not all, binder companies use low-elasticity shoulder straps.
- **Accessible sizing** designs include sizes ranging from XXS to 6XL. Reference the binder comparison chart at www.healthybinding. com to find which companies make a binder fit for your body.

By Trans, For Trans: TransTape

TransTape was created in 2016, when Kaiyote, at the age of 35, discovered and accepted that he was transgender... Like most trans men, he instantly purchased a "traditional" binder... [and] he felt more like himself but was very uncomfortable, especially in the New England heat and humidity. He knew there needed to be a better alternative to the classic binding technique which leaves most people overheated, feeling restricted and on a time limit of eight hours of use. He remembered a kinetic tape that the chiropractor used on him and that lasted a week before needing to be removed... [After experimenting to find a technique,] he knew he needed to share this [method of binding]... that allows for a full range of motion, with no restriction or compression, that was waterproof and able to be worn in the shower, ocean, and pools. TransTape has been providing [people in] the community with freedom to... transform [their] bod[y] and ease gender dysphoria while allowing them to find comfort in their skin for days on end.

– TransTape

Kinetic Tape (e.g., TransTape)

An innovative alternative to compression garments became commercially available in 2017. The company TransTape developed a method of applying kinetic tape to compress the chest tissue in an entirely new way. Kinetic tape is primarily used by physical therapists, chiropractors, and athletic trainers to aid in muscle function and recovery. It's made of 95 percent cotton and 5 percent spandex with a latex-free, hypoallergenic, medical-grade adhesive. It is waterproof and can be worn in the shower, the pool, and the ocean. Results vary, but some people wear the same application for three to four days. Unlike utility tapes or medical tape mentioned earlier in the chapter, kinetic tape is made for long-term use on the skin and does not obstruct fluids under the skin.

It is never to be used to wrap around the chest. The elastic design of the tape allows you to adhere to the tape in the center of the chest, pull the tape and chest tissue towards the armpit, and secure it. This leaves a flatter contour on the front of the chest, creating a silhouette under clothing that works nicely for many people. However, no two chests are alike so expect to experiment.

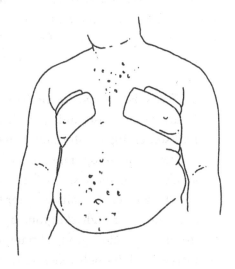

There is an "art" to taping your chest, but with tutorial videos and patience, chests of all shapes and sizes can be bound with kinetic tape. Be aware that applying the tape requires upper body mobility and a good deal of practice. Kinetic tape can be purchased from many vendors but I recommend the products and extensive instructional resources produced by the trans-owned company TransTape.

Binding with kinetic tape to exercise is completely safe for the ribs, lungs, spine, and shoulders, though, depending on the size and shape of your body, it may not provide enough support to be worn while exercising without adding an athletic compression shirt to provide extra support. Singers and musicians, who rely on full lung capacity to perform, often prefer kinetic tape because lung capacity is unaffected. For the same reason, kinetic tape can also be a good alternative for people with disabilities, medical conditions, or chronic pain for whom any compression garment causes pain.

Serious skin injury is the primary risk with the tape binding method. You must follow the instructions carefully to avoid skin damage. The tape must always be removed by saturating it with oil to prevent abrasions to the skin. A skincare routine and off-days to allow skin to recover are key to successful long-term use (see page 100 to learn more about skincare). When any skin irritation occurs, you must allow the skin to recover fully before reapplying tape to avoid skin infections.

Kinetic tape is a disposable product, so keep your finances in mind when exploring this option because you'll have to continually restock. If tape is your primary method of binding and you bind on a regular basis, this can get pricey.

By Trans, For Trans: Flavnt Streetwear

Courtney, our co-founder, saw her twin brother, Chris, struggling to find something comfortable to wear specifically in the summertime in Texas as a pre-op transgender man—and posed the question "why aren't binders more subtle?" From there we decided to make the silhouette a racerback, allowing for less coverage but still functionality, and a range of nude skin tone options to create something discreet... the input of a close group of trans masculine folks who beta-tested prototypes, and through a Kickstarter campaign we gathered the feedback of over 700 backers to help create the size range, color choices, and other creative decisions regarding the original Bareskin Binder.

– Flavnt Streetwear

Sports Bra

What's the difference between a compression sports bra and a binder? Basically, a sports bra leaves room for breast tissue and a binder doesn't. The more compressive the sports bra is, the less room it leaves for the tissue. A high-compression sports bra can be very effective in flattening the chest. But, before you go stocking up on sports bras, consider the pros and cons of this option.

Worn correctly, sports bras don't put as much strain on the lungs because the tissue is not pressed into the sternum and rib cage with the same force as a binder. Since the garment is designed and tested for athletic activity, it's safe for cardio, lifting, and playing sports. But, beware, binding with a sports bra that is too small can cause most of the same kinds of chronic pain and breathing restrictions as a binder, though long-term injury is less likely. Signs that your sports bra is too tight are similar to those experienced with binders: difficulty taking a deep breath, marks or divots on the shoulders, and irritation to the skin around the armholes.

If you are in a power struggle with a parent, spouse, or medical professional over your desire to bind, sports bras are less controversial to people opposed to binding and may be easier for you to acquire. It may not completely alleviate dysphoria but if it's the binding method accessible to you, it can be a lifesaver until your circumstances change.

Finding a sports bra to compress and flatten your chest requires being a savvy shopper.

- When looking online, search these terms:
    - "High compression" + "sports bra"
    - "No cups" + "sports bra"
    - "No pads/padding" + "sports bra"
    - "Minimizing" + "sports bra"
    - "High neck" + "sports bra"
    - "Removable inserts" + "sports bra."

- Shop on high-intensity sport sites for cycling, rock climbing, running.
- Look for elastic content above 20 percent (spandex, elastane, Lycra®).
- Zoom in on product images to look for center seams or rounded seams designed to encourage a cup shape.

Strenuous activities such as team sports, lifting weights, cardio activities, or physical labor often occur in highly gendered environments so the desire to bind may be more intense. But the right sports bra can be the safest option and still provide a moderately flat contour (see Chapter 4 for more information about binding while exercising). Over your sports bra, consider wearing a compression shirt (see page 70). Wearing a thick, dark-colored T-shirt can help to hide the appearance of chest tissue, but be careful about staying cool and hydrated when you add clothing layers.

Tight sports bras can exert more pressure and dig into muscles on the tops of the shoulders because the straps are generally made of the same powerful elastic fabric as the rest of the garment. The straps' pressure on the shoulder muscles can trigger migraines, TMJD pain, and tension headaches. Many binders use a less compressive fabric for the straps and may be a better choice for people with these conditions.

Doubling up sports bras does not pose all of the same dangers as layering binders but there are still risks so it should still be done carefully, if at all. It's important to layer sports bras that are constructed differently; this will increase the effectiveness of the flattening by compressing in different directions. It's crucial to find two where the underbust elastic bands do not overlap, otherwise it will effectively create a 360-degree elastic wrap around a small section of the rib cage. For a refresher on why this needs to be avoided, revisit the wrap binder section on page 45. Layering carelessly can cause irritated skin, bruised ribs, and painful trigger points between the ribs.

Combining a sports bra and a binder is counter-productive because the bra will encourage the chest tissue to the middle, forming the dreaded "uni-boob." When smushed together, the tissue doesn't compress as effectively. The combination of the two garments applies more pressure at the sternum which can cause inflammation. I recommend owning binders and sports bras for different activities but picking a single method to wear at a time.

It is best to stick with one sports bra, but when layering is needed, here are some strategies for doing it safely and effectively:

- Do not layer more than two sports bras.
- Wear differently shaped sports bras to allow the elastic bands and shoulder straps to sit in different places.
- To prevent "uni-boob" as much as possible, combine two sports bras with elastic panels that cover different areas.
- Wear one bra forward and one backward. This takes some experimentation. Trying them on in the store is strongly recommended.

Small-chested people can often achieve a satisfying chest contour in a high-compression sports bra. Large-chested people are often dissatisfied with their appearance. Common complaints are that the tissue is pushed to the front of the body, the tissue bulges out the side or top of the sports bra, and the sports bra creates visible cleavage. Correctly sized traditional binders are often the better choice if you experience these results.

Since sports bras are the best option for cardio, weightlifting, and contact sport activities, it's a good idea to find one that works well enough for you. If you are having a hard time finding one because of your chest size, check out companies catering to gender non-conforming people and gender-neutral attire as many have designed products to address these complaints. Also consider compression tops, described in the next section, which offer more room for displacing chest tissue than a sports bra but less compression than a binder. Up-to-date suggestions of these models and companies are available on www.healthybinding.com.

The science isn't there yet to tell us if safe binding methods have any lasting impact on rib cage development. So a well-chosen sports bra may be a good option if your bones are still developing and you are concerned that they may be more susceptible to compression. If asthma, a heart condition, anxiety disorder, disabilities, or another medical condition make binder-style chest compression too stressful on your body, a sports bra may be a good alternative for you.

Sports bras are a great way to give your body some relief on off-days when you're at home and the need for publicly expressing your gender is lower (I understand fully that being alone does not make dysphoria stop). Sports bras can hold the tissue firmly in place while giving your rib cage some rest. A sports bra for this purpose should not be overly tight, and off-days are not a time to double up. If you bind for work and school, consider sports bras for weekends and evening activities. If it's your style to wear baggy clothes, consider outfits where a sports bra will give you a sufficient flat contour. If you live in a cold climate, consider switching to sports bras when clothes and coats make your chest contour less visible. Every day out of a binder is a day for your body to rest and recover. Swapping in a sports bra occasionally gives you the resilience to bind healthily on other days. Your future self will thank you. (Read more about the importance of off-days on page 84).

Euphoria from Other Methods

I am always trying new ways to manage my chest. Lately, I've been wearing bra tops that minimize rather than highlight my chest because even when I am binding, I don't feel like I have a flat chest physique. So I've stopped searching for the right binder and have been trying to just minimize however I can. Even though there is no pretense that I have a flat chest, this is the closest I have seen my shape to how I wish I could look.

– *S, 54, Pennsylvania,* USA

Athletic Compression Shirts

Clothing-industry language is far from universal so "compression shirt" refers to multiple types of garments. It can get confusing because some brands use similar terminology to mean full-strength binders. This section discusses the ubiquitous tight-fitting compression shirts from major athletic-apparel companies. They have the elasticity of a strong swimsuit fabric and fit close to the body. Compression shirts come in many cuts and styles and vary in degrees of tightness in the elasticity. Do your research and look at the fabric specifications for 15–20 percent elastane/spandex/Lycra®.

Keep a few athletic compression shirts around for when:

- you are taking a break from the binder and need help to minimize your dysphoria
- you are wearing a sports bra for athletic activity and you need to add extra compression for smoother contours
- you only need light compression.

Compression Tops

A term that's appearing more in the market is "compression top" which refers to a garment that is more than a sports bra and less than a binder. They are similar to full elastic compression binders explained earlier in the "Healthy Binder Choices" section. They do not have a panel of non-elastic fabric but they are designed for assigned female at birth (AFAB) humans, unlike many of the full elastic options that are designed for cis men. Therefore, they are cut to allow more space for chest tissue like a sports bra. If you've ever worn a swimsuit for competitive swimming, the degree of elastic will feel more similar to that than to a sports bra. It will not tax your body in quite the same way since the tissue is not being pressed into the center of the chest with the same force as a binder. Compression tops may be a better choice for strenuous activity but it's just as important to follow sizing guidelines as it is with binders. A compression top that is too small can impede full expansion of the rib cage and apply stress to the shoulder muscles with tight straps.

By Trans, For Trans: PeeCock Products

[Binders] are the first essential need for every FTM [female to male] guy's transition journey and there were limited choices at very high price. [So,] 10 years ago we decided to make our own collection and started to sell them at reasonable prices.

– *PeeCock Products*

Correct Sizing

Reputable companies have done their part by wear-testing their products and providing clear sizing guidelines on their websites, but you have to make the choice to follow the guidance. Each company sizes its binders differently, so never assume that a large in one brand is a large in another. Always reference the sizing guide for each company individually before ordering.

Even if you do your homework and think that you have the correct size, it's important to know the following signs that you have a binder that is too small or a poor fit for your body type:

- **Shallow breathing:** You may have difficulty breathing when you first put on a new binder. The right-sized binder will feel tight (especially when new), but you should be able to take a deep breath. You *are* wearing a compression garment—so your breath in your binder will not be as deep as without one, but it should not be noticeably shallow. If it is hard to breathe, your binder is too small. Take it off immediately and contact the company to exchange for the correct size.
- **Red marks:** If your binder leaves red marks on your skin along the arm and neck seam lines, it is probably too small. It is possible that it is the recommended size but the design of that binder is ill-suited to your body.
- **Indentations:** If the shoulder straps dig into your shoulders and when you take it off you can see indentations, this is a sign that the binder isn't a good fit. Often this is the result of purchasing one smaller than your measurements but it can also mean that the design doesn't suit your body's size and shape. Since this kind of pressure into your shoulder muscles can cause headaches, it is worth finding a better fit by either returning it for a larger size or checking out other companies' products. Custom binder companies like Origami Customs and Shapeshifters are excellent options if you need something made to fit.

- **Hunching:** If putting a binder on pulls you into a hunched position where your shoulders are more bowed than they were before you put it on, it is too small. Wearing this binder will increase your risk of developing chronic pain in your ribs, chest, shoulders, and neck. It's best to take your measurements and return it for the correct size.

Growth and Change

It is important to measure yourself periodically. Anything altering your body shape—a growth spurt, fluctuation in your weight, dieting, menopause, bulking up at the gym, taking testosterone—warrants remeasuring. I recommend measuring every one to two months—or whenever the binder starts fitting differently. Write down your measurements, so you can discern if your body is changing or if your binder is losing its shape. If it's worn out, replace it. This also helps track when your body predictably fluctuates between two sizes with seasons, and having binders in both sizes means you always have a correctly fitted binder on hand.

Before you consult the sizing charts, you'll need to know your measurements. They are not difficult to take but not everyone is familiar with the process, so here is a detailed breakdown of how and what to measure.

By Trans, For Trans: For Them

As a queer, non-binary human-being, I saw thousands of companies focusing on products and services that did not speak to my experience. Wellness looks different for everyone. For Them understands and celebrates that.

– Kylo Freeman, For Them

How to Take Measurements

A cloth measuring tape and a trusted assistant is the easiest way to take your measurements. However, if you don't have one, a string and a ruler make a suitable substitute. Wrap the string around your body and mark where it comes together. Use the ruler to measure the length of the string.

If you can, enlist a trusted person to help. It's easier and generally makes for more accurate measurements. If not, make sure that you have a mirror that shows your entire torso, which will help you ensure that you are keeping the tape or string level and taut.

Tips for accurate measuring:

- Do not wear a binder, bra, or compression of any kind.
- Do not wear bulky clothing; instead wear no clothing or a thin T-shirt.
- Keep the tape or string taut, but not tight, around your body.
- Keep the tape or string parallel to the ground all the way around your body.
- Use the mirror to ensure the correct position of the tape on your body.

The brands discussed in this book ask for different measurements but there are only six measurements that could be needed. Follow these instructions to measure properly.

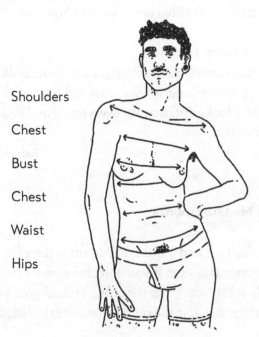

Shoulders

Chest

Bust

Chest

Waist

Hips

- **Chest or underarm:** This measures the circumference of your rib cage just above the chest tissue.

    1. Place the tape/string at the top of the armpit.
    2. Wrap it around the body, keeping it level all the way around.
    3. Record the measurement where the ends of the tape/string meet.

Tip: When measuring yourself, get the tape in place and drop your arms to hold the tape securely while you read the measurement.

- **Widest part of your chest or "bust":** This measures the circumference of the tissue that your binder will be compressing, so accuracy here is crucial to your comfort.

    1. Lift the chest tissue up so that it is level and not hanging down.
    2. Hold it in this position.
    3. Loosely wrap the tape around the widest part.
    4. Inhale a normal-sized breath and tighten the tape/string but *do not* cinch the tissue. There should be no bulging tissue on either side of the tape/string.
    5. Record the measurement where the ends of the tape/string meet, then exhale.

Tip: If you have chest tissue that hangs down, you may find it difficult to hold the tissue in place and wrap the tape or string without a person to assist.

- **Ribs or "underbust":** This measures the circumference of your rib cage just below your chest tissue.

    1. Lift your chest tissue up and out of the way.
    2. Wrap the tape where the underwire of a bra would go, keeping the tape close to the fold where your chest tissue meets your rib cage.
    3. Inhale normally.

    4. Record the measurement where the ends of the tape/string meet.

    5. Exhale.

- **Shoulder width:** This measures the broadness of your shoulders.

  1. Measure from one shoulder, across the chest, to the other shoulder without wrapping around the body.
  2. Check the mirror to ensure the tape/string is level.
  3. Record the measurement.

- **Waist:** To find the actual waist, bend to the side and notice where the body naturally creases or smushes an existing fold of your belly.

  1. Standing upright, wrap the tape/string around your body at your waist.
  2. Check the mirror to ensure the tape/string is level.
  3. Record the measurement where the ends of the tape/string meet.

- **Length:** This is for choosing the length of custom binders.

  1. Hold the tape at the top of your shoulder and allow it to hang to the floor.
  2. Record the measurement where you want to the binder to end.

By Trans, For Trans: gc2b

Founded in 2015, gc2b is a trans-owned company based in Maryland. gc2b's founder, CEO, and designer, Marli Washington, saw that the only binding options were uncomfortable and inadequate compression shirts designed for cis men. As a University of the Arts Industrial Design graduate, he used his experience in product design and his background in textiles to provide accessible, comfortable, and safe binding options designed by trans people, for trans people.

– gc2b

Donation Programs

Limited finances should not be the reason that anyone is unable to fully express their gender in daily life. Too often that is the reason that people resort to unsafe binding methods. For young people living at home, unsupportive family members may also be a barrier to acquiring a binder. Binder companies, amazing non-profits, and inspired individuals are trying to prevent that by operating binder donation programs. Donation programs and LGBTQIA+ organizations generally offer binders without parental participation and ship them in discreet packaging.

The largest organization currently distributing binders is Point of Pride which can be found at www.pointofpride.org. They partner with gc2b for their donations which they distribute free of charge worldwide. They are volunteer-run and receive thousands of requests per month so there is generally a wait time between applying and receiving your binder.

Binder donation programs are disproportionately located in the USA, Canada, and the UK, but many of the larger organizations ship internationally. Check www.healthybinding.com for an updated list of programs and contact us if you know of a resource for binder donations that should be listed.

By Trans, For Trans: Urbody

Back in 2012, when I started binding, there were very few options available... While I did find what I was looking for, it was evident from the website, models, and product descriptions that the designers and intended customers were not queer or trans individuals struggling with gender dysphoria or body dysphoria. They were garments designed on cisgender bodies with cis people's needs in mind.

As a trans non-binary person and licensed therapist who has worked extensively with gender-diverse individuals in community-based organizations and medical settings...I co-founded [Urbody] alongside my longtime friend Anna Graham (she/her), [leveraging] the knowledge and the relationships I have gained over a decade of working in transgender health.

It [is] of utmost importance to us to honor...[community] feedback...

[and to] recognize that some people want the flattest chest possible...
while others [do] not.

– *Mere Abrams, Urbody co-founder*

CHAPTER 3
DAILY PRACTICES

> Before getting top surgery, binding was an essential part of my everyday life. It allowed me to exist in my skin. Binding made even simple things, like walking around my college campus, easier and less scary because of the way my body finally felt congruent to how I imagined myself to be.
>
> – *E, 30, Pennsylvania,* USA

Binding means committing to take care of your body in ways that other folks do not have to. I know that can feel like one more thing that you have to deal with as a TGNC person, but remember that lots of life choices about personal expression come with trade-offs. Think of that femme who wears the perfect heels and stands at the party for hours knowing they'll be off their feet in house shoes the next day to nurse seriously aching feet. And how about people who wear fabulous makeup? They usually have elaborate skincare routines that non-makeup wearers don't bother with. A binder is a tool for your expression and, just like high heels or makeup, when it comes off, you need a routine that supports your ability to wear it again another day.

Throughout the years, I have observed a stark difference between my clients and students who are diligent about self-care exercises, hygiene, and rest... and those who are not. The ones that are committed admit that there's a difference in how they feel when they are keeping up with their routines. Ultimately, I see less of those clients because they don't need me for pain relief anymore.

Far too often, I don't get to meet clients until they're in serious pain or injured. This chapter is for everyone, but it is especially for those new to binding. Let's start with good daily practices and avoid problems down the road.

Time Out Is Time Well Spent

Minimizing the amount of time in your binder is the best advice for your physical health but since we know that a binder holds more significance to us than a regular item of clothing, it can be hard to take it off. I'm going to break down the benefits for you because knowing why always makes it easier for me to do something that's good for me, especially if I don't naturally want to do it. The most important reasons your body needs time outside your binder are muscle recovery, body repair, and sufficient oxygen supply.

Muscle Recovery
Imagine if you put a rubber band around your fingers and then spread your fingers apart against the tension. How many times could you do it before your hand muscles were too weak to continue? Compare that to how many times in a row you could spread your fingers without a rubber band around them.

When in a binder, your muscles have increased resistance to range of motion. Each muscle is working harder than it is designed to, and the result is fatigue. But since you have to keep breathing, holding yourself upright, and using your arms for everyday tasks, these muscles find a way to keep functioning. Coping with that demand can lead to painful trigger points, muscle strains, spasms, or recruiting alternate muscles to do the tired muscles' jobs. Generally with binding, you will feel some fatigue, soreness, and pain; but even if you do not, the binder is still placing an unhealthy demand on those muscles day in and day out.

Breaks from your binder equate to removing the rubber band from your fingers. The muscles will be tired, but they will be able to relax, soften, and move freely. This daily binder-free break is the perfect time to do the stretches and massage essential for keeping these muscles healthy, pain-free, and more resilient when you put your binder back on. Part 2 of this book is designed to help you determine the best self-care routine for you.

Body Repair

The sympathetic state of our nervous systems, known as fight-or-flight, is when your nervous system activates to respond to stress, anxiety, or danger. Humans today spend the majority of the waking hours in the sympathetic state. However, when you rest, sleep, or intentionally calm your body, you enter a parasympathetic state, known as rest-and-digest. This nickname is apt, as the parasympathetic state is the only time your body focuses inward and nurtures its vital systems. Being a human living on this earth causes a lot of wear and tear to the body; humans need time in a parasympathetic state to repair the tax that life literally puts on every cell in the body.

Shallow breathing signals to your nervous system that there is a reason to be in alert mode. In fight-or-flight mode, the nervous system tells the body that it's not safe to rest or repair yet. Binding's impact on breathing patterns can produce this message even if you are feeling relaxed. When you take your binder off and intentionally breathe more deeply, your body gets the signal that it's safe to let down its guard and starts to shift into a parasympathetic state. If you're always in your binder, your body has no choice but to keep going without the repair it needs.

Need more inspiration to relax your body? Sustained periods spent in the sympathetic state can lead to increased anxiety, weight gain, digestive issues, decreased concentration, restless sleep, and emotional regulation.

Sufficient Oxygen

It's no secret that binding makes it harder to breathe and we all know that oxygen is necessary for all functions of life. It follows then that time out of your binder taking fuller breaths that move more oxygen into the bloodstream is a good thing.

When the body is low on a resource, it will always prioritize the most essential functions and organs of survival (heart, lungs, brain), even at the expense of other vital systems. So, time out of your binder is time that these systems can get plenty of nourishing oxygen.

A key part of your healthy routine is intentional deep breathing. Make the most of the time out of your binder by learning and practicing the breathing exercises in Part 2. This added bonus of increasing your oxygen supply shifts your body into a parasympathetic state. Woo hoo—that's more rest-and-digest time!

Euphoric Tears

I cried happy tears when I saw myself in a binder with a black T-shirt on for the first time. I felt like I was seeing the first glimpses of the person I have always wanted to be. I had that warm feeling in the pit of my stomach, the first inkling of the immense euphoria and joy that I would continue to experience presenting as myself in the world. These moments where I feel powerful, feel confident, feel myself, are what fuel me through the hard times and make living as my authentic self worth it.

– Q, 23, *Washington, DC, USA*

How Many Hours Can I Bind?

For this section, "in your binder" means in your full-compression binder. Light-to-moderate compression alternate binding methods are considered "out of your binder."

Short answer: bind for as few hours as possible each day.

In most resources about binding, the recommended guideline is to bind for no more than eight hours per day. In 10 years of specializing in binding-related care, I have never found the origin of this recommendation. My guess is that it was a recommendation based on someone's common-sense estimation.

In 10 years of seeing clients for binding-related pain, I haven't traced any client's chronic pain directly to their average daily time in a binder, but I have seen many clients with problems from long stretches of binding, especially with other factors like heat and physically demanding activities. Let's frame the discussion differently: it's not about a "magic number," it's about balance, with as much off-time as possible and a commitment to self-care routines.

Suggested guidelines:

- Bind for the fewest number of hours possible.
- Switch to low-compression garments to manage dysphoria at home or in safe spaces.
- Avoid pushing yourself beyond 12 hours, except in unsafe circumstances where strangers or acquaintances cannot be trusted to respect your identity.
- Plan to take a 15+ minute break after four to five hours of binding to rest, breathe, and stretch.
- Take an off-day once per week (more on this in the next section).

Being realistic is key to being sustainable. Limiting the hours in a binder can be a serious challenge for people who have 12-hour shifts, long commutes, or 10-hour school days. It is of paramount importance to keep yourself safe physically and emotionally, and it's your job to get creative in structuring and planning your days to give your body the rest it deserves.

At times when you are struggling with severe dysphoria, removing your binder can feel unbearable. If wearing your binder overnight or for long hours keeps you safe from self-harm in a mental health crisis, that supersedes this advice. However, it should only be done until you can get crisis support. If you are in a mental health crisis, tell someone in your life or reach out to www.translifeline.org by phone, text, or chat. Wearing a binder for long hours, during strenuous activities, and overnight cannot be the ongoing solution for dysphoria. Causing serious health issues often means that *you cannot bind at all.* Part of taking care of your mental health is ensuring that you don't lose this life-saving tool from your toolbox. (If you missed it, check out the Introduction where I tell the story of how that happened to me.)

Since home is where you are most easily and safely able to be out of your binder, it's important to maximize the opportunity. If you struggle with wanting to bind even when you are not in public, consider some of the lower-compression alternatives (page 70) that can help with dysphoria and still allow you to take a break.

Science Says... Take a Day Off

There's very little research on the health impacts of binding and, so far, no studies yet that have looked at people's health over time as they bind. In the largest study done to date, 1,800 participants self-reported negative health outcomes of binding. The researchers[1] looked at duration (years spent binding), intensity (hours per day spent binding), and frequency (days per week spent binding). They found that frequency, not intensity or duration, was the factor most associated with negative health outcomes. This means that taking *at least one day off from binding each week* is what the available science tells us is most effective at reducing pain, discomfort, and injury. Binding for the least number of hours at a time is still the recommended practice, but instead of trying to shorten your days for fewer hours in your binder, concentrate your energy on organizing your week to allow for a day off from binding.

Depending on the pace of your life, your off-days may be predictable or they may vary by week. Since your health outcomes really do hinge on your commitment to giving your body rest, it is important to prioritize. If an entire day off is not possible because staying in your house isn't an option, consolidate all essential errands to a couple of hours, and reserve the rest of the day to be binder-free. The next section is full of more strategies to help you think creatively.

Plan Your Week for Relief

Just like the eight-hour rule was someone's best guess and not hard science, the following are suggestions based on 10 years of working with people on how to make binding work for their bodies and their lives. There is nothing magical about these suggestions. The power is the plan and the accountability it provides.

---

1   Peitzmeier, S., Gardner, I., Weinand, J., Corbet, A., and Acevedo, K. (2017) 'Health impact of chest binding among transgender adults: a community-engaged, cross-sectional study.' *Culture, Health & Sexuality* 19, 1, 64–75.

Make a Plan

Examine your average week. Identify situations that absolutely require you to bind and those when it is not essential for you (even if you might *want* to). Designate an off-day (or more than one!) in your week when you will not bind. And then stick to your own rules.

Give Yourself a Visual Reminder

Make a schedule and stick it to the bathroom mirror or put it in your underwear drawer. If you are creative, make art that will inspire you and remind you that you are investing in your future self. If you have limited privacy, remember that only you need to know what it means.

Find an Accountability Partner

Discuss your intentions and struggles to minimize the length of time in your binder with a trusted person in your life. Just like a gym friend or a study partner, this trusted binder-break buddy can keep you honest. Try texting them each day when you take your binder off. Share which day is your off-day and ask them to check in to make sure that you are, indeed, taking the day off from binding.

Create a "Binding Budget"

Determine the number of hours in your average week that absolutely require you to bind, then choose a number of discretionary hours per week. This sets up your "bank" of total hours that you can bind in a week. Block off your off-day and stick to it. Treat your hours just like you would a budgeted amount of money. Just as you would with a spending budget, you can negotiate with yourself about when and how it is most important to you to bind.

Hacks for Reducing Binder Time

Binder Breaks in Public

- Carry a lighter compression option to change into when you leave work or school.

- Wear an oversized coat or sweatshirt to hide your unbound chest on your commute home.
- Take your lunch break in your car or in a private room where you can remove the binder.
- Wear a binder with a hook, zipper, or Velcro closure so you can relieve the pressure without needing to remove your clothing.

Binder-less Around the House
- Wrap up in a blanket or big bathrobe.
- Plan alone time when you won't have the pressure of others seeing you.
- Do low-intensity activities that will distract you while you are taking time off of your binder, like reading, playing video games, or watching a movie.
- Have an off-day buddy, a trusted friend with whom you can be binder-free (bonus: if that friend also binds, you can help each other on your off-days).

Quick Breaks and How to Grab 'Em
- A single-person bathroom where you can remove or loosen the binder, breathe deeply, and do some stretches.
- A stall in a public bathroom (less ideal than a single-person bathroom) where you can remove the binder, breathe deeply, and do some stretches.
- A car where you can remove your binder, cool off, and breathe deeply.
- Make arrangements to use a secure room in your school or workplace where you can take off your binder.
- Wear a binder with a hook, zipper, or Velcro closure so you can take the break without needing to remove your clothing.

A Self-Care Routine You Can Stick To

An ounce of prevention is a pound of cure. This old adage could not be more true regarding binding health. Developing a routine that is as consistent as brushing your teeth is your best chance of avoiding pain from binding. And, if you do end up with acute pain, your body will have an extremely valuable head start at healing the injury, as the muscles, tendons, and cartilage will be as unrestricted as possible and able to support your body's recovery. Think of this preventative routine as an investment in your chances of not *having* to stop binding altogether.

In Part 2 of this book, you will read a lot about fascia. It supports the muscles when the body spends significant time in stressful positions. The by-product of this fascial armoring is constriction and sticky adhesions. As you bind day after day, your body gets the message that it's supposed to hold you in that compressed position. Fascia thickens to make the surface of the muscle more rigid and bonds muscles to surrounding tissue, impeding movement.

The good news is that by consistently doing exercises to thin out the rigidness and unstick the stickiness, you can release that fibrous tissue as it builds up. Muscles moving with ease helps to prevent weakness, strain, spasms, and serious injuries. By contrast, if you are not regularly addressing the fascial tissue, your body builds layers upon layers of strong fascia, making it harder to move with ease. This rigidity makes you susceptible to injury and pain and could mean a lot more time and effort to recover.

If your plan for when to do self-care exercises isn't realistic and sustainable, you won't keep up with it: you need a routine that fits your life. It's up to you—do many exercises at once each day or spread them out throughout the day or week. The important thing is to do them regularly.

Attaching new habits to existing habits or regular activities is one of the best ways to adopt new routines of self-care.

- Do diaphragm and sternum massage when you lie down at night (exercises #4 and 7).
- Do shoulder rotation in the shower (exercise #14).
- Do chin tucks at red lights (exercise #16).
- Do neck mobilization while you make coffee (exercise #18).
- Do pectoralis and serratus anterior massage while you watch TV (exercises #8 and 11).

Things will change in your body too, so set a reminder to scan your body for how your muscles, joints, skin, and breath are feeling in and out of your binder. This is vital, especially if you tend to dissociate from your body enough to ignore pain and discomfort, so you can add exercises to your routine before you develop a more significant problem.

Times that might be good reminders to do a body scan:

- Before a regular therapy appointment
- When you give yourself your testosterone shot
- On your off-day.

Dancing Euphoria

I recently went to a family wedding and I wore my binder along with dress pants and a button-up which was a far cry from the flouncy dress and long hair I wore to the last wedding! I felt *amazing*. I felt so much more able to participate and be my authentic self. I remember at the last wedding, I felt like a wallflower—I was just trying to disappear. I didn't dance, and I kept going to the bathroom to hide. This time, I felt comfortable enough in my body to be out there, talking to my family, and I even danced this time!

– M, 24, Oregon, USA

(Almost) Never Sleep in Your Binder

Sleeping in a binder will hurt. Depending on your age, your health, and the tightness of your binder, you might be mildly sore or in serious discomfort after one night in a binder. Don't let a lack of immediate pain convince you that you are not doing your body harm.

If you are like my clients over the years, you likely want to know *why? What's the harm?*

Sleep is the repair cycle of the body's daily routine. The body prioritizes the actions that enable you to function during your waking hours. It must be able to power down at night and repair the wear and tear of the day. Without this repair process, your tissues are not able to continue working to support you. In tangible terms, tissues that become weak, vulnerable, and function poorly lead to more injuries, chronic pain, autoimmune disorders, weight gain, muscle loss, headaches, and fatigue.

In your sleep, your body establishes a steady breathing cycle free from the things that cause people to breathe shallowly: binders, anxiety, and life's interferences. Quality sleep-breathing activates the diaphragm to take the deepest, most nourishing breath you get all day. And you need it because binding often causes the body to bypass the diaphragm when breathing. Unrestricted breathing enriches the blood with plenty of oxygen which nourishes the body.

Sleep is when the body repairs muscle tissue—an integral part of the muscle building/strengthening cycle. For example, if your goal is to build your pectoralis major muscle, sleeping in a binder post-workout will thwart your efforts. Strengthening muscles includes micro-tearing their fibers and repairing them so that they are stronger and bulkier. Deprive the body of the full cycle of repair, and you work against your own efforts to bulk up muscles or strengthen them for higher athletic performance.

In addition to nourishing the tissues throughout your body, unencumbered breathing helps to stimulate a crucial part of the nervous system: the vagus nerve. This nerve supports digestion, blood pressure, and respiration, and connects to nearly every organ in the body. These connections alone make stimulating the vagus nerve extremely valuable. The vagus nerve carries the messages of fight-or-flight or rest-and-digest to the body, and the deep, slow breathing of sleep stimulates the calming effect which helps the brain to recover from the effects of anxiety and trauma triggers. Given the high incidence of dysphoria, depression, anxiety, and PTSD among TGNC people, the role the vagus nerve plays in calming the nervous system may be the most compelling argument for not sleeping in your binder. If you prevent the body from sending calming messages to the brain while you sleep, you deprive yourself of one of the body's most effective ways to support healthy emotional regulation during your waking hours.

So what do I mean by "*almost never* sleep in your binder"? Your physical safety is the exception to this rule. There are times that taking off your binder could expose your trans identity to people who could hurt or bully you. These should be true exceptions, such as getting stuck sleeping in an airport or traveling with colleagues or classmates and sharing sleeping quarters. During emergencies, you want to find time to take breathing breaks from your binder in bathrooms or other private spaces.

Prevent Roll-Up

In and of themselves, full-length binders are no greater risk to your health than other styles. However, when the bottom of the binder rolls up, the compression exerted inward is multiplied. I have seen bruised or shifted lower ribs from rolled binders. This was a factor in my own experience of a serious binding injury, so take it from me, don't ignore it.

If a full-length binder is your jam but it has a tendency to roll up on you throughout the day, there are some inexpensive products designed to keep shirts tucked in that can do the trick.

- **Shirt garters or stays:** Clips that attach the bottom of your binder to a band around your thighs or to your socks, respectively.
- **Grip tape:** Elastic or fabric band that provides friction between the binder and your skin when sewn to the inside edge of the binder hem.
- **Boxers with clips or elastic bands** to attach to the bottom of your binder.

Ease Into It

Getting your first binder is exciting. Congratulations! Despite the urge to wear it for long hours, it's best to ease into it. Wear it for an hour the first day. Use this time to try on your clothes and celebrate the euphoria of this new element of your gender expression. Gradually add an hour or two each day. You may be frustrated to be binding at home or the grocery store—instead of at work or school—but it's a small sacrifice that allows your body time to acclimate. Not rushing helps you experience less discomfort or pain when you start binding for longer stretches. As you build up time wearing your binder, practice activities you do in your average daily life. If you are a barista, working long hours with your arms extended making beverages, wear it while you cook dinner to allow your body to explore similar sensations. If you will have a long walking commute, go for long walks while acclimating to your binder.

Trapped But Still Euphoric

There is nothing quite like the moment when you are trapped inside your binder, wondering if this is how you're going to die. My chest, "double Ds" that had been compressed all day like fleshy Jack-in-the-boxes, sprang forth the moment the elastic rolled up high enough. That was also the point at which the tube, made of the strongest synthetic materials known to man, constricted itself around my armpits; upper arms pressed tightly against both sides of my head, forearms flopping uselessly in the air, completely unable to see or hear anything happening around me. Luckily I was also completely drenched in sweat (from wearing my binder while merely contemplating activity) so my newly bare skin glistened in the cool air as the dank material pressed moistly against my face.

This was truly the moment I had imagined when I first bought my binder: the euphoric feeling of being constricted and smothered while simultaneously exposed and cold. After the first few times spent bumping into furniture as I flailed around the room attempting to remove the damned thing, I learned that I needed another person who was willing to wrench a compression top upwards while I emerged like a newborn giraffe dropping naked and wet to the ground below. These are the friends who you will remember decades from now, those who were willing to risk the sweaty odors to help extract you from your binder.

– R, 43, Vermont, USA

Getting In and Out of a Binder

Binders can be tricky to get on and off, especially at the beginning, but with practice, you'll figure out the method that works best for you! If you live with a person you trust, ask them for assistance because you will probably get stuck at least a couple of times.

Your skin must be dry to get a binder on. Wet, or even moist, skin will cause friction between the fabric and your skin, and the binder will roll up on itself as you pull it on. If you live in a humid climate, you may need to stand in front of a fan before getting dressed.

Different methods of putting on a binder will work for different body types. Ultimately, you'll find what works for you, but these step-by-step instructions should help you find your strategy:

Over-the-Head Method #1

Tank-style binders can be pulled over the head like a sports bra.

1. Put both arms all the way into the armholes and slide the fabric up towards your shoulders.
2. The fabric should be bunched with no folds or rolls.
3. Pull over your head so that the binder is bunched up (not rolled up) under your armpits and across your chest above the chest tissue.
4. Hook your thumbs under the edge of the binder on the front of your chest and pull the bunched-up fabric down over your chest tissue.
5. Work your thumbs to your armpits and around the side of your body, continuing to pull the bunched fabric down as you go.
6. If any bunched material remains in the center of the back, pull it down by reaching behind your back or get someone's assistance to pull it down.

If reaching behind your back is a challenge, try this: after you put your arms through—but before you put your head through—slip a belt or yoga strap through the head hole so that it hangs over the back panel of the binder. Then, in the last step when you are working the back panel fabric down, you can *tug lightly* on the belt to help work it down. Be gentle so you don't break the stitching around the neckline of the binder.

Over-the-Head Method #2:

1. Put one arm all the way in, and pull the binder over that shoulder.
2. Put your head through the head hole. This tight squeeze won't be comfortable for all body types.
3. Be sure that the binder is not rolled up on itself.
4. Put your other arm through, reaching in an upwards direction. This will require a lot of strength and strain in the shoulder and may not be best for people with large upper arms or weak/injured shoulders.
5. Pull the remaining bunched fabric down over the chest tissue.

Step-In Method

1. Turn your binder inside out and hold it in front of you by the bottom hem with the straps hanging down.
2. Step into the binder, putting your legs through the head hole.
3. Gently shimmy the binder up your body and over your hips. (The binder should still be inside out, and the shoulder straps should be below the hem.)
4. Grab the shoulder straps and shimmy the binder up your torso, turning your binder right-side out.
5. Slip each arm through the armholes one at a time, and work your arms into the holes until the shoulder straps are in place.
6. Pull down the bottom of the binder, taking care that neither the bottom nor the shoulder straps are rolled, folded, or bunched.

Side-Closure Method #1

1. Clasp the bottom two hooks or zip a couple of inches of the zipper (be sure the zipper pull is in the locked position).
2. Pull the binder over your head gently so you don't overstress the clasped hooks or zipper.
3. Pull the binder down over your chest tissue and then clasp the remaining hooks or zip the remaining zipper under your armpit.

Side-Closure Method #2

1. Put your head and arms through the armholes.
2. Pull the binder down over your chest.
3. Rotate the binder around your body until the zipper is in the center of the chest.
4. Zip or clasp the binder (it may be helpful to leave the top couple of inches undone at this point).
5. Rotate the binder into place.
6. Put your arms through the armholes.
7. Finish zipping or clasping, if needed.

Kinetic Tape Application

The basic method of applying kinetic tape as a binding method is to spread tissue toward the armpit and use strips of body-safe tape to secure the tissue, leaving a flat appearance at the center of the chest. The method is easy once you get the hang of it but is unique to each body. Rather than provide instructions here, I encourage you to visit www.transtape.life for graphic instructions, tips, and video tutorials. Be prepared to experiment until you get the right system for your particular chest.

Arranging Your Tissue

Three ways to arrange chest tissue in a binder

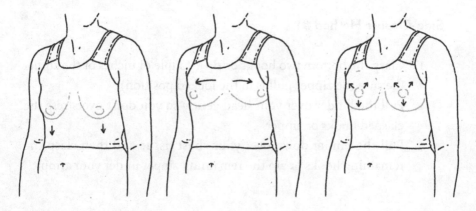

How you arrange the chest tissue varies based on the shape, size, and density of your chest. Experiment with squishing the tissue in different directions to see what gives you the flattest results.

There are three basic ways to arrange the tissue: towards the armpits, towards the toes, or smushed in place. Depending on the size of your chest, your ideal tissue placement will vary. It's important to manage your expectations based on your chest size. Larger-chested people will not be able to achieve a completely flat chest even with the tightest binder. You will be able to achieve a flatter contour than what you can achieve without a binder, but, depending on the dimensions of the rest of your body, you may not be able to achieve a cis-assumed appearance.

Small-to-medium-chested people and people with chests that have lost their density from testosterone or age may find that they do not need to arrange the tissue much because the binder compresses the tissue in place, like a pancake, and this achieves a flat contour.

Medium-to-large-chested people will probably need to rearrange the tissue. Separating the tissue and moving it towards each armpit will create a flatter section on the center of the chest but might make certain clothes fit differently in the arms. Pressing the tissue downward will leave the armpit area less congested and will create a barrel-chested look with a flat contour. This method can achieve an especially seamless contour for people with generous bellies because the chest tissue and the belly fat create a continuous flat contour. Avoid bringing the tissue upwards as this can accentuate the chest and give a "uni-boob" effect.

Large-to-very-large-chested people will want to use a combination of arranging towards the armpit and towards the toes. Often, large-chested people achieve a barrel-chested contour by arranging the tissue smoothly in all directions so that the chest, arms, and belly appear without any bulges of tissue.

People with pendulous chests may have an issue with their tissue bulging out at the bottom of the binder. If your chest tissue is not very dense, you should be able to pull up and towards the armpit which might resolve the issue. If you still hang out the bottom, it is best to avoid full-length binders with spandex abdominal fabric below the compression panel because they can accentuate the tissue that bulges. In these cases, a binder with compression mesh on the entire front panel (like those made by Underworks) is a good option.

I often get asked about whether arranging the tissue towards the toes will impact the outcomes for top surgery. In my research, I have found that there is a difference of opinion among plastic surgeons. The concern is that sustained stretching of the skin as the tissue is pulled downward could degrade the elasticity of the skin. Generally, healthy young skin has excellent elasticity and is not too susceptible unless a person has a hypermobility spectrum disorder impacting the integrity of collagen in their skin. As we age, elasticity in our skin decreases, and the risk of stretching skin increases. However, successful top surgeries have been done on chests of all shapes, sizes, and ages, and regardless of binding, there is often natural stretching of the skin from the growth and weight of the chest. It is up to each person to determine how comfortable they are with the risks of skin stretching since there is no definitive research, but I generally advise people to worry less about that outcome and focus more on what arrangement of tissue helps them to feel the best in their body.

Skin Irritation

In a study of 1,273 people who bind, skin irritation was reported by 76.3 percent.[2] It can range from mild to severe, and the pain and discomfort of it can be a serious hindrance to living your life. Preventative steps keep your skin irritation-free and your binder on your body, instead of in your drawer waiting for your abrasions to heal.

Properly caring for your skin when it is out of a binder will improve the integrity of the skin and make it less likely to become irritated or infected (see the "Skincare" section on page 100). However, even with the best hygiene, binding can irritate the skin. Two common factors that

---

2   Peitzmeier, S., Gardner, I., Weinand, J., Corbet, A., and Acevedo, K. (2017) 'Health impact of chest binding among transgender adults: a community-engaged, cross-sectional study.' *Culture, Health & Sexuality* 19, 1, 64–75.

exacerbate mild skin problems are the binder rubbing against the skin and sweating. If you are having serious skin irritation, review the "Skin Conditions" section in Chapter 5 to be sure your symptoms are not that of an infection that needs medical attention.

If the binder is rubbing or cutting into your skin, wearing a thin cotton tank top underneath works well for lots of folks. If possible, wear a non-ribbed tank undershirt with armholes the same size or smaller than your binder. Make sure to situate the fabric of the shirt between your irritated skin and the edge of the binder. Smooth the shirt out under the binder because creases or bunches can cause irritation. If the armholes are leaving red, chafed skin, your binder is either too small or not a good style for your body. Check to ensure you're wearing the correct size based on the sizing guidelines of the company. It's possible that the size is correct, but the design isn't a good fit for your body's size and shape. If you have the means to do so, purchase a different style.

Chances are high that sweat will accumulate under your binder, and when skin stays moist for long periods of time, it becomes softer and easier to damage. Keeping the skin dry can go a long way to preventing cuts, scrapes, or existing irritations (like acne) from becoming raw and irritated.

Antiperspirant can be used on the skin under the binder to help minimize the amount of sweat that your body is producing. If you are getting a heat rash or red irritated skin, this is an excellent option.

- Get a stick antiperspirant made for sensitive skin. Gels and aerosols have more ingredients that can irritate your skin.
- Be sure to apply the antiperspirant wherever skin touches skin, especially in the fold under the bottom of the chest tissue.
- Be careful to purchase antiperspirant (the thing that prevents sweating) and not deodorant (the thing that makes you smell good).

Products to reduce friction are becoming more common and can be a good solution for areas where skin is rubbing and blistering.

- Apply to areas where rubbing is occurring or where you see red, irritated skin when you take your binder off.

- These products are often marketed for thighs rubbing together, so try search terms such as "chub rub" and "thigh chafing."
- Cyclists and runners know plenty about chafing; check out solutions used by athletes.

Powder is a powerful ally in reducing sweat, as it absorbs moisture produced by your body.

- Cornstarch-based powders absorb moisture and can help reduce the amount of moisture from sweat that accumulates against the skin (avoid powders with talc).
- If your skin itches or irritates, a medicated powder can absorb moisture and soothe skin (these are usually made with menthol and zinc oxide).
- Preventative powders for athlete's foot (not treatment medications) can be effective at absorbing moisture and preventing fungal growth.
- Always apply the powder to completely dry skin—if you have a lot of chest tissue with a lot of skin-on-skin contact, you will need to allow that skin to air-dry completely before dusting it with powder.
- If it is extremely hot and you are sweating profusely, carry a small bottle of powder so you can take a break and reapply (remember to let your skin dry before a reapplication).

See Chapter 5 for complete guidance on what to do when different skin irritations occur, but keep the following in mind:

- A binder should never be worn over an open sore or scrape that has broken the skin, because infection can occur very quickly (covering the sore with a band-aid does not prevent the infection).
- Acne under the area of your binder, especially where the chest tissue is compressed against the body and sweat is trapped, can easily become infected because bacteria will fester (if you experience chronic acne, find suggestions for treatment in the acne section of Chapter 5).

Garment Care

Binders are undergarments that spend long hours absorbing sweat, dirt, and bacteria from your body. It is extremely important to keep them clean, so you are not wearing a petri dish of bodily secretions on the daily.

When to Wash

- The more you sweat in your binder, the more it needs to be washed.
- Wash a sweaty binder after one or two days of wear.
- Wash your binder if it is visibly dirty.
- During cool or cold times of year when you are not sweating as much, you can get away with washing it one to two times per week.

Some people can afford to buy only one binder and find it challenging to find time to wash it before they wear it again. An alcohol spray down and overnight dry can tide you over an extra day or two, however, it's critical to create a routine where you can remove and wash your binder with enough time to let it dry before the next day. Another great reason to take regular off-days!

How to Wash

- Wash in cold water—do not use warm or hot water as this will cause the fabric to break down more quickly.
- In the washing machine, use the delicate cycle or wash in a garment bag with the rest of your clothes.
- When handwashing your binder, work the detergent into the fabric thoroughly and always rinse it completely.
- To prevent irritation from chemicals, be sure that no soap remains in the fabric and use free and clear detergents to reduce the irritants that might bother your skin and lead to irritation under the binder.
- Rather than wringing the water out of your binder directly, roll it in a dry towel and squeeze the water out.
- Hang your binder to dry.
- Don't put your binder in a hot dryer; the extreme heat will cause it to stretch out more quickly.

- For speed drying, squeeze the water out with a towel and then use the *air-only* cycle in the dryer which uses no heat or drape the binder over a fan.
- Don't wear your binder before it's completely dry—the extra moisture is a recipe for a fungal infection.
- Never bleach your binder, because the chlorine will break down the elastic in the fabric.

Skincare

Keeping the surface of your skin clean is one of the easiest and most affordable ways to prevent skin irritation. A binder is going to hold all of the dirt, bacteria, and other infection agents against your skin, so always put your binder on clean skin. Shower or wash with a cloth the area that is under the binder, including the upper back, and then let it dry completely before putting on your binder. After a day of binding, showering to thoroughly clean the body is best. If you do not have access to a shower every day, use a washcloth with soap to thoroughly clean the skin covered by your binder and in your armpits. Be sure to completely rinse the soap off the skin to prevent irritation from the residue.

Establish a daily routine that cares for your skin. Even if you have hardy skin, it's best to use a gentle soap, ideally one made for cleansing sensitive skin. Wash before and after a day of binding. If you have acne, it is best to find a routine that helps to prevent and control outbreaks; see Chapter 5 for more information about skincare for acne. After cleaning the skin, you need to moisturize to help prevent the skin from breaking when it gets rubbed or irritated. You can use a moisturizing lotion; it's generally best to use one with little to no perfume or dyes, or an oil like almond, jojoba, or shea butter.

Most people's chest skin is thinner and more sensitive than the rest of the skin on their body, especially where there is skin-on-skin contact. You do not want to scrub or exfoliate delicate skin because that can make the skin more vulnerable to irritation when you bind. If your skin is not sensitive to exfoliation and is prone to dry, flakey texture, exfoliating once per week can help keep pore-blocking dead skin cells from adding to the build-up on the surface of your skin, but be careful not to overdo it. The abrasive nature of exfoliation makes it a great thing to do on an off-day from binding or a day when your activity level will be low.

If your skin is red, rubbed raw, or irritated from a day of binding, pat your skin dry or air-dry rather than rubbing it with a rough towel to avoid any further irritation. This irritation is an indication that you may be wearing a binder that is too small or a poor fit for your body type so revisit Chapter 2 to explore other options.

Dysphoria is an insidious beast and dissociation causes some people to simply avoid washing their chests altogether or to wear their binder in the shower. Not washing the skin of your chest, armpits, and back can lead to uncomfortable irritation and impact your ability to bind. Wearing your binder in the shower prevents you from getting clean and likely hastens the breaking down of your binder's fabric. If seeing your chest in the shower is a struggle, try wearing a baggy T-shirt in the shower and soap up the skin by reaching under the shirt or pulling your arms inside the shirt. Be certain you've thoroughly rinsed, so soap residue doesn't later irritate your skin.

When you remove your binder, do a quick check for irritation. Spotting mild abrasions from rubbing before the surface of the skin breaks allows you to address the problem and save yourself from a more serious (and painful) skin issue later on. See Chapter 5 for more information about caring for skin irritated by binding.

Skincare for Kinetic Tape

This form of tape is designed for safe, long-term use on the skin. It can help to avoid many of the irritations that come from sweat and rubbing, however, you must be even more vigilant about the skincare routine. Even though the tape is designed specifically for this use, it's most often applied to ankles, knees, and arms, where the skin isn't as thin or delicate as the chest. Being careless when removing the tape can very easily tear the upper layers of the skin, leaving raw and painful sores. These sores will prevent you from wearing tape or a garment binder until they are healed, which can take up to a week.

Use oil to break down the adhesive before you remove the strips of tape. TransTape sells a removal oil specifically formulated for this purpose and is body and environment safe and a healing salve to help restore the skin between applications. Most body-safe oils, such as jojoba, almond, and sesame, work just fine for removing the tape too. Saturate the strips of tape with the oil and allow it to sit for at least five minutes before slowly peeling back the tape. If it pulls the skin, you need more time or more oil.

In addition to care of the skin when applying and removing the tape, adopt a regular skincare routine for your chest because even safe adhesive applied to the skin regularly will disrupt the regular functioning of the skin such that it requires extra attention to stay healthy.

CHAPTER 4
AN ACTIVE LIFE

Binding let me enjoy summer more, despite enduring binders stuck to my skin with sweat. I've loved swimming since I was a kid, and now I could swim again! (With a looser swim binder for safety.) I even joined a softball team in a local queer league, where all my teammates called me the right pronouns and supported me.

– L, 34, Washington, DC, USA

There are four factors that have to be considered when you are evaluating whether and how to participate in activities that push your physical body: breathing, muscle constriction, heat, and access to relief. Continuing to participate in the activities you love is vital, and binding is simply a factor that you need to consider. With a little extra thought and planning, you can be safe while binding with most activities. However, not taking the risks into consideration can lead to skin problems, muscle strain and weakness and, in rare cases, serious injury. Take on the extra responsibility to prepare and then live your best life!

Music, dance, sports, art, exercise, and recreation—the good stuff that enriches our lives. These activities give us a sense of community, inspire us, and require movement that produces uplifting neurotransmitters that combat depression, anxiety, and, you guessed it, dysphoria. Too often, clients tell me that when they started binding, they quit doing activities that brought them joy. Misinformation out there has scared some of my clients into believing they *have* to quit all physical activities if they bind. This is false, and this section is all about setting the record straight.

Are there **increased risks** when binding during strenuous activities? **Yes**.

Do people who bind need to take **extra precautions** to not injure themselves when participating in strenuous activities? **Yes**.

Should people who bind **abstain** from the physically demanding activities that bring them joy? **No**.

12 Tips to Keep Moving and Stay Safe

1) Least Restricting Binding Garment Possible
Consider wearing:

- a compression shirt or minimizing sports bra
- a binder one size larger than your usual size
- kinetic tape
- an older, stretched-out binder.

2) Fewest Layers Possible
When exercising in a binder it is critical that you prevent heat exhaustion by wearing the most breathable clothing possible for the activity. Wearing multiple layers over a binder is a common strategy for improving the flat appearance of the chest but in physically strenuous activities, especially in warm or hot conditions, this should be avoided.

When wearing tape during strenuous physical activity, layers are OK. It is still a good idea to minimize layering in hot weather.

If you bind regularly, you are likely relying on your chest muscles to do most of the work of respiration which will result in more breathing fatigue and more difficulty keeping your body cool.

3) Breathability
Not all binders are made of the same materials or have the same number

of layers of fabric. Choosing a binder with breathable fabric mesh or moisture-wicking fabric can be an excellent strategy for avoiding overheating.

If the tape binding method can provide enough binding for your body and the activity, breathing is less restricted and the risk of overheating is reduced.

4) Manage Sweat

Heat rash is common in hot weather, especially in areas where skin folds can trap moisture. So remove your sweaty binder as soon as possible.

If you are not safe or comfortable being without a binder after your workout, then pack a clean one in your gym bag and change.

If you are using a tape method of binding, sweat will accumulate under the tape, especially where there is skin-on-skin contact. Since tape is waterproof, a thorough shower can be sufficient to rinse the sweat from those areas. However, if you experience irritation or smell pungent body odor, you may need to wear each application of tape for a shorter period of time in order to keep the skin clean and healthy.

5) Fabric Irritation

Choose a workout binder that does not irritate your skin along the edges of the shoulder straps or armholes. Increased movement of your body means increased movement of the binder *on* your body. If the armholes cut in a little tight during regular wear, they will cause a more serious skin irritation during strenuous activities. Skin irritation can be painful but it can also quickly develop into infections if the irritated skin is ignored.

6) Fabric Rolling

Full-length binders have a tendency to roll up, forming a highly compressive roll of fabric at the waist/low rib cage. This is never a good thing but with the rapid and forceful expansion of the rib cage during strenuous activity, it can quickly cause painful lower rib problems. See page 90 for suggestions about preventing the binder from rolling up and if you are unable to prevent it, change to a half-length binder, especially when you are being active.

7) Range of Motion

Binders compress muscle tissue and constrict the movement of the shoulders and the shoulder blades. If the activity requires a lot of arm movement and strength, it is important to consider which type of binder will allow for the most movement. If the pressure of the binder prevents you from broadening your shoulders, clasping your hands above your head, or placing your arms behind your back, it can prevent you from correctly developing the desired strength and coordination. If this is the case, wear a larger size binder to exercise.

Exercises that loosen the muscle tissue and release the fascia around the scapula and spine will help reduce this restriction (exercises #13–15, 21–23).

8) Quick Release

Binders that have hook, Velcro, or zipper closures can support participation in strenuous activities because you can quickly release the pressure and take a breather. This style of binder can be excellent for anyone, but people who have asthma attacks, panic attacks, or a high risk of heat exhaustion should heavily consider it as an option.

9) Tape Alternative

Since kinetic tape does not compress the rib cage it poses no risk to the body during physically strenuous activities. If it provides you with enough support, it is the safest way to bind during physical exertion, especially cardio activities.

10) Wash After Use

Binders worn for strenuous physical activity should be washed after each use. Sweat and dirt accumulating in the fabric can cause the skin under the binder to become irritated or develop bacterial or fungal infections.

11) Practice Breathing Daily

Strenuous activity requires deeper and/or more rapid breathing, and wearing a binder teaches your body to breathe more shallowly. To be safe and successful in the activities that you love, you need to condition your body to breathe deeply using the most powerful muscle of respiration: the diaphragm. Commit yourself to doing five minutes of breathing exercise every day as part of your commitment to the sport, hobby, art, or recreation that you love.

12) Know Your Limits

Are you new to the activity? Are you out of shape? Is it allergy season? Pace yourself.

Getting Enough Oxygen

Cardiovascular exercise, or "cardio," is any activity that sustains an elevated heart rate throughout the activity. Cardio exercise increases the need for oxygen so muscles of respiration must work harder to expand the chest cavity to get a sufficient amount of air. The body is most efficient when it relies on the diaphragm muscle to breathe but recruits smaller chest muscles to help when cardio activity demands more oxygen. Chest breathing, or relying primarily on the smaller muscles to expand the lungs, doubles the challenge of keeping up with cardio breathing because the weaker muscles must expand the chest against the pressure of the binder without much help from the diaphragm. If cardio activities are a thing that brings you joy, then training your body to breathe deeply is the extra preparation that you need to do in order for the activity to be safe and sustainable.

Check out the section on breathing in Part 2 and learn about developing and maintaining healthy breathing muscles. Teaching yourself a new way to breathe will be key to getting sufficient air while keeping up with your team, belting out your solo, or beating your personal best. If you intend to play or perform in a binder, then I recommend you practice in a binder to condition your body.

When doing any cardio activity, it is best to wear a binder one size larger or sports bra. Sprinting down the field is not the time to wear the binder you would wear to flatten out in a button-down and bow tie. Being active in a binder may mean that you have to trade adequate oxygen for a slightly bulkier, but still flatter, chest appearance.

General Advice

- Have a post-game or post-performance binder to change into so that you are not sitting in a sweaty binder which can make the skin more vulnerable.
- Wear a binder one size larger or sports bra when you are doing strenuous activities.
- For less cardio-intensive activities, a stretched-out binder is an option.
- When playing in the heat, review recommendations in Chapter 5 about binding healthily in the heat.

Tape-Binding Euphoria

2017 was the first time I used TransTape to bind my chest and I cried. The ability to bind my chest one time and it'll last for three to five days straight was a huge game changer for me. This meant I could live my life without fear of people outing me based on the sports bra straps crowding my neck or traditional binder lines that are noticeable through my shirt. The whole experience could be bottled up into one word: Freedom. I'm able to live, shower, and sleep feeling affirmed without having to plan my day based on when I can bind. I'm able to exercise and play more sports without feeling claustrophobic when I start to sweat and breathe heavily in my binder. Wearing this made me feel comfortable enough to swim shirtless without having to achieve top surgery first!

– A, 26, Kingsport, Tennessee, USA

Activity-Specific Advice

Cardiovascular Activities

Running, cycling, dancing, aerobics, circuit training, Vinyasa Yoga, marching band, and other activities that get you huffin' and puffin'.

- The most important thing to remember in cardio activity is that you need to be able to get maximum breath capacity.

- Wear a binder one size larger or sports bra.
- Models with quick-release options are great for situations where you are having a hard time catching your breath.
- If you become light-headed, dizzy, or unable to catch your breath beyond typical cardio breathing, stop the activity to catch your breath. This is likely a sign that your binder is too tight.
- Exercise recommendations:
  - Breathing Series (exercises #1–5)
  - Sternum Massage (exercise #7)
  - Pectoralis Muscles Massage and Trigger Point Release (exercise #8 and 9)
  - Serratus Anterior Massage (exercise #11)
  - Anterior Torso Release (exercise #23)

Shoulder-Intensive Activities
Competitive swimming, water polo, rowing, baseball/softball, volleyball, golf.

- Wear a binder one size larger or sports bra.
- For less cardio-intensive activities, a stretched-out binder is an option.
- To minimize compression on the shoulder blade, choose a binder with average swimsuit spandex on the back.
- Avoid binders with power mesh or other highly compressive fabric on the back as this restricts full movement of the shoulder blades which can impact muscle strength, especially in the rotator cuff, trapezius, pectoralis minor, rhomboids, serratus anterior, deltoids, biceps, levator scapulae, and latissimus dorsi.
- A racerback binder can give maximum range of mobility to the shoulder blades. Be mindful as straps of a racerback binder can dig into shoulder and neck muscles, causing muscle fatigue and trigger points. If you are experiencing headaches, this might be the cause.
- Tank binders are acceptable options as long as the back panel is average spandex and you can achieve sufficient range of motion in the arms.
- Exercise recommendations:
  - Breathing Series (exercises #1–5)

- Serratus Anterior Massage (exercise #11)
- Rotator Cuff Trigger Point Release (exercise #13)
- Shoulder Rotation (exercise #14)
- Scapular Mobilization (exercise #15)
- Trapezius and Levator Scapula Trigger Point Release (exercise #20)
- Thoracic Mobilization (exercise #21)

Recreational Swimming

- Wear a stretched-out binder or purchase one size up for swimming.
- Check on the binder company site that the binder is waterproof or check www.healthybinding.com for a list of waterproof binder options.
- Dedicate a binder to be your "swim binder" because the fabric may break down more quickly in saltwater or chlorine.
- Exercise recommendations:
  - Breathing Series (exercises #1–5)

Open-Water Sports

Open-water swimming, waterskiing, surfing.

- Wear a binder one size larger or sports bra.
- Choose a quick release for situations where you cannot easily take a break to catch your breath if you are in distress. A binder with hook, Velcro, or zipper closures allows quick release to immediately increase your lung capacity.
- Exercise recommendations:
  - Breathing Series (exercises #1–5)
  - Pectoralis Muscles Massage and Trigger Point Release (exercises #8 and 9)
  - Serratus Anterior Massage (exercise #11)
  - Thoracic Mobilization (exercise #21)
  - Thoracic Opener (exercise #22)
  - Anterior Torso Release (exercise #23)

Running Euphoria

When the gym became an unsafe place for me, I began running outside all year around. I started out running while wearing two sports bras, but the bands crushed my ribs and my chest shape still caused me dysphoria. I decided to find a binder that I could safely run in. I searched for a while and finally found a brand of binders that shaped my chest beautifully while compressing my ribs less than a standard sports bra. Running became a joy rather than a source of dysphoria—to move my body through rain, snow, and sunshine, with relentless forward motion, being one with nature. It let me feel like everything was going to be OK in the end; it gave me hope for the future.

– A, 35, Massachusetts, USA

Running-Intensive Sports
Soccer, basketball, field hockey, rugby, etc.

- See the recommendations in the "Cardiovascular Activities" section above.
- Wear a binder one size larger or sports bra.
- Additional exercise recommendations:
    - Chest Opener (exercise #6)
    - Thoracic Opener (exercise #22)
    - Anterior Torso Release (exercise #23)

Walking, Hiking, Camping
- It is generally OK to bind in a properly sized binder.
- Beware of your fitness level and consider a quick-release option if you think that you might need help catching your breath.
- When camping, have a plan for not sleeping in/taking your binder off.

Cycling
- See the recommendations in the "Cardiovascular Activities" section above.

- Wear a binder one size larger or sports bra.
- The rounded upper-body posture can impact the openness of the front of the chest and result in additional constriction in the chest. Post-ride self-care can help to mitigate this impact.
- Additional exercise recommendations:
  - Chest Opener (exercise #6)
  - Serratus Anterior Massage (exercise #11)
  - Chin Tuck (exercise #16)
  - Neck Mobilization (exercise #18)
  - Trapezius and Levator Scapula Trigger Point Release (exercise #20)
  - Thoracic Mobilization (exercise #21)
  - Thoracic Opener (exercise #22)
  - Anterior Torso Release (exercise #23)

Weightlifting

- Wear a binder one size larger or sports bra.
- Choose a style that exposes as much of your shoulder blades as possible.
- Be mindful of proper form and building strength on the front and the back of the body.
- Exercise recommendations:
  - Breathing Series (exercises #1–5)
  - Chest Opener (exercise #6)
  - Serratus Anterior Massage (exercise #11)
  - Rotator Cuff Trigger Point Release (exercise #13)
  - Shoulder Rotation (exercise #14)
  - Scapular Mobilization (exercise #15)
  - Trapezius and Levator Scapula Trigger Point Release (exercise #20)
  - Thoracic Mobilization (exercise #21)
  - Anterior Torso Release (exercise #23)

Rock Climbing

- Wear a binder one size larger, a stretched-out binder, or a sports bra.

- Exercise recommendations:
    - Breathing Series (exercises #1–5)
    - Chest Opener (exercise #6)
    - Serratus Anterior Massage (exercise #11)
    - Rotator Cuff Trigger Point Release (exercise #13)
    - Shoulder Rotation (exercise #14)
    - Scapular Mobilization (exercise #15)
    - Trapezius and Levator Scapula Trigger Point Release (exercise #20)
    - Thoracic Mobilization (exercise #21)
    - Anterior Torso Release (exercise #23)

Hatha/Gentle Yoga

- It is generally OK to bind in a properly sized binder. Wear a binder one size larger, a stretched-out binder, or a sports bra for more easeful breathing.
- Pranayama, the breath practice in Yoga, might be more difficult in a binder. Practicing this breathing in a binder is a way to strengthen your deep breathing muscles.

Vinyasa/Flow Yoga

- See the recommendations in the "Cardiovascular Activities" section above.
- Wear a binder one size larger or sports bra.
- Allow yourself to pause to catch your breath when you need it.

Drag King Euphoria

I didn't [bind my chest] to battle body dysphoria, I did it for the stage. For years, as a drag king, I chestbound unsafely with things that were not meant for that purpose. There weren't many products on the market that offered that type of illusion while allowing you to breathe easily and have full range of motion. That was until I discovered Trans-Tape. It was a game changer because it allowed my rib cage to fully expand so I could dance vigorously during my numbers. It came in a skin tone color so I could go shirtless and push my illusion. And it was waterproof to withstand my sweat during those long Pride festivals in June!

– Q, 45, Massachusetts, USA

Performance

Acting, Public Speaking, Singing, Playing an Instrument.

- Consult voice coaching and speech therapy resources to learn to project from your diaphragm. Regardless of binding, the secret to projecting one's voice is the diaphragm; binding can just make it a little harder to belt out at the mic.
- If you intend to perform in a binder, practice in a binder.
- Regularly release your diaphragm muscle.
- Exercise recommendations:
  - Breathing Series (exercises #1–3)
  - Diaphragm Massage and Release (exercises #4–5)
  - Chest Opener (exercise #6)
  - Rib Cage Trigger Point Release (exercise #10)
  - Lateral Torso Release (exercise #12)
  - Anterior Torso Release (exercise #23)

Sexual Activity

- The temptation to overbind is understandably high in intimate moments. Resist wearing a binder that is too small and never resort to forms of risky binding.
- See recommendations in the "Cardiovascular Activities" section above.

Physical Labor

- **For jobs where you cannot easily take a break:** Consider a quick-release binder so you can catch your breath if you are in distress. A binder with hook, Velcro, or zipper closures allows quick release to discreetly increase your lung capacity.
- **For jobs requiring cardio activity:**
  - Wear a binder one size larger or sports bra.

- See the recommendations in the "Cardiovascular Activities" section above.
- **For jobs that are not cardio-intensive,** a stretched-out binder is an option.
- **For jobs requiring arms to be outstretched, overhead for long periods, or forceful shoulder exertion:** See shoulder intensive activity recommendations
- **For jobs in extreme heat:** Review the recommendations in Chapter 5 about binding healthily in the heat.

HAVE A PLAN

Wearing a binder in strenuous activity adds a risk, and it is up to you to be prepared.

Consider the environment, people, resources, and demands of the activity:

- Where could you go to remove your binder quickly?
- What is the nearest place that you can go to cool down?
- How will you stay hydrated?
- Will you be able to stop participating in the activity if you need to?
- Is there anyone there who knows that you bind and can be your advocate if you get injured or pass out?
- Is there a coach or instructor that you need to talk to in advance in case you need to stop for a reason related to binding?

CHAPTER 5
HEALTH RISKS OF BINDING

My binding journey introduced me to gender euphoria in a time of my life when my trans identity had only ever been a devastating secret. To finally make a choice that honored my identity after years of complete dissociation from self was the first time I had ever felt agency and ownership over my body. Once I was able to wear a truly safe binder, I looked into the mirror and realized for the very first time that my identity didn't have to hurt me anymore. This was the beginning of my process of accepting my true self and finally sharing it with the world.

– *W, 23, Chicago, IL, USA*

Does the mere thought of going to the doctor heighten your anxiety? Statistically speaking, if you are reading this book, it probably does. In addition to all of the reasons that cisgender people dread the doctor, you have to worry whether your gender identity will be respected.

You're not alone.

Sadly, the lack of understanding in the medical profession about TGNC people means that TGNC folks avoid seeking medical attention or get sub-par care when they do. As you likely know from personal experience, even well-meaning providers can do harm when uninformed about the practice of binding. If you have sought care for muscle, respiratory, or skin issues from binding, your providers may have blamed *you* because you bind and, without discussion, ordered you to stop. All too often, doctors don't understand the life-saving role binding plays in our lives. Being dismissed and blamed is enough to swear off doctors completely. I get it. Since avoiding medical care can be an extremely dangerous choice, this chapter aims to help you determine if you should consult a doctor.

PAGING EVERY SINGLE DOCTOR!

We need our doctors to be educated about binding.

We need doctors to understand that binders are life-saving gender-affirming care.

We need doctors to understand that most conditions do not require permanently stopping binding.

We need doctors to know that prohibiting us from binding can seriously endanger our mental health.

We need doctors to work with us on a harm-reduction approach.

Most patients aren't going to stop wearing binders, so the sooner doctors accept this truth, and the fact that our well-being depends on doing so, the sooner we can make informed decisions. If you, as a doctor or healthcare professional, discount the importance binding plays in our quality of life and safety, we will likely feel shamed, invalidated, and patronized. This will further reinforce our distrust of medical care—a vicious cycle with dangerous, sometimes lethal results. Did you know that 24 percent of us avoided going to the doctor for necessary medical care in the last year because of fear of being mistreated as a transgender person?[1]

Are you a medical provider? Thank you for prioritizing TGNC health. Please share this with your colleagues.

Do you know a medical provider? Please suggest they read this book.

1   James, S. E., Herman, J., Keisling, M., Mottet, L., and Anafi, M. (2015) U.S. Transgender Survey (USTS). Inter-university Consortium for Political and Social Research [distributor], 2019-05-22. https://doi.org/10.3886/ICPSR37229.v1

Consider this chapter as a starting point to understand the variety of health problems that can result from binding. I am not a doctor. This is not medical advice. Think of this more like a medical encyclopedia lovingly curated for you so you don't have to face the overwhelm of anxiety-fueled late-night Googling.

Each condition mentioned is one I've seen in my own clients as a result of binding, in first-hand accounts from students in my workshops, or has been documented in research of transmasculine health. Again, not a doctor, and everything I suggest could be found by sifting through reliable medical websites. You'll find the basics of the condition and suggestions about how to bind responsibly to avoid complications.

Some rare complications of binding—thoracic outlet syndrome, cellulitis, and heat stroke—are serious and require immediate medical attention. For less serious conditions that do still require medical treatment, I've detailed what to expect going into doctor's appointments so you can better prepare for potentially triggering exams and plan how to answer difficult questions. If you are going to see a provider you don't know or are in an area where doctors are ignorant of or hostile towards transgender health, it may be helpful to review Chapter 6, "Navigating Appointments with Health and Wellness Providers." Additional resources to help educate health providers are at www.healthybinding.com.

This chapter is divided into three sections:

- Section 1 outlines conditions related to overheating.
- Section 2 provides guidance for binding with chronic conditions.
- Section 3 covers acute illnesses related to respiratory, neurological, skeletal, and skin conditions.

HOW TO USE THIS CHAPTER

1. Read Section 1 on heat-related conditions because every person who binds needs to be prepared for these at all times.
2. Review Section 2 on chronic conditions if any apply to you.
3. Use Section 3 as a reference for when unusual symptoms arise.

4. If you are having musculoskeletal pain, exercises in Part 2 will guide you through managing the pain on your own.

Section 1: Heat-Related Conditions

The risks associated with binding in the heat are easily downplayed because we are familiar with being hot and that tends to make us underestimate its danger.

Sweating is the body's temperature control system. As sweat evaporates, skin cools. Like other garments that cover a large surface area of the skin, binding garments disrupt this system. The thick fabric of your binder against your skin collects, traps, and stores body heat. The binder itself forms a barrier between your sweaty skin and the air. Once this crucial control system fails, the body's temperature can rise rapidly. You'll get hotter faster and take increasingly longer to cool down.

In addition to binders, it's common for transmasculine folks to wear extra layers to obscure the contours of the body. While it's an excellent strategy, you have to be realistic and strategic about just how much layering your body can tolerate in hot environments. Exposure to extreme heat can easily cause dehydration, heat exhaustion, and heat stroke. While the symptoms are generally mild to moderate, severe cases can damage the brain or other vital organs. With forethought, this is an easily managed risk of binding.

High-risk environments include:

- hot, humid climates
- jobs that require working in the heat without breaks—for example inside kitchens and outdoors in the sun
- locations with no shade or respite from the sun
- anywhere outdoors where you do physically exhausting activity during hot weather (sports, commuting by bike or foot, playing with kids).

12 Tips for Hot Weather

You can't change the weather, but you can change how you prepare for it.

1) Wear One Layer

If you can't wear just one layer over your binder, be ready and able to remove layers if you experience symptoms of heat exhaustion.

2) Rock a Cooling Fabric

Let us thank the textile wizards who created this amazing fabric that stays cool to the touch when wet. If the fabric has "PVA cooling technology" or "evaporative cooling," it will get 15–20° cooler than the surrounding air when wet. That's an excellent way to drop your body temperature in a hurry. It is available in a variety of easily applied and easily worn options: towels, headbands, durags, vests, tank tops, hard-hat inserts, and more. To activate the cooling technology, get the fabric wet from any water source. If you bind, I recommend keeping one of these lifesavers in your work bag, locker, backpack, car, desk drawer, etc.

3) Hydrate, Wisely

Drinking water is essential to staying cool. Your body will be losing a lot of water by sweating and you need to be replacing that water constantly. If you are going to be out in the heat, think ahead about how you will have enough water for the entire time that you are out. This may mean carrying a large jug, asking ahead about where you can refill your water bottle, or preparing to purchase bottled water as needed.

4) Thirst Is the Alarm

Don't wait to get thirsty. By the time your body alerts you with thirst, you are already dehydrated. Keep a steady flow of fluids before, during, and after being in the heat.

5) Choose Your Beverages Wisely

Alcohol has a diuretic effect causing increased urination. Beverages with a lot of sugar and caffeine are dehydrating. Avoid drinking alcohol and sugary, caffeinated sodas in environments where you are unable to keep yourself cool and well hydrated. Binding shouldn't be a reason to abstain from celebrations with your community, so if you are drinking, have ready access to water and employ the "1 for 1 rule": for every ounce of soda or alcoholic beverage have one ounce of water.

6) Keep It Light and Breezy

Wear light colors that reflect, rather than absorb, heat. Choose clothes that allow the moist air to come into contact with your skin.

7) Get Outside at Dawn or Dusk

Watch the sunrise as you bike early in the day or play a pick-up game in the evening. Basically, if you're doing something outside that causes you to sweat and elevates your heart rate, try doing it in the morning or the evening hours when the temperatures are usually cooler and the heat from the sun less intense.

8) Take It Easy

Make an effort to cool off between games or jobs. The cumulative effect increases the risk of heat-related illnesses. Even if this means just grabbing some shade in the park or stepping into an air-conditioned grocery store, do it!

9) Don't Get Burned

Wear and reapply sunscreen because sunburns increase dehydration and the heat from your skin makes it harder to cool down. Rashguard swimsuits are also a great choice and cover your binder.

10) Plan Your Cool Down

Before you go out, know how you will get out of the sun. Is there an indoor area where you can cool off? Is there shade? A car with air conditioning? A body of water to submerge yourself in or a fountain to run through?

Then be proactive and take cooling breaks. Drink water before you get back out in the heat.

11) If You Know, You Know

Part of binding responsibly is knowing the difference between dehydration (mild–moderate), heat exhaustion (serious), and heat stroke (very serious). Lucky for you, you can find everything you need to know in the next few pages!

12) Worst-Case Scenario

Mentally and logistically prepare for the fact that a medical emergency may necessitate removing your binder.

MAKE A GO-BAG

A handy go-bag is one already well stocked with cooling equipment and ready to grab anytime you plan to bind when going out in hot conditions. Keep your go-bag in your backpack, glove compartment, locker, or desk so you can be just as spontaneous as your friends. Here's a packing list for your go-bag:

- A binding alternative (sports bra, compression tank, or kinetic tape) in case you need to take off your binder
- Reusable water bottle
- Electrolyte packets, chews, drops, or gel which can give you quick access to electrolytes in any situation
- Cooling towel ("PVA cooling technology" or "evaporative cooling")
- Instant disposable ice pack from first aid supplies
- Quick reference card with symptoms and interventions of heat-related illnesses (keep laminated in case the bag gets wet)

Dehydration

Being able to preempt dehydration is your best defense against it. Double bonus: staying hydrated is the best defense against more serious heat-related conditions.

- Thirst
- Dry lips and tongue
- Headache
- Weakness or dizziness
- Nausea
- Muscle cramps

These warning signs announce the first stage of the heat-related illness spectrum. It is vital to consume water as soon as you recognize any of these symptoms. Consuming a combination of water and electrolytes can help your body maximize its ability to maintain hydration. Remaining in the heat without fluid intake very likely leads to heat exhaustion.

Heat Exhaustion

The milder form of heat-related illness is heat exhaustion. Being in hot temperatures with poor hydration, especially day after day, brings it on. Binding turns up the dial by trapping heat in layers of clothing and caus- ing excessive sweating (loss of fluid). You must be conscientious when in a binder to not ignore signs of heat exhaustion. Doing so will allow them to escalate to the much more dangerous illness: heat stroke.

KNOW THE SYMPTOMS

- Excessive thirst
- Nausea
- Fainting
- Cool, clammy skin
- Weakness
- Muscle aches or cramping
- Heavy sweating
- Fast, weak pulse
- Dizziness

INTERVENTIONS FOR HEAT EXHAUSTION

- Get to the coolest place possible
- Loosen clothing to allow airflow to your skin

- Remove your binder if it is safe
- Take sips (not gulps) of water or a sports drink
- Get into a cool body of water

WHEN TO SEEK MEDICAL ATTENTION
- You vomit or dry heave
- Your symptoms worsen
- Your symptoms have not improved after one hour

Heat Stroke
The most serious heat-related illness is heat stroke. This occurs when the body's ability to sweat fails entirely and is completely unable to control its temperature. Body temperature rises quickly, and the body becomes incapable of cooling. Temperatures may rise to 106°F or higher over the course of 30 minutes.

Heat stroke can cause organ failure, brain damage, and death if the person does not receive emergency medical attention.

KNOW THE SYMPTOMS
- Hot, red, and dry skin
- Very high body temperature (103+ degrees)
- Rapid, strong pulse
- Confusion
- Shortness of breath
- Nausea and vomiting
- Headache
- Dizziness
- Loss of consciousness

WHAT TO DO FOR HEAT STROKE
Generally, the person experiencing heat stroke is too delirious to take the following actions so it is crucial that a trusted person be knowledgable in case you are unable to advocate for yourself.

- Call for emergency medical support immediately.

- Get the person to the coolest place possible.
- Loosen clothing to allow airflow to the skin.
- Remove the binder.
- Get into a cool body of water.
- Or spray the skin with water and fan the body.
- Do not push fluids on the person.

TREATMENT AND RECOVERY

Treatment for heat-related conditions is to cool down the person and address any complications. It will be necessary to rehydrate the body. The severity of the situation will determine how exactly to do this, whether it be by slowly sipping water, drinking water with electrolytes, or receiving intravenous fluids. Dehydration causes body aches, headaches, nausea, and muscle cramps—stubborn symptoms that hang around until your body is fully rehydrated.

After a moderate-to-severe heat-related event, you will need to rest and allow your body to recover from what has been an extremely taxing attack. You will need to conserve energy, rehydrate, and stay in a cool environment. Treat yourself like a mushroom. Get in a dark, cool space and stay moist.

BEING PREPARED FOR EMERGENCY MEDICAL ATTENTION

If your heat-related illness requires emergency medical attention, assume the emergency medical technicians (EMTs) will remove your clothing to cool you down, especially if you are confused, dizzy, or losing consciousness.

If you need emergency medical attention, you will likely be sick and disoriented. Having EMTs remove your binder with no one there to advocate for your safety could make a bad situation much worse. That's why you need someone to speak up for you. It's critical to appoint a trusted friend, coach, or coworker to be your advocate if something goes wrong. Make sure that they know the signs of heat exhaustion and stroke. If you are stealth, cis-assumed, or not out, this informed confidant is a must-have. In most heat-related emergencies, removing a person's clothing is the first step. Your advocate is the person who can intervene in these situations to maintain your privacy as much as possible.

MEDICATIONS AND HEAT OFTEN DON'T MIX!

Many prescription meds act as accelerants, stoking your internal fire and putting you at risk for overheating.

Take a minute, right now, to check the list below before you're out in the heat and it's too late. Drugs for depression, anxiety, attention deficit hyperactivity disorder (ADHD), and more can increase your risk of heat-related illness.

Medications and Intoxicants that Increase Risk of Heat-Related Illness:

- Alcohol is a diuretic and increases urination, causing the body to lose water more quickly.
    - All forms of beer, wine, cider, mead, and spirits.
- Antihistamines and anticholinergic drugs decrease the body's ability to sweat.
    - Over-the-counter meds and prescriptions used to treat colds, as well as sinus and respiratory infections.
- Benzodiazepines bond to receptors in your brain and can impact your body's temperature-regulating center.
    - Prescribed for anxiety.
- Beta-blockers and calcium-channel blockers reduce blood pressure which slows blood flow to the skin which is integral to heat leaving the body.
    - Prescribed for high blood pressure and migraines.
- Diuretics, often called water pills, reduce blood pressure and increase urination which dehydrates the body.
    - Prescribed for high blood pressure and edema or swelling.
    - Caffeine has a diuretic effect, especially when consumed in high doses found in energy drinks, caffeine pills, and multiple espressos.
- Laxatives combat constipation by pulling water from elsewhere in the body to flush the intestinal tract, effectively dehydrating the body.

- Phenothiazines (anti-psychotics) affect the temperature-regulating center of the brain.
- Stimulants, including some prescription drugs used to treat ADHD, increase metabolism and raise internal body temperature. (Stimulants are also vasoconstrictors.)
  - Cocaine (powder and crack), methamphetamines ("meth"), and non-prescription use of amphetamines ("study drugs") will all dangerously increase the risk of overheating.
- Vasoconstrictors constrict blood vessels, slowing blood flow to the skin and making it release heat.
  - Triptans and other migraine medication.
  - Prescription and non-prescription opioids.

IS DRY MOUTH DEHYDRATION IN DISGUISE?

Since dry mouth is a side effect of both cannabis and dehydration, it is not far-fetched to assume that cannabis is causing dehydration. However, dry mouth is from cannabis's effect on the salivary glands and not necessarily an indication of the body's need for water.

When consuming cannabis in heat, be careful because dry mouth can make you dismiss your thirst even when it *is* your body alerting you to dehydration. Your best bet when using cannabis in the heat is to keep a water bottle nearby and drink consistently, whether you are feeling thirsty or not.

Section 2: Binding with Chronic Conditions

Asthma

SYMPTOMS

Asthma causes swelling and/or constriction in the airways of the lungs. Symptoms, ranging from mild to severe, include:

- Shortness of breath
- Chest tightness or pain

- Wheezing
- Coughing or wheezing attacks

IMPACT OF BINDING

The compression that a binder exerts on chest tissue limits the ability of the upper rib cage to expand when the lungs fill with air. The muscles enabling respiration then must work harder to resist the binder's pressure. (Read more about the impact on breathing in Chapter 8.) With asthma, getting a full breath may already be a challenge; binding exacerbates the difficulty, especially if your symptoms flare.

If you think that you may have asthma and you bind, it is essential that you consult with a doctor to create a plan for how to treat your symptoms when they flare. Treatment often includes the prescription of a rescue inhaler for asthma attacks, and it's imperative that you carry it with you anytime that you are wearing your binder.

If you know that you have asthma, realize that wearing a binder causes additional pressure on the lungs during deep inhalation. Consult with a doctor to create a plan for how to treat your symptoms when they flare. Depending on the severity of your symptoms, you may need to adjust when you bind, making sure to plan for events when binding endangers your physical health.

BINDING RECOMMENDATIONS

- Wear a binder with side or front closures that allows you to quickly ease the pressure for easier breathing.
- Own two sizes of binder and wear the larger when in situations likely to trigger an asthma flare.
- Bind with the kinetic tape method of binding instead of a garment binder.
- If exercise triggers your asthma, consider not binding at all during cardio activity.
- If binding during cardio activity, always wear a loose or oversized binder.
- If allergens trigger your asthma, consider not binding or loosely binding during peak allergy season.

- Regularly do:
  - the Breathing Series (exercises #1–3)
  - Diaphragm Massage and Diaphragm Release (exercises #4–5).

CONSULT WITH YOUR DOCTOR

If you already have a diagnosis of chronic asthma when you begin binding, inform your doctor about this change. Review the sections "Communicating with Your Provider" and "In the Appointment" in Chapter 6 for advice on navigating these conversations.

Hypermobility Spectrum Disorders (i.e., Hypermobile Ehlers-Danlos Syndrome)

If you have or suspect you have HSD, please read the following guidance before doing any of the exercises in Part 2 of this book.

Hypermobility spectrum disorders (HSD) are a cluster of disorders affecting the body's connective tissue which is responsible for holding all structures in the body in their proper places. With HSD, this "glue" becomes fragile and stretchy, allowing joints to extend beyond normal range of motion like when a person is "double-jointed." HSD is more serious than just being unusually flexible and can cause pain ranging from a moderate disruption to daily living to severe pain and substantial disability.

MUSCULOSKELETAL HSD SYMPTOMS
- Beyond typical range of motion in joints
- Joint pain and instability, including partial dislocations
- Tendonitis or bursitis
- Frequent soft tissue overuse injuries

IMPACT OF BINDING

There is a vast array of symptoms of HSD including vascular, visceral, ocular, and more. This book addresses only the effects binding has on the musculoskeletal system.

The pressure that binding puts on the rib cage, spine, and shoulder joints can lead to painful subluxations (partial dislocations) of the joints, inflammation in the tendons or bursas (shock-absorbing pillows) of the joints, and hyper-engagement of the muscles surrounding the joint. In essence, the body of a person with HSD will have more difficulty withstanding the compression of a binder added to their already lax joints without experiencing significant pain.

BINDING RECOMMENDATIONS

- Wear a binder one size larger than your measurements.
- Consider athletic compression shirts (spandex similar to swimsuit compression) instead of traditional binders.
- Try kinetic tape binding for a no-compression method—be aware of potential tearing if you experience skin fragility.
- Limit the duration and frequency of binding to when joint pain is manageable.
- Avoid binding in situations that frequently cause spine, rib, or shoulder displacement issues as these might be exacerbated by compression.
- If binding is primarily impacting pain in your cervical spine, shoulders, or collarbones, a strapless binder might be an appropriate option (I generally recommend against strapless binders but in this case it can be supportive if not overly tight).

EXERCISE RECOMMENDATIONS

- It is important to avoid stretching exercises as that can make your joints more vulnerable to pain and dislocation.
- Self-massage is generally safe and effective—try:
    - Sternum Massage (exercise #7)
    - Pectoralis Muscles Massage (exercise #8)
    - Occiput Massage (exercise #17)
    - SCM Massage and Trigger Point Release (exercise #19).
- Work with a physical therapist familiar with HSD to create a safe regimen of exercises that support your body.

CONSULT WITH YOUR DOCTOR

If you are experiencing moderate-to-severe pain from hypermobile joints, you should be under the care of a doctor. If you already have a diagnosis of HSD and intend to begin binding, inform your doctor about this change. It is best for you to discuss your intention to bind with your doctor and make a plan for what will support your body. Depending on your unique case, working with a physical therapist may increase your ability to bind in select situations. Additionally, employing a combination of the suggestions above can support you in achieving some degree of your desired gender expression. Alternating binding methods is a strategy for reducing repetitive strain.

Be prepared to be told to stop binding. Review the section "Communicating with Your Provider" in Chapter 6 for advice on navigating these conversations. For additional advice on receiving treatment for HSD and for self-managing HSD, visit www.ehlers-danlos.org.

Gastroesophageal Reflux Disease (GERD)

Most people experience occasional acid reflux or heartburn. However, multiple occurrences per week usually suggest a condition called gastro-esophageal reflux disease (GERD). The sphincter which opens and closes to allow food to pass into the stomach becomes weakened, allowing acid to backflow from the stomach and irritating and inflaming the esophagus.

SYMPTOMS

- Burning in the chest, especially after eating
- Regurgitation of stomach contents
- Sour taste in the throat
- Chest pain
- Sensation of a lump in the throat
- Laryngitis

IMPACT OF BINDING

Many people who experience heartburn, acid reflux, or GERD symptoms before binding will find that the compression of the upper abdomen with binding exacerbates their symptoms. Tight, restrictive garments increase pressure on the esophageal sphincter, increasing the likelihood that acid will travel upward from the stomach.

BINDING RECOMMENDATIONS

- Follow sizing guidelines to be sure you are wearing the correct size.
- Try a binder that is one size larger to reduce overall pressure on the abdomen.
- Avoid full-length binders which compress more surface area of your abdomen.
- Wear a binder with side or front closures so you can release the pressure without removing your binder when symptoms flare.
- Remove your binder whenever possible to release the pressure on the abdomen.
- When symptoms flare, remove your binder.
- Prioritize taking days off from binding.
- When eating while binding, eat more slowly, eat smaller portions, and avoid heartburn-inducing foods.

DIET RECOMMENDATIONS

- **Foods to avoid:** Fried and greasy foods, cheese, carbonation, tomato-based sauces, foods with chilis and pepper.
- **Foods to eat:** Wholegrains, high-fiber vegetables, bananas, melons, cauliflower, fennel, nuts, and watery fruits and vegetables.
- **Home remedy:** Ginger tea or ginger chews can calm heartburn because ginger has a high pH and anti-inflammatory properties.

EXERCISE RECOMMENDATIONS

- Avoid doing exercises while GERD symptoms are flared
- Diaphragm Massage and Release (exercises #4 and #5)
- Anterior Torso Release (exercise #23)

CONSULT WITH YOUR DOCTOR

If you are already under a doctor's care for GERD and binding makes the condition worse, make an appointment to discuss increasing or changing medications. If you are not comfortable disclosing that you bind, explain that it is worse when you are wearing a sports bra. The important thing is to make sure the doctor understands that tight clothing on your abdomen is exacerbating the problem.

Review the section "Communicating with Your Provider" in Chapter 6 for advice on navigating these conversations.

Irritable Bowel Syndrome (IBS) and Inflammatory Bowel Disease (IBD) (i.e., Crohn's Disease and Ulcerative Colitis)

While IBS and IBD are two different conditions of the gastrointestinal (GI) tract, both cause painful swelling in the abdomen.

SYMPTOMS
- Abdominal swelling or distention
- Abdominal pain and cramping
- Diarrhea and/or constipation

IMPACT OF BINDING
Especially during a flare of GI symptoms, people with IBS and IBD may find that the compression of the upper abdomen with binding exacerbates their symptoms.

BINDING RECOMMENDATIONS
- Follow sizing guidelines to be sure you are wearing the correct size.
- Size up one size if the compression irritates your intestinal symptoms.
- Avoid full-length binders which compress more surface area of your abdomen.
- Wear a binder with side or front closures so you can release the pressure without removing your binder during sudden cramping or bouts of diarrhea.
- Remove your binder whenever possible to release the pressure on the abdomen.
- Avoid binding when the abdomen is especially distended or is tender to the touch.
- Prioritize taking days off from binding.

EXERCISE RECOMMENDATIONS

- Avoid doing any exercises that cause abdominal pain or discomfort, especially when IBS and IBD symptoms are flared.
- Focus on self-massage and trigger point release exercises.
- To facilitate less constriction in the abdomen do:
  - Diaphragm Massage (exercise #4) when not in a flare
  - Anterior Torso Release (exercise #23) which provides relief for some people with IBD and IBS symptoms.

CONSULT WITH YOUR DOCTOR

If you are under the care of a doctor for IBS or IBD and binding is making your symptoms worse, make an appointment to discuss additional medication or diet changes that could improve your symptoms. Be prepared to be told to stop binding altogether and take a binder to the appointment to assist in this conversation. Review the sections "Communicating with Your Provider" and "In the Appointment" in Chapter 6 for advice on navigating these conversations.

Migraines and Cervicogenic Headaches

Migraines, a disease that impacts the nervous system, can cause intense and severe headache pain. Cervicogenic headaches are caused by pain that refers pain to the head from a specific area in the neck. In both cases, increased muscle tension in the neck can be a trigger for the headache.

SYMPTOMS

- Severe headache pain, often on one side of the head
- Light and sound sensitivity
- Nausea and vomiting (migraine)
- Variety of less common symptoms, such as vertigo or auras

IMPACT OF BINDING

Shoulder straps of binders exert pressure on the muscles at the base of the neck which can be a trigger for headaches (note that shoulder straps in many sports bras and traditional bras have more compressive straps than binders). Increasing the tension in these muscles can agitate the cervical spine and cause pain in the cranial muscles. The tighter the straps, the more they dig into these muscles. The shoulder straps of many binders are made of average spandex which will apply the least pressure, and others are made of the highly compressive fabric that compresses the chest tissue. Binder straps are either tank or racerback style. The shape of the racerback straps applies more pressure to an area notorious for trigger points that refer pain to the cranial muscles and can set off a migraine or increase the intensity of headache pain. See Chapter 8 to learn more about binding and headache pain.

Wearing a smaller size than your measurements indicate will result in shoulder straps digging more deeply into these muscles. Wearing a too-small binder will pull the shoulders into a bowed position which causes Forward Head Posture (FHP) that pinches the occipital muscles at the base of the skull and overstretches the muscles on the front of the neck, both of which are heavily correlated to migraine and cervicogenic headache pain.

BINDING RECOMMENDATIONS

- Wear only your true size according to the size guide of the specific binder you purchase.
- Choose binders with straps made of spandex with elasticity similar to a swimsuit to exert less pressure over the shoulders than those made of power mesh.
- Do not wear any binder where the shoulder straps are made of power mesh (common in Underworks/Xbody models).
- Avoid racerback binders and sports bras.
- Use kinetic tape methods of binding to eliminate shoulder straps entirely when flares are at a peak.

EXERCISE RECOMMENDATIONS

- Chin Tuck (exercise #16)
- Occiput Massage (exercise #17)
- Neck Mobilization (exercise #18)
- SCM Massage and Trigger Point Release (exercise #19)
- Trapezius and Levator Scapula Trigger Point Release (exercise #20)

CONSULT WITH YOUR DOCTOR

If you are under the care of a doctor for headaches and binding is making your symptoms worse, make an appointment to discuss additional medication or other therapies which could provide support. Be prepared to be told to stop binding altogether and take a binder to the appointment to assist in this conversation. Review the sections "Communicating with Your Provider" and "In the Appointment" in Chapter 6 for advice on navigating these conversations.

Other treatments which can be helpful for chronic headaches are acupuncture, therapeutic massage, craniosacral therapy, chiropractics, and physical therapy.

Temporomandibular Joint Disorder (TMJD)

TMJD impacts the jaw joint due to inflammation of the tissue inside the ball-and-socket joint which allows you to open your mouth and to chew. Pain in this joint can result from multiple factors, including several habits related to stress and trauma: teeth grinding, jaw clenching, FHP, and nail or lip biting. Pain in the jaw joint can also be felt as referred pain from trigger points in neck muscles. Referral pain from these trigger points can be the sole source of TMJD or it can intensify the pain that already exists from the physical factors in the joint.

SYMPTOMS

- Pain located in the joint just in front of the ears
- Clicking, grinding, or popping noise when opening or closing the mouth
- Difficulty opening the mouth fully

IMPACT OF BINDING

Pressure from shoulder straps into the trapezius, scalene, sternocleidomastoid (SCM), and platysma muscles can cause trigger points to form which radiate pain to the jaw. For people with persistent jaw pain, choosing a binder that minimizes or eliminates compression of the muscles under the shoulder straps might be necessary.

FHP (read more about this in Chapter 8) can develop due to rolling shoulders and hunching to hide the appearance of your chest. Wearing a binder that is too small can increase this posture, putting the SCM muscle in an overstretched position. In this posture, the SCM can develop painful trigger points that will result in jaw pain.

BINDING RECOMMENDATIONS

- Avoid binders with shoulder straps made of the same high-compression power mesh as the chest panel.
- Avoid wearing sports bras with straps made of strong elastic fabric that dig into shoulder muscles.
- Avoid racerback designs (binders or sports bras) because they dig into the trapezius muscle more than tank styles.
- Choose binders in which the straps are made of a spandex with elasticity similar to a swimsuit to exert less pressure over the shoulders.
- Avoid binding or have a looser binder on hand for days when jaw pain is severe.
- Consider using kinetic tape methods of binding to eliminate shoulder straps entirely.

EXERCISE RECOMMENDATIONS

- Chin Tuck (exercise #16)
- Occiput Massage (exercise #17)
- Neck Mobilization (exercise #18)
- SCM Massage and Trigger Point Release (exercise #19)
- Trapezius and Levator Scapula Trigger Point Release (exercise #20)

CONSULT WITH YOUR DOCTOR

If you are under the care of a doctor for TMJD and binding is making your symptoms worse, discuss new therapies which might be helpful. Review the sections "Communicating with Your Provider" and "In the Appointment" in Chapter 6 for advice on navigating these conversations.

Other treatments which can be helpful for TMJD are acupuncture, intraoral massage, craniosacral therapy, and dry needling.

Sensory Processing Disorder

Sensory processing disorder is a condition that impacts how the brain interprets information from the senses. This can impact all or any of the senses and can be mild to severe.

SYMPTOMS

- Intense experiences of sensory stimuli—sounds, light, touch, taste, textures
- Reaction to stimuli can range from a mild irritant to extreme pain

IMPACT OF BINDER

The sensory information that comes from the skin in contact with the binder can be a disruptive factor for people with sensory processing disorders. Some of the things that can prevent people with sensory sensitivities from binding are exposed seams, rough fabrics, tags, zippers, Velcro, and hook closures.

BINDER SUGGESTIONS

- Choose tank-style binders to avoid zippers, Velcro, and hooks.
- Shop from companies that specialize in binders for sensory sensitivities, including Amor Binders and For Them.

Arthritis

Arthritis is a cluster of more than 100 different disorders that causes joint inflammation. These conditions cause pain, swelling, and stiffness in joints throughout the body. They can be hereditary and/or autoimmune.

SYMPTOMS

- Joint pain, swelling, and stiffness that persists
- Fatigue in joints
- Depending on the condition, pain and inflammation throughout the body

IMPACT OF BINDING

The pressure that binding puts on the rib cage, spine, and shoulder joints can lead to pain that triggers or exacerbates arthritis symptoms in the shoulders, sternum, cervical and thoracic spine, and jaw.

BINDING RECOMMENDATIONS

- During flare-ups, avoid binding or wear a loose or oversized binding option.
- Wear athletic compression shirts (spandex similar to swimsuit compression) instead of traditional binders.
- For chronic sustained arthritis, especially in the spine, choose a low-compression method of binding.
- Use kinetic tape binding method for a no-compression binding.

EXERCISE RECOMMENDATIONS

- Focus on exercises that target muscles and trigger points.
- Avoid any exercises which target joints where you have arthritis.
- If an exercise causes pain in your joints, stop and consult a physical therapist for support.

CONSULT WITH YOUR DOCTOR

If you are under the ongoing care of a rheumatologist to manage an arthritis condition, it is a good idea to update them on the fact that you have started to bind, especially if you experience a change or worsening of your arthritis symptoms. Take a binder to the appointment to assist in this conversation. Review the sections "Communicating with Your Provider" and "In the Appointment" in Chapter 6 for advice on navigating these conversations.

Section 3: Acute Illnesses

Respiratory Conditions
Colds, Bronchitis, and Allergies

Bronchitis, common colds, and seasonal allergies are mild conditions that impact the respiratory system. When experiencing a cough, congestion, frequent sneezing, or chest tightness, it is important to limit binding to critical situations. The chest constriction from binding can make it harder to clear mucus from the lungs, increasing the severity and duration of the illness or causing it to progress to pneumonia.

Wearing a binder when coughing, sneezing, and wheezing can strain muscles and inflame cartilage in the rib cage, chest, and back. These injuries can be painful enough to prevent you from binding once you are well, so best let your body heal without the burden of the binder.

Pneumonia

Pneumonia is a respiratory infection that causes inflammation in the lungs, causing mucus to collect and fluid to fill the sacs in the lungs where oxygen exchange occurs. If the body cannot clear the fluids, serious infection, which can require hospitalization, will develop.

SYMPTOMS

- Cough, which may produce greenish, yellow, or bloody mucus
- Fever, sweating, shaking, and chills
- Shortness of breath
- Rapid, shallow breathing
- Sharp or stabbing chest pain that gets worse when you breathe deeply or cough
- Bluish color in your lips and fingertips
- Loss of appetite, low energy, and fatigue

See a doctor right away if you have a cough accompanied by another symptom listed above. Get emergency medical attention if you have bluish color in your lips or fingertips or sharp, stabbing chest pain.

IMPACT OF BINDING

Binding reduces your ability to fight off respiratory infections. When lungs are compressed by a binder, they cannot fill to capacity. The passageways inside the lungs are like a tree with progressively smaller branches. Wearing a binder can mean that airflow is not reaching the smallest branches, or bronchioles. It is possible for a less serious respiratory infection (i.e., common cold or influenza) to turn into pneumonia when the bacteria or virus fills the bronchioles with mucus. When forced to work against the added pressure of your binder, your body cannot cough as deeply in order to get the mucus out.

Unfortunately, people who bind are more likely to ignore symptoms of pneumonia because:

- restricted breathing can seem like a normal part of binding, so the shortness of breath or rapid, shallow breathing of pneumonia goes unnoticed
- appointments for chest infections are avoided because they require an exam of the chest and could lead to questions about binding.

PREVENT AND REDUCE RISK

Binding Recommendations

- Each time you remove your binder, take three to five deep, rib-expanding breaths (see exercises #1–3) and cough to help clear fluid from your lungs.
- When you have a cough or flu-like symptoms, remove your binder as soon as it's safe to do so, then minimize or eliminate time in the binder until symptoms subside.
- Build strength in respiratory muscles by doing breathing exercises as part of your daily routine (exercises #1–5).

If You Develop Pneumonia:

- Do not bind until the infection has completely cleared.
- Constriction will make it harder to get a full breath and cough deeply enough to clear mucus from your lungs.
- Coughing fits when the rib cage is compressed can also result in painful trigger points and rib dislocation or displacement.

Other Suggestions

- Wash your hands!
- Get the flu shot.
- Talk to your doctor about whether a pneumonia vaccine is right for you.

- If you smoke or are immunocompromised, the American Lung Association considers you high risk and recommends talking to your doctor about the pneumonia vaccine.
- Smoking and binding increases risks of respiratory infections—consider getting support to stop smoking from a smoking-cessation program.

Treatment and Recovery

Since the most common form of pneumonia is bacterial, your doctor will likely prescribe antibiotics. For viral pneumonia, you may be prescribed antivirals or be instructed to manage symptoms and rest until your body fights off the infection. Since treatment is different for bacterial and viral pneumonia, you must seek medical care to confirm the source of your infection.

Recovery from pneumonia requires a lot of rest. Some patients on antibiotics are able to return to daily activities in about a week, but others need a month or more to recover. It is crucial that your body be able to rest and heal without the added stress of the binder, so you will need to abstain from binding during recovery. Wearing a binder can cause relapse and should be avoided until you are not experiencing congestion, coughing, or wheezing. It's best to abstain from smoking (both tobacco and cannabis) and vaping during respiratory infections.

PREPARING FOR A DOCTOR VISIT

For most people who bind, going to the doctor is hard enough without it being a visit to specifically address your chest area. Since pneumonia will not go away on its own and catching it early is important, you will need to make a doctor's appointment.

A visit for pneumonia will include questions about your medical history, risk factors, and exposure. It is up to you whether to divulge that you bind. The treatment is not likely to change, either way. In addition to the questions, the physical exam will include listening to your lungs with a stethoscope placed on your chest and back. The doctor may need to shift the dense chest tissue to the side to listen to specific areas of your lungs. This is one of the key diagnostic measures as there are often crackling, bubbling, and rumbling sounds when you inhale. You will not be able to wear your binder during this exam. Your chest will remain covered during this exam. I recommend wearing a button-down shirt to the exam to enable you to limit your exposure.

Not every visit to the doctor for pneumonia will involve a chest X-ray, but many do. The purpose is to look for the location and extent of inflammation in your lungs. During a chest X-ray, you will probably be given a medical gown to wear and will need to remove your top. You will not be able to wear a binder during this procedure. You will lie down and the X-ray technician will position the machine directly at your chest. An X-ray procedure is brief, but it is wise to prepare, as the technician will be focused on your chest intently as they position the arm of the X-ray machine.

SMOKING

The US Transgender Survey in 2015[2] showed that transgender adults have higher rates of smoking tobacco than cisgender peers, with the highest rates among transgender people who are non-visual conformers.

I was a pack-a-day smoker for six years after suffering harassment for coming out as queer and still struggling to understand my gender identity. Coping strategies are important—smoking was mine—and it isn't always the right time to stop.

But we need to be honest with ourselves. Smoking tobacco and diminished lung health go hand in hand, because smoking compromises lung function, reduces immune system response, and adds to lung inflammation, all of which can make pneumonia and other respiratory conditions more severe. Data on lung health and cannabis smoking and vaping is still emerging, but it is likely that inhalation is an irritant to bronchial passageways.

2 James, S. E., Herman, J., Keisling, M., Mottet, L., and Anafi, M. (2015) U.S. Transgender Survey (USTS). Inter-university Consortium for Political and Social Research [distributor], 2019-05-22. https://doi.org/10.3886/ICPSR37229.v1

If you smoke or vape and bind regularly, I strongly encourage you to seek support to stop or reduce your use.

Where to Get Support

- If you live in a city with a LGBTQIA+ health or service organization, see if it offers smoking-cessation programs.
- If you do not have local access to a LGBTQIA+ smoking-cessation group, online support for LGBTQIA+ people is available at:
  - https://smokefree.gov/lgbt-and-smoking
  - https://www.becomeanex.org

If stopping smoking isn't possible now, support your lung health with daily breathing exercises and exercises to open the chest and rib cage (exercises #1–12).

If you develop a respiratory disease and feel unable to abstain from smoking tobacco while you are sick, talk to your doctor about measures to curb nicotine withdrawal while you recover. If you use cannabis regularly, edible options can allow your lungs to rest while still providing the effects of cannabis.

COVID-19 or SARS-CoV-2

The SARS-COV-2 virus can cause bronchitis, pneumonia, and acute respiratory distress syndrome (ARDS) which vary in severity but all impact the lungs' ability to clear fluids. Resulting symptoms include coughing, congestion, fluid in the lungs, shortness of breath, and, in extreme cases, failure of the respiratory system, resulting in death.

Unlike traditional forms of bronchitis and pneumonia, it can take longer for the lungs to recover, resulting in symptoms and scarring that can last as long as a year. If you at high risk for a serious case of COVID-19, binding could increase your risk, and I recommend binding only in essential situations.

It will take years for science to fully understand long-COVID but the chronic symptoms can include lingering respiratory symptoms which may require changes in your binding routine until they resolve. Other long-COVID symptoms—persistent fatigue, headaches, dizziness, tingling sensations, and stomach pain—can be exacerbated by binding. It is important to pay attention to and track symptoms if you are experiencing long-COVID so that you have accurate information to share with doctors.

SYMPTOMS

- Fever or chills
- Cough
- Shortness of breath or difficulty breathing
- Fatigue
- Muscle or body aches
- Headache
- New loss of taste or smell
- Sore throat
- Congestion or runny nose
- Nausea, vomiting, or diarrhea

IMPACT OF BINDING

As with pneumonia, people who bind are more likely to ignore symptoms of COVID because:

- restricted breathing can seem normal, so the shortness of breath and rapid, shallow breathing go unnoticed and treatment is delayed
- appointments for chest infections require an exam of the chest and could lead to questions about binding—see Chapter 6 for help talking to medical professionals about binding.

Binding while experiencing any respiratory infection puts you at risk for getting a more severe infection. Since a severe COVID infection can have long-term health implications and be life-threatening, it's important to pay special attention to your lung health if you are exposed to COVID and/ or test positive.

Binding while your body is fighting off a COVID infection reduces your ability to fight off the virus and can allow it to spread more quickly.

The compression of the binder means that your body is less able to cough powerfully enough to get the fluids out. This could accelerate a mild case of COVID into a more serious case.

Binding while experiencing symptoms of coughing, sneezing, or wheezing can strain muscles, inflame cartilage, and lead to rib displacement, all of which can require lengthy recovery periods when binding is not generally possible due to pain.

PREVENT AND REDUCE RISK

- When you remove your binder, take three to five deep, rib-expanding breaths (exercise #1) and cough to help clear any fluid in your lungs.
- Make breathing exercises part of your daily routine to strengthen the body's ability to draw air deeply into the lungs and expel mucus that accumulates, especially if you are at high risk for COVID.
- Abstain from tobacco or cannabis smoking and vaping during respiratory infections.

If You Develop COVID Symptoms

- If you are exposed to COVID, binding less during the incubation period is advised, in case your body is in the early stages of fighting a respiratory infection.
- If you experience any COVID symptoms, remove your binder as soon as it's safe to do so and get tested.
- If you test positive, avoid binding during isolation to support your body in successfully fighting off the disease.
- If you test negative but are having respiratory symptoms, wait until the symptoms abate before resuming binding.
- If you must bind to avoid a threat of violence, bind for the shortest amount of time possible and wear the loosest binder that you have.

Avoid Exposure

- Get vaccinated and boosted unless a medical condition prevents it.
- Wear a mask, especially in crowded indoor environments.
- Socialize in well-ventilated settings, outdoors when possible.

- Wash your hands well and often.

TREATMENT AND RECOVERY

For most cases of COVID, treatment and recovery require you to rest, hydrate, and treat the fever and cold symptoms with over-the-counter medications. It is crucial that your body be able to rest and heal without the added stress of the binder so you will need to abstain from binding while recovering.

Adhere to the local recommendations for how long to isolate in order to prevent spreading the disease to others.

Seek immediate medical attention if you have any of the following symptoms:

- Trouble getting an adequate breath
- Persistent pain or pressure in the chest
- New confusion
- Inability to wake or stay awake
- Pale, gray, or blue-colored skin, lips, or nail beds, depending on skin tone

PREPARING FOR A DOCTOR VISIT

Your doctor will ask about your exposure to the virus and your risk factors. They may also ask questions about your medical history. It is up to you whether or not to divulge that you bind, and the treatment is not likely to change.

If you are having serious respiratory symptoms, the doctor will need to assess them to determine the severity of the infection. This will include listening to your lungs with a stethoscope on your chest and back, and around the densest part of your chest tissue. They may need to shift the dense chest tissue to the side to listen to specific areas of your lungs. This is one of the key diagnostic measures as there are often crackling, bubbling, and rumbling sounds when you inhale. You will not be able to wear your binder during this exam and your chest should remain covered during this exam. I recommend wearing a button-down shirt to limit your exposure during the exam.

At this point in the progression of the virus, you should not be binding so prepare to interact with the medical staff without a binder. Your doctors will be running tests to determine the extent that the virus has impacted your respiratory system, so expect that the assessments will focus on your chest area.

If your symptoms lead to hospitalization, a variety of treatments may be tried based on what's available in your geographic location. Due to the contagious nature of the disease, prepare to be your own medical advocate and reach out virtually to your network for support. For tips on navigating medical appointments, see Chapter 6.

Skin Infections

Tinea Corporis or Ringworm

You may be familiar with athlete's foot, the name given to the itchy fungal infection that attacks the feet. Tinea corporis is the same fungus, just on your torso. It's usually referred to as ringworm, but don't worry, there is no worm involved! This fungal infection can be a complication of binding, especially if excess sweat saturates your binder.

SYMPTOMS

Tinea corporis causes a red, itchy rash under your binder that can present as:

- An inflamed area with patches of pimple-like bumps
- Red inflamed skin with flaky edges
- Red inflamed ring-like patches (hence "ringworm")
- Intense itching

IMPACT OF BINDING

Binder-sweat is a way of life. especially for anyone binding in a hot, humid climate, and heavy sweating is a risk factor of tinea corporis. Because tinea corporis is a fungus, it's more likely to grow in the skin folds that result from smushing chest tissue inside of a binder. Wearing a clean binder is key in preventing the fungus from growing on your skin. Binders that get sweaty one day should not be worn again the next day.

PREVENT AND REDUCE RISK

- Wash your binders regularly. If you sweat enough in your binder that it is wet, wash it before its next wear.
- Apply a non-talc powder with Miconazole Nitrate under your binder to reduce sweating and prevent fungal growth, especially in skin folds.
- Do not use cortisone cream; it can make the fungal infection worse.
- If you have "athlete's foot," "jock itch," or fungal infections of the nails, treat the infection right away. It is the same fungus as tinea corporis, so take extreme care not to transfer it to your torso. Carry hand sanitizer and wash your hands any time you touch the infected part of your body.

TREATMENT AND RECOVERY

Once a doctor rules out a more serious skin infection, you will be prescribed anti-fungal medication, which may be prescription or over-the-counter. Be sure to use it as long as directed, not just until the infection is not visible or painful.

PREPARING FOR A DOCTOR VISIT

Fungal infections are diagnosed by a visual inspection of the rash which will require you to expose the infected area of your chest. In rare cases the doctor will need to take a sample of the flaky skin to evaluate in a lab.

Consider wearing no undergarment under a loose T-shirt or button-down that easily allows you to expose the affected skin without having to remove your top. If you are uneasy about the exposure of an in-person visit, this is an excellent opportunity for a telehealth visit. Some providers may even be willing to evaluate the rash from a photo.

For help navigating doctor visits, see Chapter 6.

Acne

Most people get some form of acne in their lifetime. It's caused by pores getting clogged with the overproduction of sebum, the oily substance produced to lubricate the hair follicle. When the pores are clogged by the sebum and dead skin cells, it usually causes a mild form of acne. When bacteria gets involved, then moderate and severe acne can occur. If you are taking testosterone as part of medical transition, you may experience moderate-to-severe acne that you did not experience before taking testosterone because the hormone increases sebum production.

SYMPTOMS

Acne includes six forms:

- Mild, non-inflammatory acne
  - Whiteheads (closed clogged pores)
  - Blackheads (open clogged pores)
- Moderate inflammatory acne
  - Small red, tender bumps (papules)
  - Pimples (pustules), which are papules with pus at their tips
- Severe inflammatory acne
  - Large, solid, painful lumps under the skin (nodules)
  - Painful, pus-filled lumps under the skin (cystic lesions)

IMPACT OF BINDING

Friction from the binder and the oils trapped against your skin underneath it increases the risk of acne breakouts. Even when they're not in a binder, the chest, upper back, and abdomen are among the areas most likely to develop acne. When oils and bacteria on the skin are in the moist environment of a binder, the conditions are prime for infections that cause moderate-to-severe inflammatory acne.

Dysphoria can lead people to avoid touching their chest at all, including in the shower. While it may be psychologically painful to do, it's critical that you wash your chest, especially in folds of skin, in order to prevent painful acne that could prevent you from binding in the future. See Chapter 3 for more about skincare.

PREVENT AND REDUCE RISK

- Regardless of the presence of acne, people who bind need to cleanse the skin covered by their binder daily.

- Take days off from binding to give the skin time to air out and recover.

TREATMENT AND RECOVERY

The following recommendations are for people with no history of skin disorders. If you have any underlying skin disorders, consult your dermatologist before addressing any acne that develops under your binder.

If mild acne occurs, over-the-counter skin washes are an excellent option. For non-inflammatory acne, try salicylic acid, sulfur, and tea tree oil. If you have sensitive skin, sulfur is the least likely to irritate.

For inflammatory acne, benzoyl peroxide is an effective way to treat the bacteria that contributes to the formation of papules, pustules, and some mild lesions. If, after six weeks, you do not see improvement, consult your primary care provider or a dermatologist.

For severe acne, you need to see your primary care provider or a dermatologist so that a regimen can be tailored to your needs and medications can be prescribed as needed.

PREPARING FOR A DOCTOR VISIT

If you develop moderate acne that doesn't clear up within six weeks of over-the-counter treatment or severe acne, a doctor will need to examine the acne to determine a course of treatment. Depending on where the outbreak is, you may be able to lift only a portion of your shirt or gown to limit exposing your chest. Wearing a button-down with no binder underneath will allow you to expose part of your torso without exposing the entire chest. The doctor will probably want to examine the entire outbreak, so if any of it is obscured by your binder, don't wear it to the appointment. This way, you avoid any discussion of your binder or your gender identity unless you choose to disclose it. For more tips about how to discuss limiting exposure of your body with your doctor, see Chapter 6.

Cellulitis

This is a rare complication and requires urgent medical attention.
Cellulitis is one of many infections caused by the bacteria Group A Strep (Streptococcus) and it is generally assumed that the infection gets into the

body through breaks in the skin and causes an infection that can become serious very quickly. Breaks in the skin can be from injuries (scratches, cuts, abrasions), sores, raw skin, infected acne pustules, or flares of skin conditions (eczema, ringworm).

SYMPTOMS

- Red, swollen, and painful skin
- Hot and tender to the touch
- Bumpy or blistered texture
- Fever and chills (in some cases)

If you are experiencing these symptoms, see a doctor urgently to avoid a more serious infection. If you develop a fever in addition to rash symptoms, seek emergency medical attention.

IMPACT OF BINDING

Cuts, scratches, sores, acne, rashes, and irritations can all result in broken skin. When they occur on the chest and upper back, they're covered by your binder. Group A Strep is a common bacteria that lives on our skin without doing harm, but when it gets into the body it causes cellulitis. A binder and a skin wound can create the perfect environment for this to occur.

Dysphoria and fear of transphobia deter many people who bind from seeking medical attention when they experience cellulitis, especially because exposing their chest will be necessary for care. Since cellulitis can quickly escalate to something serious, the lack of healthcare can result in dangerous infections. This is a situation where it is too high risk to avoid seeking care.

PREVENT AND REDUCE RISK

- If you have broken skin on the area that will be covered by your binder, do not bind until it is healed.
- When you do get a minor break in the skin, clean it and keep it clean as it heals.

- Oozing, bleeding, or sutured skin should never be covered with a binder.
- Wash the skin under your binder on a daily basis.
- Wash your binder regularly to keep your binder free of bacteria.
- If you have an open wound or active skin infection, avoid hot tubs, swimming pools, and natural bodies of water (e.g., lakes, rivers, oceans).

TREATMENT AND RECOVERY

Cellulitis is generally treatable with oral antibiotics. Serious cases may require intravenous (IV) antibiotics. As with any course of antibiotics, it is important to finish the entire course as prescribed. Not finishing the medication can result in developing antibiotic-resistant streptococcus in your body.

PREPARING FOR A DOCTOR VISIT

If the rash is accompanied by a fever, this infection may require a visit to the emergency room which is often more distressing than seeing your familiar medical provider, so take someone with you to be your medical advocate (for more on navigating emergency medical care, see Chapter 6). One or more medical providers will likely examine your chest while in emergency care. It's important that you tell them about wearing a sweat-trapping undergarment since the chest is not a common area for cellulitis and they may not immediately diagnose it as such. For advice about how to inform doctors about binding, see Chapter 6.

Heat Rash

Heat rash, common in people who bind, is rarely serious. It can, however, be uncomfortable and require a break from binding for hours or days. When sweat gets trapped in the sweat glands, the skin reacts with a rash.

SYMPTOMS

There are multiple types of heat rash with varying symptoms. All manifestations can occur after being hot and sweaty.

- Small, clear, fluid-filled bumps that burst easily
- Small, red bumps that itch or feel prickly
- Small, red bumps that become inflamed and pus-filled (uncommon)
- Small, firm, flesh-colored bumps (very uncommon)

IMPACT OF BINDING

Wearing a binder adds a layer of clothing which increases the amount of heat trapped close to your body. When sweat is trapped under your binder it cannot cool your skin because it can't evaporate. With sweat trapped under the binder and against your skin, the likelihood that sweat gets trapped in the sweat glands increases.

Heat rash is an irritation to the skin and, though not serious, may make it uncomfortable to bind in the hours and days after it occurs. Anytime your skin is red and painful, it is best to prioritize finding a place where you can be without your binder while your skin recovers. Resuming binding before the skin has recovered could irritate the rash and lead to more serious skin problems. See Section 1, "Heat-Related Conditions" at the beginning of this chapter for tips on navigating hot weather safely in a binder.

PREVENT AND REDUCE RISK

The main way to avoid heat rash is to cool down your body and your skin. If you're planning on being in the sun and/or heat, make a plan for how to cool off and pack a go-bag to help you to do so (see page 122).

This plan should include:

- access to cold water to drink
- cool, loose-fitting clothes (other than your binder, of course)
- a place where you can go to cool down
- a place where you can go to safely remove your binder.

See Section 1, "Heat-Related Conditions" for tips and strategies for staying cool and being prepared in the heat.

TREATMENT AND RECOVERY

Heat rash resolves on its own when you are able to cool your body temperature and air out the area of the rash. It can take a few hours or up to two days for the skin to recover. If it stays red and painful longer than two days, consult a doctor.

The first thing you need to do is get out of the heat, drink water, and cool down. As soon as it is safe, take off your binder and allow the skin to breathe. Place a cool compress or cool moisture-activated fabric on the rash to cool the body (i.e., "PVA cooling technology"). Take a cool bath with a non-drying soap. Allow the skin to air-dry. Avoid fabrics and activities that will cause friction until the skin is no longer sensitive from the rash.

Circulatory and Neurological Conditions
Thoracic Outlet Syndrome (TOS)
A rare complication and some cases require emergency medical attention.

TOS is a condition of compression of the nerve, artery, and veins that travel from the neck into the arm. These structures must pass through several narrow passages between neck muscles, the first rib, the collarbone, and the scapula before getting to the arm. Any of the three can get impinged, or pinched, in one of these passages. The symptoms of TOS appear in the upper arm, the wrist, and the muscles of the hand.

There are two main types of TOS: neurogenic and vascular. In neurogenic TOS, the nerve bundle to the arm is impinged, while in vascular TOS the vein or artery gets impinged. While it accounts for just 5 percent of all TOS cases, vascular TOS is an acute condition requiring immediate medical attention. The majority of cases of TOS impact the nerve, causing discomfort and pain, and should be addressed by seeing a physical therapist, chiropractor, osteopath, or massage therapist.

SYMPTOMS

Vascular TOS (5 percent of cases)
- Bluish color in the hand and/or arm
- Pale hand and/or arm
- The hand and/or arm is unexpectedly cool to the touch

- Swelling in the hand and/or arm
- Painful tingling in the hand and/or arm (more intense than pins and needles)
- Bulging, swollen, or visible veins in the neck

Neurogenic TOS (95 percent of cases)
- Tingling in the fingers/hand that gets worse when the arms are held overhead
- Unexplained weakness in the arm or grip
- Pain in the arm, especially the wrist or elbow

IMPACT OF BINDING

It is likely that people who experience vascular TOS in combination with binding have a predisposition based on the congenital growth of the bones or muscles in the neck. However, since most people don't know about the presence of these bone growths until TOS occurs, binding can add the additional compression needed for the onset of symptoms.

A person's first rib is just under the collarbone, in the same neighborhood as the dozens of small muscles that stabilize the head, aid in respiration, and allow for full shoulder mobility. The criss-crossing of these muscles, bones, and tendons creates small passageways through which nerves and blood vessels must pass.

In neurogenic TOS, dysphoria hunching and chronic upper chest breathing can force the muscles between the clavicles, first ribs, and scapula to adapt in ways that narrow these passages to apply squeezing pressure which causes pain, tingling, or aching in the arm. Binders which are too small cause people to further round their shoulders forward, raising the first rib and further narrowing the passages. FHP (read more about FHP in Chapter 8), a direct result of a rounded posture, a history of trauma to the cervical spine, a family history of TOS, and strenuous activity that requires the arms to be overhead or in full extension for long periods, can all make a person more vulnerable to TOS.

High-Risk Activities
- Work with the hands overhead (e.g., mechanic, server)

- Work with the arms extended for long periods (e.g., hair stylist)
- Sports demanding strenuous action with extended, externally rotated arms (swimmers, baseball pitchers, tennis players)
- Sitting in slumped posture at a computer, on the phone, driving for long hours
- Lifting weights, especially without proper form

PREVENT AND REDUCE RISK

- Know the warning signs of vascular TOS and seek medical attention immediately if you experience them.
- If you notice any of the signs of vascular TOS, remove your binder and do chest-opening exercises.
- Build muscles to maintain a posture of broad shoulders and neutral neck posture.
- Train the body to breathe deeply using the diaphragm muscles rather than relying on the upper chest muscles (exercises #1–5).
- If you begin experiencing tingling in the arm or hand, start this series of exercises:
  - Chest Opener (exercise #6)
  - Pectoralis Muscles Trigger Point Release (exercise #9)
  - Chin Tuck (exercise #16)
  - SCM Massage and Trigger Point Release (exercise #19)
  - Trapezius and Levator Scapula Trigger Point Release (exercise #20)
  - Thoracic Mobilization (exercise #21)

TREATMENT AND RECOVERY

Vascular TOS requires emergency medical attention because the impingement of the vein or artery can cause blood clots or restrict adequate blood flow to the arm. Treatments include blood-thinning medication and thrombolysis (unblocking the vein) and the surgical removal of the atypical bone or muscle tissue.

For mild-to-moderate neurogenic TOS, treatment is physical therapy to improve posture and neural mobility, and build strength in weak muscles to reduce the likelihood of the narrow passages compressing the nerves.

Severe cases of neurogenic TOS can require surgery to relieve pressure, though this is rare.

PREPARING FOR A DOCTOR VISIT

If you have symptoms of vascular TOS, you will need emergency medical attention, likely at an emergency room. These emergency visits, with unknown healthcare workers, can be more distressing than seeing your regular medical provider. Given the repeated explanations needed of binding and gender identity during an emergency visit, take someone to be your medical advocate. It's crucial the doctor knows you wear a binder, since any compression of the upper chest is vital information to have when making an accurate diagnosis of this serious condition. See Chapter 6 for tips on discussing binding with doctors.

For tests, you will generally be in a hospital gown and can minimize exposure of your chest since the collarbone/shoulder region is the primary area of concern. Common tests for evaluation include ultrasound, nerve block, chest X-ray, CT scan, MRI, or nerve conduction studies. You should be able to keep your chest covered through all examinations and tests.

If you have symptoms of neurogenic TOS, the doctor will take a thorough medical history. It is best that you tell the doctor you bind. Not doing so could lead to a false diagnosis. See Chapter 6 for advice on talking to doctors about binding.

After taking your medical history, your doctor will ask you to move in ways that recreate the symptoms. You will be able to remain clothed. Have your binder with you, in case the doctor needs to see it worn, to determine if it's a contributing factor.

To rule out other conditions that can be misdiagnosed as neurogenic TOS, the doctor might order an ultrasound, nerve block, chest X-ray, MRI, or nerve conduction study. You may need to change into a gown but should be able to remain with your chest covered through all such tests.

Physical therapy is the most common and successful course of treatment for neurogenic TOS. It is hard to predict what a physical therapy visit will look like, but it should include you explaining your binding practice to the provider. Be prepared that for most rehabilitation exercises, you will not be able to wear your binder. See Chapter 6 for more information about talking with physical therapists about binding.

Skeletal Conditions

Rib Misalignment or Dislocation

Ribs, to accommodate the expansion of the lungs, are in constant motion and designed to be extra fluid at the joints with the spine and the sternum. Stable under normal forces, the rib joints shift to absorb extra forces. However, if they're unable to shift due to compression, the ribs are at risk of misalignment or partial dislocation, called subluxation.

The severity of the movement of the rib and the amount of discomfort caused can range from mild to severe. It can be caused by mundane activities, such as twisting to reach for something or a coughing/sneezing fit. When a rib displaces, the muscles that surround the head of the rib will contract and tighten to stabilize the rib and prevent further shifting. In some cases, it is the muscle contraction that causes the most pain, and in others, the rib itself can generate the pain. In either scenario, the pain will change or intensify with deep breathing, coughing, laughing, sneezing, or twisting. Depending on the affected rib(s), arm movement can also cause pain.

SYMPTOMS

- Rib pain centered at the spine or along the sternum, generally tender to the touch
- Stabbing chest pain when laughing, coughing, or sneezing
- Pain that radiates around the rib cage
- Dense knotted muscle, sometimes visibly in contraction, along the spine that developed at the same time as the pain
- Ache or sharp pain with deep inhalation
- Pain when twisting at the waist to look over the shoulder
- Pain with large arm movement, particularly overhead

IMPACT OF BINDING

When tight compression is exerted onto the rib cage, the joints that attach the ribs to the spine and sternum are forced to work against extra resistance to support breathing and movement. Since the body is extremely adaptable, it will find ways to continue to move and breathe even under the greatest strain. To adapt, the rib can shift in the vertebral (at the spine) or the sternal (at the sternum) joint to decrease that resistance.

Ideally when this displacement occurs, a person rests and does gentle movement to allow the rib to re-situate in the normal position. However, it's more common that a person continues to bind and the body slowly accepts the abnormal position of the rib as the new normal. The muscles and fascia will then tighten and thicken to support the out-of-place rib, resulting in chronic pain that can no longer be resolved by rest and gentle movement. The longer it's ignored, the more entrenched the pattern becomes. The abnormal positioning of bone, muscle, and fascia causes painful inflammation, and yet, many people come to accept they just have a chronic pain that they have to "just live with."

Wearing binders to do strenuous cardio, sports, weightlifting, and physical labor does not need to be something you avoid. However, you can reduce your chances of dislocating a rib by wearing a looser fitting binder that is either stretched out or one size larger than your measurements. If you are comfortable, wearing a sports bra for these activities reduces the risk of this injury. See Chapter 4 for more about binding safely while doing strenuous activities.

WHEN TO SEEK EMERGENCY MEDICAL ATTENTION FOR RIB PAIN

- If you experience stabbing chest pain, you should seek emergency medical attention to rule out any serious cardiac symptoms. ALWAYS.
- If pain in your ribs or with breathing develops after a physical trauma, such as a punch, car accident, or fall, you need emergency care to rule out rib fractures and damage to internal organs.

PREVENT AND REDUCE RISK

- Never use a wrap binding method.
- Do not layer multiple binders.
- Wear a binder that is properly sized based on your measurements.
- Avoid binders with equal compression 360 degrees around the body.
- Avoid wearing a tight binder while you do strenuous work or workouts, as doing so increases your risk of displacing a rib (see Chapter 4 for more on binding in strenuous activities).
- Remove a binder during panic attacks and asthma attacks when

rapid, erratic breathing is often coupled with a rounding of the shoulders into a protective position.

- Do not bind while experiencing sickness or allergies that involve heavy coughing, sneezing fits, or vomiting.
- When playing contact sports, doing aerobic activity, or doing strenuous physical labor, wear a loose or oversized binder.
- Consider binding with kinetic tape which is a non-compressive option.
- Regularly do the following exercises before any displacement occurs:
  - Breathing Series (see exercises #1–5)
  - Chest Opener (see exercise #6)
  - Sternum Massage (see exercise #7)
  - Thoracic Mobilization (see exercise #21)
  - Thoracic Opener (see exercise #22)

TREATMENT AND RECOVERY

Rib misalignment/displacement can resolve on its own if caught early. You will need to take time off from binding and strenuous activity to allow your body to rest. The exercises above will help the muscles to relax and allow the rib to reset. When the problem is allowed to persist, the muscles and fascia will need to be released from the protective pattern by a chiropractor, osteopath, or massage therapist.

If you do not have access to one of these practitioners, these self-treatment exercises are an alternative. It is important to start very gently and reduce intensity if you feel any pain. Too much too fast can cause the muscles to constrict and the pain to increase.

Recommended exercises:

- Quadruped Breathing (exercise #3)
- Sternum Massage (exercise #7)
- Rib Cage Trigger Point Release (exercise #10)
- Serratus Anterior Massage (exercise #11)
- Thoracic Mobilization (exercise #21)
- Anterior Torso Release (exercise #23)

When you experience relief from the rib resetting into alignment, don't jump back into full-time binder wearing. You are still recovering and should wear your binder only for essential situations. The compression of the binder can push the still-tender rib out of alignment before it has had a chance to stabilize in the new position. If this happens, remove the binder and do the exercises above. If you feel no improvement in three days, see the chiropractor, osteopath, or massage therapist to have the rib adjusted again.

PREPARING FOR A DOCTOR VISIT

Chiropractors and osteopaths are the best doctors to see for a misaligned rib. You will be able to leave on loose-fitting clothes during any adjustment or muscle manipulation. The chiropractor or osteopath may feel along the spine, sternum, and rib cage for tender spots. They may need to put their hand in your armpit to palpate the upper ribs. Not binding during the adjustment will allow the tissues full freedom to adjust but if removing it feels unsafe, wearing it does not risk serious harm. It can be helpful to take your binder with you to the appointment so that the doctor can clearly understand its effect on the rib cage.

Chiropractic adjustments can (but do not always) involve close body-to-body contact, as the chiropractor uses their body to twist or fold yours to adjust the bones. If you are a trauma survivor or are a person who struggles with close bodily contact, be aware that this might be a triggering treatment for you. Consider seeing an osteopath or massage therapist instead.

An osteopath is a medical doctor who takes a holistic approach to treatment and will generally take a thorough history to discover what might be contributing to the pain. It's important to be honest about when and how often you bind. Have the binder with you to help the doctor better understand its impact on your body and movement. Treatment varies from osteopath to osteopath but generally focuses on the soft tissue that's immobilizing instead of adjusting the rib itself.

Therapeutic massage therapists, too, can be helpful in the treatment of misaligned ribs. Not all massage therapists do "rib work" for misalignment, so ask ahead of time. Depending on the type of massage, you might be asked to undress or to dress in loose clothing and lie on a massage table. If you are undressed, you will be draped in a sheet and only the body part being treated should be exposed. Though it depends on the therapist, it is unlikely that massage for a misaligned rib can be done while wearing a binder; however, you will want to show it to the therapist who will likely be unfamiliar with the garment. Since you'll change out of your clothes after discussing your condition with the therapist, you can wear the binder to your appointment.

Slipping Rib Syndrome

Slipping rib syndrome generally affects the lower ribs (8 to 10), which are connected to the sternum by long strips of cartilage. When this cartilage sustains enough stress it can break, leaving a loose tip of the rib which can slip around. This slippage can make a clicking or popping sound. Often, when you touch the area, you can feel rib movement that isn't present on the other side. This loose tip can slip under the cartilage of the ribs above or below, causing irritation, inflammation, and pain. Several of my clients with hypermobility spectrum disorders have a palpable slipping rib, but it causes minimal to no pain.

SYMPTOMS

Since the rib can slip in and out of irritating positions, these symptoms might come and go with certain activities or movements.

- Sharp stabbing pain in the mid-abdomen off-center on the side of the slipping rib
- Sharp stabbing pain wrapping around the side onto the back
- Sharp pain or shifting rib when taking a deep breath that fills the lower rib cage or belly
- When fingers are curled under the edge of the rib cage (exercise #4), you feel the cartilage of the ribs shift or click under your fingers.
- Pain which comes and goes in sharp and alarming pangs
- Wearing a binder causes the pain to occur/increase

WHEN TO SEEK EMERGENCY MEDICAL ATTENTION

- Any fever accompanied by sharp, abdominal pain
- Lower-right abdominal pain, rule out appendicitis
- Right-side pain under the ribs, rule out liver and gallbladder disorders, especially if you have any history or high risk
- Stabbing pain under the left lower ribs accompanied by any stomach symptoms, rule out ulcers or gastritis

IMPACT OF BINDING

Compression exerted on the low ribs by certain kinds of binding can impede those ribs from properly adapting to movement the way they would if they were free to move. Binders that put the most pressure on the lower ribs are full-length binders and binders that compress 360 degrees around the body.

Full-length binders pose a higher risk when the fabric rolls up, effectively exerting two or three times the intended compression on the ribs at your waist. Then the lower ribs are under sustained inward pressure and the cartilage is forced to absorb any additional shock to the rib cage. In this situation, a load-bearing twist, hard cough, or minor impact to the waist could exceed what the cartilage can absorb and cause it to break.

PREVENT AND REDUCE RISK

- Do not allow your binder to roll up. If this is a problem, see Chapter 3 for more on preventing roll-up.
- Do not layer multiple binders.
- Wear a binder properly sized based on your measurements.
- Avoid binders with equal compression 360 degrees around the body.
- Consider binding with kinetic tape which is a non-compressive option.
- Avoid physical labor or working out in a tight binder, see Chapter 4 about safely binding with strenuous activity.
- Avoid playing contact sports in a binder.
- If you experience discomfort (without stabbing pain) in the lower rib cage, especially on one side, do deep breathing exercises three

or more times per day to help resist the force of compression and stabilize the rib (exercises #1–3).

TREATMENT AND RECOVERY

Unfortunately, slipping rib syndrome cannot repair itself because the cartilage has broken and separated. Working with a physical therapist to strengthen other muscles will minimize slipping and make pain manageable. When the clicking sensation is present without pain, working with a physical therapist can prevent the condition from becoming a pain. If the pain is severe and impeding daily life, see an orthopedist who can evaluate you for surgery to repair the broken cartilage, though this intervention is rare.

If it's painful, then there is inflammation which needs time to heal. You must take a break from your binder to rest and recover. NSAIDs (non-steroidal anti-inflammatory drugs) (oral or topical), Arnica Montana (homeopathic), and turmeric (dietary) can help reduce inflammation.

Regardless of pain level, it is important to explore different shapes, styles, and brands of binders to find one that is less constricting on the lower ribs and allows you to bind pain-free. A custom binder is an option if you are unable to find one that works for your body.

PREPARING FOR A DOCTOR VISIT

A doctor will use the "hook test" to assess this condition which involves gently curling fingers under the edge of the rib cage and giving a slight pull. If you see a doctor for slipping rib syndrome, explain that you bind, to ensure a correct diagnosis and treatment plan. Two reasons not to wear your binder during the appointment: it may be too painful and the doctor will evaluate you better without it; if you arrive wearing a binder, the doctor will probably want you to remove it for evaluation. I recommend taking a binder with you to your appointment because most doctors are unfamiliar and may make incorrect assumptions about binding. See Chapter 6 for tips on discussing binding with doctors.

Since symptoms of slipping rib syndrome can resemble other conditions, the doctor may order imaging tests (X-ray or MRI) to rule out other conditions. During such tests, you will most likely not be able to wear a binder and will need to change into a standard hospital gown. If surgery is required, you will be unable to bind while in the hospital. Having surgery can be an extremely vulnerable experience, both physically and emotionally. Be sure to have a person with you to be your medical advocate.

The physical therapist will also assess the slippage by doing a "hook test." This should be done fully clothed. It's best not to wear a binder while being evaluated for this condition. If you are concerned about doing physical therapy appointments without a binder, ask your physical therapist if doing the strength-building exercises will be impeded by wearing a loose binder. See Chapter 6 for tips on talking to physical therapists.

Costochondritis or Tietze's Syndrome

Costochondritis is the inflammation of the cartilage that attaches the upper ribs directly to the sternum. It results from irritation of those joints and it can be both painful and slow to heal. Tietze's syndrome is essentially costochondritis with swelling at the joint that causes a raised and tender area along the sternum. Constriction around the rib cage exerts pressure on the thoracic vertebrae, increasing the pressure where the ribs attach to the sternum, causing the cartilage there to become inflamed. Depression of the sternum by the compression of dense chest tissue for sustained periods of time can cause the cartilage to become inflamed in response to the strain. A person is at highest risk for this condition when tight binding is coupled with repetitive movements of the torso and infrequent off-days.

SYMPTOMS

- Sharp pain at the sternum and/or pain elsewhere in the upper rib cage
- Aching or unrelenting feeling of pressure at the sternum
- One or more tender and swollen areas along the sternum
- Pain along the edge of the sternum
- Pain that worsens when you take a deep breath, especially high in the chest
- Painful to cough, sneeze, or project your voice

WHEN TO SEEK EMERGENCY MEDICAL ATTENTION

Anytime that you experience sharp chest pain, you should seek emergency medical attention to rule out serious cardiac symptoms.

IMPACT OF BINDING

In order to compress the chest tissue, a binder must depress the sternum which causes a slight concave shape to the front of the chest and can limit the mobility of the thoracic spine where the ribs connect. Since the ribs attach to the sternum, this is an unnatural position for those rib joints, and limitation at the spine immobilizes ribs at the vertebrae. In turn, the rib-to-sternum joint must work considerably harder to accommodate the motions of respiration. Eventually, fatigue in these overworked tissues causes inflammation in the cartilage along the sternum. Once this inflammation starts, continued binding agitates the strained cartilage and causes the condition to worsen.

PREVENT AND REDUCE RISK

- Wear the correct binder size and never double or triple up.
- Make these exercises routine:
    - Breathing Series (exercises #1–5)
    - Chest Opener (exercise #6)
    - Sternum Massage (exercise #7)
    - Thoracic Mobilization (exercise #21)
    - Thoracic Opener (exercise #22)
    - Anterior Torso Release (exercise #23)
- Take breaks from your binder whenever you feel an aching sensation around your sternum.

TREATMENT AND RECOVERY

Costochondritis heals very slowly but responds well to self-treatment.

- First and foremost, see a doctor to rule out serious cardiac conditions.
- Rest, rest, and rest some more.
- Limit binding to situations in which your personal safety is a concern.

- Use anti-inflammatory medications such as NSAIDs (oral or topical), Arnica Montana (homeopathic), or turmeric (dietary).
- Apply heat and/or ice to manage the pain.
- Do the following exercises to encourage healing:
  - Breathing Series (exercises #1–5)
  - Chest Opener (exercise #6)
  - Sternum Massage (exercise #7)
  - Pectoralis Muscles Massage (exercise #9)
  - Serratus Anterior Massage (exercise #11)
  - Thoracic Mobilization (exercise #21)
  - Thoracic Opener (exercise #22)
  - Anterior Torso Release (exercise #23)
- Refrain from movements (including the exercises above) that cause pain.

Physical therapy, massage therapy, and acupuncture can support healing and complement self-treatment. In all treatments, the goal should be to relieve pain, mobilize the thoracic spine, address trigger points throughout the thoracic region, and improve posture.

When the pain of costochondritis is impacting your daily life and regular exercises and/or physical therapy are not working, you may need to see an orthopedist who can help to address the inflammation.

PREPARING FOR A DOCTOR VISIT

It will be helpful to tell your doctor, physical therapist, massage therapist, or acupuncturist about your binding to avoid confusion in diagnosis or treatment.

Assessments will likely involve palpation of the ribs on the front, sides, and back of your body. You will remain clothed or draped with a sheet for this treatment but your binder should not be on for these evaluations. If you have swelling on the surface consistent with Tietze's syndrome, a doctor will need to examine and palpate that swelling. Depending on where this is on your sternum, you may need to expose the entire sternum, which will require spreading the chest tissue. I recommend wearing a button-down shirt. See Chapter 6 for more tips for navigating doctor's appointments.

Depending on the treatment, your therapist may need to access the skin on your chest and rib cage. Be clear with the therapist if you are uncomfortable being exposed and ask them to support you. It doesn't have to become a discussion about your gender—just say that you're modest.

Rib Fractures (Cracked or Broken)

Rare complication associated with unsafe wrap binding methods.

Rib fractures related to binding are extremely rare and when they do occur the rib is generally cracked but the pieces of the bone have not separated. Fully broken ribs occur as a result of severe physical traumas like car accidents. The prognosis for healing and full return to activity is good, however, the injury is quite painful and can take two or more months to heal. During that recovery period, binding is not possible.

SYMPTOMS

Sudden rib or chest pain after the following:

- Physical trauma to the torso (car accident, fall, sports injury)
- A coughing fit or days of a persistent cough while binding
- Sudden exertion while binding, especially when twisting is involved

Increased pain when:

- lying on the injured side
- breathing
- coughing, sneezing, laughing
- twisting or bending.

WHEN TO SEEK EMERGENCY MEDICAL ATTENTION

Anytime that you experience sharp chest pain, you should seek emergency medical attention to rule out serious cardiac symptoms.

Broken (not cracked) ribs require medical attention to ensure that they are not endangering other tissue and will heal properly.

IMPACT OF BINDING

It is rare, but binding can cause cracked ribs from severe coughing, asthma attacks, and sudden physical exertion. Long-term binding needs a self-care regimen that helps to support the rib cage's flexibility and alignment. Without it, the rib cage is compensating and repositioning itself to cope with the compression. Therefore, a situation that adds force to the rib cage, like a violent coughing fit, may cause injury more often in people who bind.

Full breaks are rarely caused by binding and appear to be limited to binding with utility tape and other non-pliable materials. Lung/spleen/liver punctures, which are complications from severe rib fractures sustained in traumas like car accidents and sports injuries, are not caused by ribs which crack by overexertion under binder compression.

PREVENT AND REDUCE RISK

- Develop and stick to a regular practice of stretching, breathing exercises, and self-massage to help keep your rib cage healthy and flexible.
- Recommended exercises:
    - Breathing Series (exercises #1–5)
    - Rib Cage Trigger Point Release (exercise #10)
    - Serratus Anterior Massage (exercise #11)
    - Scapular Mobilization (exercise #15)
    - Thoracic Opener (exercise #22)
    - Anterior Torso Release (exercise #23)
- When suffering from a serious cough, do not bind until the coughing fits cease completely.
- When doing strenuous work or working out, avoid wearing a tight binder. See Chapter 4 for advice about healthy binding while doing strenuous activity.

TREATMENT AND RECOVERY

Rib fractures are extremely painful, and medical attention is warranted. Depending on your pain level, seek emergency care or, if it's tolerable, wait to see your physician.

Pain management is the primary treatment for cracked ribs. NSAIDs or narcotic pain medication are common prescriptions. Apply ice immediately following the incident and avoid heat. After swelling has subsided, both ice and heat can provide relief to the aching pain.

Even though it will be painful, it's critical to keep taking the fullest breaths possible to nourish your body and avoid respiratory infections. Do not bind until the rib is healed, and since binding with a rib fracture is excruciating, you may naturally avoid it. Fractured ribs heal on their own, but it can be two months or more before the pain has subsided enough for binding to be tolerable.

PREPARING FOR A DOCTOR VISIT

The diagnosis of a rib fracture will be based on a history of symptoms and any recent trauma to the body. For this reason, it is essential that your doctor understands the role that binding may have played (see Chapter 6 to prepare for the discussion). The doctor will feel the painful area but should be able to do so without removing any clothing. The doctor will probably order an X-ray, during which you may be asked to change into a hospital gown. The X-ray technician will maneuver the X-ray machine to point to your chest, sides, and back which may be uncomfortable but will be a quick procedure.

CHAPTER 6

NAVIGATING APPOINTMENTS WITH HEALTH AND WELLNESS PROVIDERS

> The body holds shame, fear, pain, and trauma-like memories written on the skin. When trans people receive support, our bodies are taught a different story. They are taught to walk in the world unapologetically. When someone feels safe being their whole self, the person who emerges is an engaging and thriving artwork.
>
> – *G, 35, Maryland, USA*

Communicating With Your Provider

You Are in Control

- Ultimately, it is always up to you whether or not to divulge that you bind.
- If you are feeling anxious about discussing binding or your TGNC identity, you can bring another person into the exam room for your appointment—if they can't be there with you, consider having them on speakerphone or video call to help you talk to the doctor.

- At any point, you can ask the provider to pause to give you a moment to collect your thoughts.
- You can leave an appointment at any time for any reason—if you feel harassed or are feeling too vulnerable to continue, get up and politely inform the provider that you have decided not to complete the appointment.

The Blame Game

Finding a trusted provider is extremely difficult. Hopefully, you have a healthcare provider who respects you and listens to what you need. Unfortunately, finding a trusted provider is difficult and may take some time, effort, and luck. It's wise to emotionally prepare to have your condition blamed on your binding and to be told that the solution is to just stop binding. Decide ahead of time how you would want to respond to this advice.

Here are some things that you could say:

- I wish that discontinuing binding was an option for me but it's not. I am looking for your advice as to how to best treat my issue while continuing some sort of chest compression.
- I rely on binding for my mental health, so that option would not work for me. What other treatments can you recommend?
- My binder is integral to my safety at work/school/home. Are there lab tests, imaging studies, or other diagnostic procedures we could do to see if something else could be causing my issue?
- I am having (*symptom*) which I think is being made worse by the chest binder that I wear. I am looking for your advice as to how to best treat my issue while continuing some sort of chest compression.
- Binding is not a fashion choice; it is a garment I wear to control dysphoria.
- I was concerned that you might say that so I brought you some material to read about the safety of binding (give them an info sheet from www.healthybinding.com).
- I'd like for us to discuss some other treatment options beyond discontinuing binding since that is not realistic for me at this time.

- I am open to making changes to how I bind but not discontinuing binding; can we discuss some strategies?
- I think that it's best for me to see a different provider who can work together with me on this.

Not Disclosing Binding

It is always your choice whether you disclose your binding.

Keep in mind that disclosing and explaining your binding practices may be integral to getting an accurate diagnosis when you're being seen for:

- a respiratory condition
- a musculoskeletal pain impacting your torso
- a skin condition affected by your binder
- emergency medicine.

Communicate Similar Information

Carefully consider whether manipulating the truth in this way will serve your long-term goals with the provider. For example, full disclosure to a physical therapist that you are working closely with on rehabilitating from a rib or spine problem might be more important than a doctor at urgent care. If the safest choice is to avoid discussing your gender identity, these may be ways to communicate adequately with your provider:

- If you are assumed to be a cis woman:
  - say that you wear tight sports bras or compressive under- shirts every day (skeletal or respiratory pain)
  - say that you've had to wear a sweaty sports bra or compres- sion undershirt like Under Armor for long periods of time (skin problems).
- If you are assumed to be a cis man:
  - say that you have gynecomastia, a condition that causes breast tissue in men, and that you wear a compression shirt to conceal it.

Educate Your Provider

- Clearly and confidently explain that your binder is not a fashion choice; it's an essential part of your mental health care.
- Download a copy of the applicable info sheet from www. healthybinding.com and ask the provider to read it at the beginning of your appointment. Tell them you are happy to wait while they review it.
- Bring someone with you to do the explaining if you feel like it will be difficult for you. Make a plan ahead of the appointment about how they can advocate and best support you in the appointment.

In the Appointment

Make a Plan

Consider these questions when deciding whether to wear your binder to an appointment:

- Based on the reason for your visit, will the provider be:
    - visually examining your chest
    - physically examining your chest
    - listening to your breathing?
- Will you be able to change out of your binder before checking in for your appointment?
    - Remember to get there early so you have plenty of time.
- Will the provider be asking you to do any range-of-motion exercises?
    - If so, it's usually best to do them without the limitation of the binder.
- Will the binder be covering any skin that needs to be examined?
- Will you be disclosing to the provider that you bind?
    - If not, remove it before the appointment to avoid being forced to disclose in case there is an unanticipated reason for them to examine your torso.

- Will it be helpful for the provider to see what the binder is like on your body?
- If you decide to go to the appointment without a binder:
  - mentally prepare to interact without your binder with medical assistants, reception staff, and other patients in the waiting room, as well as your provider
  - consider taking a bulky clothing layer with you to hide your chest
  - consider wearing a sports bra or an athletic compression shirt.

Dress for an Easier Exam

If you are going to need to expose a part of your torso, avoid tight clothing and wear a loose T-shirt or button-down that easily allows you to expose the affected area while showing the least amount of your body.

Cis-Assumed Trans Men

To avoid being outed by your binder, you can always ask to remain covered even if a provider assumes that you will be comfortable being examined shirtless. You don't have to explain why. If you need to explain your binder, say that you bind to conceal gynecomastia, a condition that causes breast-like tissue to form in men.

Bring a Binder

Bring a binder to your appointment to help the provider understand what you are referring to. Often, providers imagine corsets or ACE bandage wraps, and they are less judgmental when they see the actual binder.

Alternative Appointment Options

Ask about doing a telehealth visit. If you are going to need to expose your chest or torso, it may be easier to be at home. Ask if they can evaluate your condition from photos, especially for skin disorders.

A telehealth visit can also be a safer way to initially interact with (or interview) a potential provider. If they are not affirming or you are triggered, you can end the visit more easily than leaving an in-person appointment.

Chronic Conditions

If you live with a chronic illness, to protect your long-term health you will want to inform your doctor about your binding. Plan to educate them and take a binder with you for them to inspect. Depending on your condition, you might need to discuss your plans to bind with the doctor ahead of time. Ask them to work with you to make a plan that will support your body and allow you to bind more safely.

Navigating Testing

You are generally required to change into a medical gown for any imaging tests of your torso (ultrasound, chest X-ray, CT scan, MRI, nerve conduction studies). In most cases, you will be advised to remove your binder. You are entitled to discuss this with the technician, but they may not have the authority to allow you to keep it on. Your chest will remain covered by the medical gown.

Other Types of Care

Emergency Care
- Emergency medicine often requires repeated explanations of binding and gender so, if at all possible, have someone with you to be your medical advocate.
- If you are not out as trans and are engaging in extreme sports, contact sports, or other activities with high risk of physical injury, disclose to a buddy or coach that you bind so they can be your advocate if you are unconscious or delirious. They will need to:
    - intervene to maintain your privacy as much as possible
    - advocate for your safety if bystanders or emergency responders react negatively to you being transgender
    - accompany you to emergency medical treatment.

Physical Therapy
- Download and share the physical therapist info sheet from www.healthybinding.com.

- Physical therapy does not require the removal of clothing unless they need direct contact with the skin for dry needling, ultrasound, TENS, or another similar treatment.
- If you are concerned about doing physical therapy exercises without a binder in public, ask your physical therapist about wearing a loose binder.
- Take a full-strength binder with you to show the physical therapist (most physical therapists are unfamiliar with binders and may assume incorrectly how the garment is impacting your body).

Chiropractic Care
- This is generally done without removing any clothing.
- Follow the guidance above for physical therapy.
- It is generally not advisable to wear a binder during the adjustment but you are entitled to discuss it with your chiropractor.
- Chiropractic adjustments can (but do not always) involve close body-to-body contact with the chiropractor as they use their body to twist or fold your body in order to adjust the bones. If you are a trauma survivor or struggle with close bodily contact and think that this might be triggering for you, consider seeing an osteopath instead.

Bodywork
- Download and share the massage therapist info sheet from www.healthybinding.com.
- Some bodywork is done with the client undressed under a sheet and blanket.
  - You will be given privacy to undress and get on the massage table. You are not required to take off more clothing than you want to, so if you want to keep your shirt or binder on, inform the bodyworker before they leave the room.
  - You will remain covered by the sheet and blanket, and only the body parts that are being massaged will be exposed—tell your bodyworker any parts of your body that you don't want touched, and they must respect your boundaries.

- Some bodywork is done in loose-fitting clothing.
  - You will be given privacy to change out of your binder and into those clothes if needed.
- You can stop any session at any time if you feel uncomfortable. Simply tell the bodyworker that you need to end the session. You are not required to give a reason.
- Since you will be given the opportunity to change during your appointment, you can wear your binder to the appointment if that is most comfortable.
- If you are seeing a bodyworker specifically to address a binding issue, take a full-strength binder with you to show them. Most bodyworkers are unfamiliar and may assume incorrectly how the garment is impacting your body.
- Ask the therapist as many questions as you want so that you feel comfortable with the session before it begins.

PART 2

SELF-TREATING AND PREVENTING PAIN

The goal of Part 2 of this book is to empower you to keep your muscles and joints pain-free and to self-treat your pain and discomfort when it occurs. Each exercise is broken down for you in clear, easy-to-follow instructions with tips along the way to help you succeed. Since many of these exercises are things that manual therapists typically do *for* you, there are some tools, techniques, and basic anatomy that you'll need to learn in order to be your own bodyworker.

Tips for getting the most out of Part 2:

- Familiarize yourself with the techniques section in Chapter 7 and then refer back as needed.

- Use the tools section in Chapter 7 to buy or make things that will support you in your exercises.

- Read about binding's impact on the body and take note of which symptoms are familiar to what you are experiencing.

- Use the recommendations in Chapter 8 and the symptom index at the end of the book to choose exercises.

- Check out variations to ensure that you are choosing the form of the exercise best suited to your body.

- Don't overdo it, especially when you are trying the exercise for the first time—too much too fast can irritate inflamed tissue and cause more discomfort.

- Heed the medical warnings and avoid any exercises that cause other conditions to worsen.

- Use the frequency recommendations to make a daily or weekly plan for your exercises and do your best to stick to it.

- Make notes about what works for you and any variations that support your body's unique needs.

- Look for these symbols to help you get the most out of the exercises:

Variations on form that can help you find what works best for your body.

Pointers on how to be sure that you're doing it correctly.

Notes will give you extra information that may be helpful to understanding the exercise.

Warnings about any health conditions or symptoms to watch out for.

Ideas about how to make the exercise more enriching or integrate it as part of your daily routine.

CHAPTER 7
TECHNIQUES AND TOOLS

Techniques Used in Exercises

Knowledge of fascia is essential to understanding the techniques used in this book to reduce restriction and pain by releasing adhesions in fascial tissue. Fascia is a connective tissue that is literally everywhere in the body—surrounding each muscle, bone, organ, and layer of skin. On a microscopic level it is a fabric of exceptionally strong fibers which form web-like sheets that wrap all of the tissues in the body in form-fitting casings of fascia, like sausage casings. These wrappings are dynamic, meaning that they respond to stress by changing their thickness and consistency. It is at the root of much of the pain and movement limitations caused by wearing a binder so it is crucial to understand the basics of how it works in order to understand how the exercises in this book can support your body.

For better and worse, fascia adapts to how we use our bodies. Inactivity and overuse are the two most common behaviors that cause fascia to react. When it receives the message that a muscle needs to hold a position for a long time, it will thicken to provide strength. If a muscle is overtaxed by extreme or repetitive motions, the fascia will create adhesions deep in the muscle called trigger points. When the body is sedentary, the fascia grows like cobwebs and incases tissue in its immobilized state.

Think of a violinist using neck muscles to grip their instrument with their chin. Fascia will respond by making the fascial sheet thicker and stronger around those muscles so it can act like support beams, allowing the muscles to hold the violin for longer periods of time with less effort. However, fascia doesn't know which positions are helpful and which are harmful to physical health. Hunching your shoulders day after day to hide your chest will also cause fascia to thicken and reinforce the muscles in that posture. These patterns of fascia in the body don't turn on and off; they are present when the violinist is trying to watch TV or the slumped person is trying to sit up straight at their desk. As a result, restrictive fascia can lead to limited range of motion and, often, chronic pain.

Fascia needs movement to stay slippery, adaptable, and pliable or else layers of tissue stop sliding and become stuck to one another, resulting in partially immobilized muscles, tendons, ligaments, and bones. Fascia is also responsive to our behaviors so the restriction creates a vicious cycle: the less we move, the more fascia immobilizes our muscles and joints which means we move less. The great news is that by understanding fascia, the same principles that cause immobility can be used to allow the musculoskeletal system to avoid restriction and discomfort. The exercises that follow use a series of techniques described below to free up the thick, sticky fascia that's been inhibiting full, fluid movement in your body and restore it to pliable and elastic tissue that can provide the appropriate amount of support.

Self Myofascial Release (SMR)

SMR is a technique that allows you to untangle the restrictive connective tissue holding your muscles and joints in uncomfortable positions. Fascia gets thicker and stickier when muscles, tendons, and joints are under strain, and doing regular SMR can prevent this build-up of restriction.

SMR Using Gravity

This is a passive release which means you aren't doing anything; you're just letting the myofascial release happen. The force of gravity does the work by pulling one part of your body towards the ground, slowly pulling apart the web-like fascial fibers as if they are cotton candy.

1. Position your body according to the instructions in the exercise and make sure that you have enough support to remain in that position for 3–5 minutes.
2. Find the point of resistance where you can feel the tautness of the tissue or as far as your body part will go in that direction without effort.
3. Allow the weight of your body to rest at the point of resistance.
4. Breathe deeply and let gravity gently pull your body towards the ground for at least 3 minutes.
5. Don't be concerned if you feel a slight burning sensation under the skin—this is a sign that the technique is working.

SMR Using Pressure AKA Trigger Point Release

Pressure applied *slowly* into the restricted tissue is an effective way to get the muscle fibers to "let go" and relax. A restriction in the tissue may be a trigger point (i.e., knot) or it may be an area of the muscle where fascia has gotten thick and sticky. When applied to a trigger point, this technique can provide relief to restricted tissue, as well as relieving pain referred to other parts of the body.

Depending on the location of the restriction, you may use a fingertip, pad of your finger, or a ball.

1. Locate a spot in your muscle that is more tender than the surrounding tissue.

> Pads of fingers are less intense than fingertips for applying pressure.

2. Slowly apply enough pressure to feel pain and then back off slightly until what you feel is tender but not quite painful.

> Applying too much pressure can make the body fight back rather than relax the tissue.

3. Hold for 30 seconds while taking deep breaths, then release for 5–10 seconds to assess any change in tenderness.
   - *If the tenderness has gone,* move on to other parts of the muscle.
   - *If the tenderness has reduced but not gone,* slightly increase the pressure until it is uncomfortable but just shy of painful. Hold for another 30 seconds.
   - *If the tenderness has not changed,* hold at the same pressure for another 30 seconds.
   - *If the tenderness has decreased but is still not gone,* let the tissue rest and do another round the following day.
4. Do easy movements with that part of your body to allow the muscle fibers to adjust to the untangling.

Active SMR

In this technique, you actively move muscle, tendon, and/or fascia away from a stationary part of your body, pulling the tissue taut to the point where the stretch equals the resistance. The result is a lengthening of the muscle tissue like pulling taffy, which can release the stickiness of restrictive fascia that has accumulated in the muscle or tendon. Like the gravity release, you will need to hold stretches for sustained periods but the difference is that gravity can't do the work for you. As you hold your body part at the point of resistance, notice your fascia allowing you to deepen the stretch the longer you sustain the position.

Be careful not to rush or overdo active SMR stretches because the fascia will tighten up if you engage it too fast or stretch too hard. Holding stretches at the endpoint of movement is what allows fascia to release. Don't work against yourself—take it slow and feel your body expand and open.

Muscle Softening

The goal of this technique is to soothe and relax the muscle through gentle self-massage, heat, and movement. If you discover a spot that is more tender when you pass over it, you have likely located a trigger point. For now, your goal is softening, so lighten up as you pass over that spot. Come back to it later and do trigger point release for a different kind of relief. Softening muscle tissue encourages more blood flow into the muscle so it will get warmer and/or pinker as you rub it.

Depending on the body part, muscle softening can be done with your fingers, whole hand, or a soft ball. Applying heat is a tool to soften muscle tissue and can be done before and/or after muscle softening. See the "Tools Used in Exercises" section for more information on balls and heat packs.

Using fingers:

1. Use the pads (not tips) of your fingers in slow circles or to apply gentle alternating pressure similar to the way that cats knead with their paws.

Using hand/palm:

1. Use the palm of your hand to gently squeeze and slowly knead the tissue.

Using a ball:

1. Place the ball on your body and place the palm of your hand over the ball.
2. Apply light pressure, being careful not to cause pain or discomfort.
3. Move your hand in small circles, moving the ball across the surface of the muscle.

Mobilization

These exercises actively move the restricted muscles, increasing movement in restricted joints. Moving the muscle slowly through its range of motion can free up the immobilized fibers and encourage them to move more fluidly. Follow the instructions for each exercise and pay close attention to your form so that you are targeting the correct muscle(s). These exercises may be coupled with SMR techniques to allow for maximum freedom in the stretched tissue.

Integrated Expansive Breathing

Muscles deep in the rib cage are hard to reach, and focused expansive breathing is a technique which can stretch and strengthen these vulnerable muscles. Expansive breathing is an exercise that directs the air you inhale to certain areas in order to stretch or activate abdominal muscles. It can be hard to do if you are unaccustomed to it, so here are a few tips:

- It may be difficult at first because your brain is not used to communicating with these muscles.
- Be patient and keep focusing on "sending air" to the desired area of your body until your brain begins to communicate with those muscles.
- Apply light pressure to the area to give you awareness of where you want to direct air.
- You have 20,000 breaths per day to practice and you can do it wherever you are!

Tools Used in Exercises

- **Balls:**
    - 1 soft palm-sized ball: foam, air-filled, or rubber like tennis ball, or racquetball.
    - 1 firm palm-sized rubber ball: density can range from tennis to lacrosse.
    - Price: set of three for under $10.
    - (Also see DIY options below.)
- **"Peanut":**
    - A trigger point release tool of two palm-sized rubber balls fused together.

- Price range: $15–$20 and up.
- Search: "peanut ball trigger point."
- (See DIY options below.)

- **Foam Roller:**
  - 36-inch recommended (long enough to reach from your tailbone to the back of your head); any density is OK.
  - Price: $20 and up.
  - (See DIY options below.)

- **Hands:**
  - Convenient tools that you have wherever you go!
  - Fingertips apply focused pressure.
  - Pads of fingers apply gentler yet focused pressure.
  - Palms apply flat pressure over a ball to provide focused pressure of a larger area.
  - Kneading with palms softens muscle tissue without pointed pressure.
  - Price: free!

DIY Tools

SOCK BALL

Making your own ball for SMR requires raiding your sock drawer. To make your own trigger point ball, you'll need:

- 1–2 pairs of old socks
- thick paper
- sturdy tape.

1. Ball up the paper into a tight ball and stuff it in the toe of the sock.
2. Twist the sock as close to the paper as you can and then turn the sock inside out.
3. Repeat this until you run out of sock.
4. If your ball needs to be bigger, put the entire ball into the toe of a new sock and continue the process.
5. When you've reached your desired size, wrap tape around the ball to keep it tight and round. Try to keep the surface as smooth as possible.

TOWEL ROLLER

To make your own prop to use as in place of a foam roller you'll need:

- sturdy tape
- 2–4 towels, the thicker the better
- yoga mat (optional).

1. Fold a large towel or yoga mat in half and roll it very tightly on the long side to make a firm, dense core for your roller.
2. Apply tape to keep it tight.
3. Fold the towel to match the size of the core and wrap it as tightly as possible.
4. Continue wrapping towels around the core until the roll is 8 inches in diameter.
5. Wrap tape around the roll to ensure that it stays tight and dense.

HOMEMADE PEANUT

A peanut is basically two rubber balls fused in the middle. To make yours, you need:

- 2 rubber balls
- sock
- sturdy tape.

1. Drop both balls in the toe of the sock.
2. Tie a knot as close to the balls as possible.
3. Wrap tape in many directions around the sock to secure the balls in a stable peanut shape.

HEAT PACK

Heat softens and soothes muscle tissue. To make your own moist heat pack, you need:

- thick sock
- 3 or more cups of rice.

1. Fill the sock with rice.
2. Tie a knot at the end of the sock.
3. Microwave for 2 minutes.
4. Apply moist heat to sore muscles.
5. Reuse again and again.

CHAPTER 8

IMPACT OF BINDING AND DYSPHORIA ON YOUR ANATOMY

Breathing

Watch an infant breathe. It seems effortless: their belly rises, their rib cage expands, and then the chest and belly deflate smoothly. That's because babies are born breathing diaphragmatically, meaning they use the diaphragm muscle to draw a full and easeful breath that fills all of the lobes of their lungs. As we grow up, we respond to emotional and environmental stressors by using the diaphragm muscle less and relying instead on secondary muscles of respiration that primarily draw air into the upper chest. By the time most people begin wearing a binder, their breathing pattern is already shallower than human bodies are designed for.

Wearing a binder applies inward pressure to the rib cage which inhibits vital rib expansion required for filling the lungs with the maximum amount of air. Breathing diaphragmatically spreads open the spaces between the ribs by pushing from the inside. By contrast, chest breathing is shallower and uses much weaker secondary muscles of respiration which must expand the rib cage by pulling ribs from the outside. Compression of a binder increases resistance for deep breathing so the muscles fatigue more easily, and eventually the body stops expecting full lung expansion

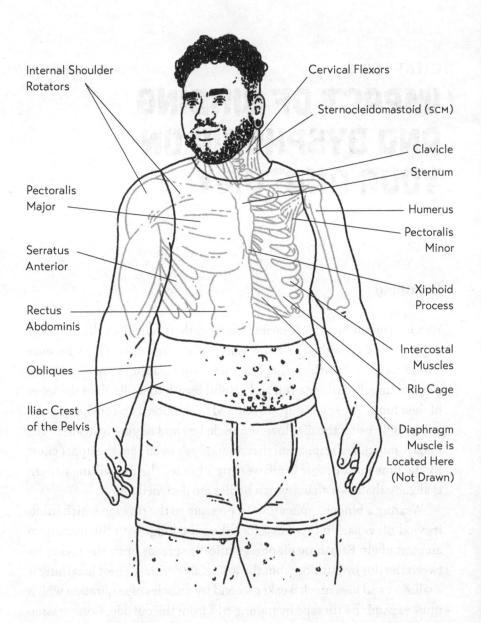

Internal Shoulder Rotators

Cervical Flexors

Sternocleidomastoid (SCM)

Clavicle

Sternum

Pectoralis Major

Humerus

Pectoralis Minor

Serratus Anterior

Xiphoid Process

Rectus Abdominis

Obliques

Intercostal Muscles

Rib Cage

Iliac Crest of the Pelvis

Diaphragm Muscle is Located Here (Not Drawn)

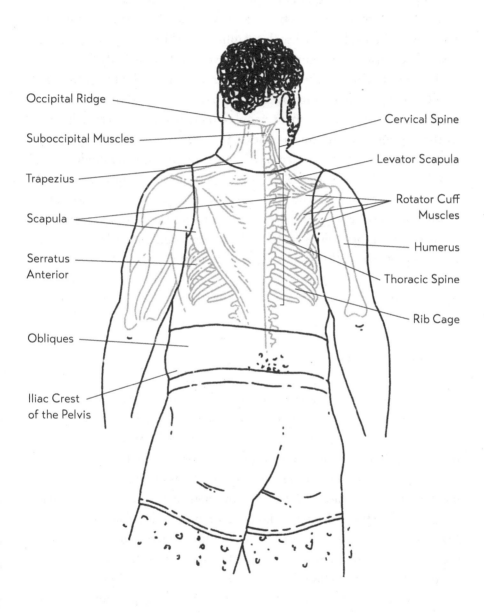

Occipital Ridge

Suboccipital Muscles

Trapezius

Scapula

Serratus
Anterior

Obliques

Iliac Crest
of the Pelvis

Cervical Spine

Levator Scapula

Rotator Cuff
Muscles

Humerus

Thoracic Spine

Rib Cage

and recalibrates to make chest breathing the norm. These weaker, secondary muscles fatigue under the pressure, and this distress causes much of the upper chest pain experienced when binding. Pushing ribs from the inside is more efficient and effective than pulling from the outside and reminds the body of how to use the diaphragm to breathe, resulting in less tax on the muscles and more oxygen to every cell in the body.

In order to draw in the maximum amount of air, the lungs expand in all directions, including towards the back. Even without the added compression of the binder, many people experience a tension and rigidity of the rib cage muscles on the backside of the body. This is especially true when the body is rounded into a hunching position by modern life, dysphoria, and/or a binder. Binders with 360-degree compression cause the most restriction on lateral expansion and wrap binders can cause these ribs to become displaced and the muscles to atrophy. Pushing the ribs on the backside of the body apart from the inside lengthens and loosens the muscles that inhibit the expansion of ribs where they attach to the spine.

- Related exercises: #1, 2, 3, 4, 5, 6

Pectoralis Muscles

You have two pectoralis muscles (commonly referred to as 'pecs'). As you can see in the anatomy diagrams above, they are entirely covered by the compression panel of a binder, so in order to move the arms, they expend more energy contracting against the counterforce of the binder.

When binding, people often develop the habits of hunching and moving their upper torso less. The lack of movement activates fascia's adhesive effect, bonding these chest muscles to other muscles, cartilage, and bones. An overly tight binder will draw the shoulders deeper into a hunched posture. This reinforcement and immobilizing causes the following: pec major pulls your arms/shoulders toward the center, rounding the chest; pec minor pulls your shoulders forward into a hunching position; serratus anterior decreases shoulder range of motion by inhibiting shoulder blade movement (read more in the "Intercostal and Serratus Anterior Muscles" section later in this chapter). Breaking up these adhesions and lengthening the muscle fibers can ease chest constriction, relieve shoulder pain, increase breath capacity, and improve upright posture.

The armholes can also dig into the muscle, further straining them. In response, the pectoralis muscles tighten, and fascia, an adhesive connective tissue, bonds them to the rib cage and sternum. The result is fatigue, dull aching pain, or tenderness throughout the pec muscles, shoulders, and arms, and increased rounding of the shoulders.

Dysphoria-hunching and chronic chest breathing already require the pecs, especially pec minor, to tighten and lock into a shortened position even before you add the resistance of the binder. Relying on upper chest muscles to breathe overtaxes the pec minor, causing the fascia to fortify against the strain which increases tenderness, stiffness, and formation of trigger points in the pec muscles.

In response to these pressures, fascia, a thick connective tissue throughout the muscle, responds to the strain and fatigue by forming trigger points, which feel like tender "knots," and can cause pain to refer across the upper chest, to the front of the shoulder, and/or down the inside of the arm (see Trigger point diagram #9 on page 246). Trigger points form in muscles throughout the body from all kinds of daily stressors, and while they can be painful, they are not dangerous to our health. Untangling the tissue of these trigger points can relieve a wide range of chest pain.

When dangerously tight binders are worn, all of these conditions are exacerbated and pain can develop. Properly sized binders may cause soreness in the pecs but this can be safely addressed by softening the tissue to relieve muscle aches, tightness, and stiffness and improve range of motion in the arms.

- Related exercises: #6, 7, 8, 9

Sternum

The sternum is the flat bone in the center of the chest and is the central attachment for the bones, cartilage, and muscles of the rib cage. The rib-to-sternum joints are designed to allow the sternum to depress slightly and then spring back up. This elasticity allows the rib cage to create a slightly concave space into which chest tissue can displace to achieve a flatter chest contour. However, the sternum was not designed to remain depressed for long periods of time so in order to cope, the body forms a thick sheet of fascial tissue. The build-up of this fascia then restricts movement of the sternum and ribs, the pec muscles in breathing, arm range of motion, and upper spine mobility. In a properly sized binder, this constriction is not excessive, and any discomfort that develops can be easily managed with exercises. Unsafe binding methods, detailed in Chapter 2, increase the compression against the sternum to unsafe levels which can lead to long-term pain and in, rare cases, rib and sternum injury.

- Related exercises: #4, 5, 6, 7, 10, 19, 23

Intercostal and Serratus Anterior Muscles

Intercostal muscles are located *between* the ribs and enable the ribs to stretch apart and come back together as you move and breathe. Serratus anterior helps to expand the rib cage by pulling ribs from the outside with finger-like sections *on the surface* of the ribs on the side of the body (under the armpit). Under constriction of a binder, these two muscles must work against additional resistance to move the ribs apart. The fascial system senses this overexertion and it forms trigger points which can cause aching pain in the armpit, sharp pain that can feel like a broken rib, tingling down the pinky side of the arm, or pain between the shoulder blades (see Trigger point diagram #10 on page 250). Fits of coughing, sneezing, or vomiting, especially while wearing a binder, often cause intercostal trigger points to form suddenly.

Serratus anterior attaches under the scapula and is one of the muscles responsible for moving and stabilizing the scapula which enables your arm to reach forward and lift weight above the head. Binders can cause the muscles to become weaker, stuck in place by fascia, and to form painful trigger points, but with safe binding methods, this muscle can be massaged to maintain proper functioning. (Check Trigger point diagram #11 on page 254 to see if you may be experiencing referred pain from serratus anterior.) Wrap binders can cause the serratus anterior to be so immobilized that it dangerously atrophies and becomes too weak to properly perform its function for breathing, rib expansion, and shoulder movement.

- Related exercises: #10, 11, 13, 14, 15

Lateral Torso

There is a chain of muscles from your armpit to your hip bone that get shortened and constricted from sedentary lifestyle and can be intensified by reduced torso movement that commonly develops with binding. Primary muscles impacted are obliques, serratus anterior, rotator cuff muscles, and the external intercostals. Muscles working less (sedentary) and working more (overexerting to counter the resistance of a binder) are conditions that cause the fascia of these side-body muscles to thicken and bond together. This reduces flexibility and impacts posture, back pain, core weakness, and range of motion at the waist. While most binding will cause these muscles to shorten some, 360-degree compression decreases torso movement much more than binders with lower compression in the back panel, and I see marked increase in these symptoms.

- Related exercises: #11, 12, 22

Rotator Cuff Muscles

The rotator cuff consists of four muscles responsible for stability of the scapula and movement of the arm (see the anatomy diagram in exercise #13 to see the location of infraspinatus, supraspinatus, subscapularis, and teres minor). Maintaining strength and flexibility in each of the four muscles is vital for preventing injury and maintaining full shoulder range of motion. Wearing a binder constricts the movement of the scapula which each of these muscles attach to and so they must exert more force against the compression. Binders with 360-degree compression place so much pressure on the scapula that the rotator cuff muscles are unable to fully activate and become weak over time. Binders with back panels made of low-compression fabric allow for adequate movement of the scapula, and weak rotator cuff muscles are rare. For people who do activities with lots of big arm movement, racerback styles allow for the greatest amount of scapular motion with the least amount of restriction.

When the rotator cuff muscles are forced to strain against the binder, the fascial system increases the thickness and stickiness of the connective tissue inside these muscles which decreases strength of the muscles and can form painful trigger points. These tender points in the rotator cuff muscles and the areas where they refer pain are shown in Trigger point diagram #13 on page 264. Treating trigger points has the potential to relieve pain felt locally throughout the upper body. Whenever you are experiencing pain or tingling in the shoulder or arm, it is worth addressing trigger points to see if the pain is being referred from a rotator cuff muscle.

- Related exercises: #13, 14, 15, 21

Shoulder Rotation

If you have difficulty holding your shoulders back and down or getting the "squared off" shoulder posture that is associated with masculine gender expression, you are struggling with weakness and constriction in the muscles responsible for rotating the shoulder forward and back. Dysphoria hunching and wearing overly tight binders cause the muscles that rotate the shoulder forward to become locked in a short position and the muscles that rotate them back to be constantly overstretched. Overstretched muscles become weak and painful over time. Movement of these muscles will free up the muscle fibers and restore them to proper balance. In most people of transmasculine identities, these muscles have been in this position for many years so be patient as you mobilize the tissue; range of motion will be restored to these muscles.

- Related exercises: #6, 8, 9, 11, 13, 14, 15, 20

Scapular Mobility

Under ideal conditions, the scapula moves freely over the surface of the backside of the rib cage controlled by the actions of 17 different muscles. Without a freely moving scapula, full range of motion in the shoulder joint is not possible and that limitation can be felt as shoulder pain, reduced arm range of motion, neck or upper back stiffness, or general shoulder tightness.

Binders with 360-degree compression place so much pressure on the scapula that the rotator cuff muscles are unable to fully activate and become weak over time. Binders with back panels made of low-compression fabric allow for adequate movement of the scapula, and weak rotator cuff muscles are rare. For people who do activities with lots of big arm movement, racerback styles allow for the greatest amount of scapular motion with the least amount of restriction.

The back panel of a binder exerts additional pressure over the scapula which forces those muscles to exert more energy to move the scapula. Binders with low-compression back panels are safer for scapular mobility than binders using 360-degree compression which restricts scapular movement much more. However, regularly mobilizing these muscles to keep them strong can allow you to wear either style safely.

- Related exercises: #8, 11, 12, 13, 14, 15, 20

Headache Pain

Hunching, rounding the shoulders, and elevating the shoulders are common for people with chest dysphoria, trauma, and/or generalized anxiety. Wearing a binder encourages and exacerbates these postures.

Under these circumstances, the head shifts forward so that it is not in proper alignment with the spine, a condition called Forward Head Posture (FHP) which increases the amount of exertion by the neck muscles to support the weight of the head. FHP causes tightness, facial thickening, and trigger points to develop in neck muscles connected to the base of the skull (aka occipital ridge) and can refer pain into the head and face which we experience as tension headaches, and for migraine sufferers, they can trigger migraines.

Elevating the shoulders is a bracing posture that humans do naturally when anxious or hypervigilant, meaning that they have sustained periods of time when their nervous system is alert to danger. Muscles can adopt this position as the new normal such that the trapezius ("traps") and levator scapula muscles must maintain constant contraction. Wearing binders with straps made of high-compression fabric (or any undergarment with tight elastic straps) forces them to overexert against the resistance of the compression. Shoulder straps, especially those in racerback styles, are also perfectly located to apply pressure to trigger points and intensify pain referred to the head and face. Non-compressive straps in tank-style binders are recommended for people with chronic head, neck, jaw, and face pain.

When the fascia thickens and the muscles become less pliable, it causes tension to increase at the occipital ridge where these tiny muscles attach. Tension along the occipital ridge causes headaches by applying pressure to nerves which service muscles on the head and face. Common patterns for headaches caused by occipital tension can be seen on the "Headache referral pain patterns" diagram in exercise #17 and are: a band of pressure above the ears, aching or gripping on the forehead, and aching pain in the eye sockets.

If you struggle with headaches when you bind, regular maintenance of these neck muscles can reduce or eliminate headache pain, allowing even migraine sufferers to bind safely. Releasing trigger points in the sterno-cleidomastoids (SCM) and occipital muscles can provide immediate relief to acute head and face pain.

- Related exercises: #1, 16, 17, 18, 19, 20, 21, 23

Neck Muscles

The dysphoria hunch causes the head to shift forward so that it is not in proper alignment with the spine. This is called FHP and over time this will weaken the deep cervical muscles which the body relies on to retract the head. Weak cervical muscles cause the head to fall forward which establishes a vicious cycle, encouraging more FHP, slouching, and hunching. Overly tight binders will increase the hunching and slouching already common in many transmasculine bodies.

FHP results in the thoracic spine becoming kyphotic (an exaggerated forward curve), together with the cervical spine becoming lordotic (an exaggerated backward curve) or losing its curve. Since FHP is not a natural head position, muscles on the front and sides of the neck are also in an unnatural position, causing overstretched tissue, muscle weakness, and chronic muscle tightness. Cervical flexors, responsible for tucking your chin to your chest, become overstretched and profoundly weakened. Scalenes and SCMs, responsible for side-to-side and rotational movements of the head, tighten into cable-like muscles on the sides of the neck. Under these circumstances, fascia thickens and bonds these small but essential neck muscles to one another which reduces the range of motion and forms trigger points which can refer pain to the head, ear, jaw, chest, shoulder, and upper arm.

Scalenes and the SCMs originate on the skull and connect to the first and second ribs and collarbones. In chronic chest breathing (common in transmasculine individuals and exacerbated by binding), these muscles get recruited to raise the rib cage for inhalation. The scalenes and SCMs are only intended to function this way only in short bursts so they become chronically fatigued which further thickens fascia and restricts range of motion. Learning to engage the diaphragm in breathing before, during, and after binding is essential for relieving this pain-inducing pattern.

Reversing the cycle requires strengthening the deep neck muscles—cervical flexors and extensors. Counteracting the weakness caused by FHP will improve the neck's strength, flexibility, and function and balance the head on the spine.

- Related exercises: #3, 7, 16, 17, 18, 19, 20, 21, 23

SCM Muscle

The appearance of unwanted chest tissue in puberty often results in the dysphoria hunch for many transmasculine people and FHP develops at a much younger age than it does for their cis peers. The SCM is the largest muscle on the front of the neck and attaches to the skull to the collarbone and sternum. In FHP, the skull shifts forward on the spine and juts out past the rib cage, and the SCM becomes overstretched. Chest breathing, chronic elevating of the shoulders, clenching the jaw, grinding the teeth, and extended periods of looking down at screens all exacerbate the strain on the SCM. These habits and FHP are both common for people who do not bind.

The fascia bonds the SCM to surrounding muscles which impacts neck movement, swallowing, chewing, and projecting the voice. In response to the strain and restriction, trigger points form in the SCM which are linked to many forms of headache pain (see Trigger point diagram #19 on page 290). Research shows that SCM tension is a migraine trigger and reducing chronic tension and releasing trigger points can reduce migraine pain and frequency. It can also be an effective intervention in head and jaw pain when it is acute.

- Related exercises: #16, 19

Upper Trapezius and Levator Scapula

The trapezius muscle, or "trap," is a large kite-shaped muscle on the back with three distinct sections: upper, middle, and lower. The upper trapezius forms a triangle from the base of the skull to the edge of the shoulder joint to the spine. It functions to stabilize the neck, assist in head motion, and move the shoulder blade to facilitate arm movement. The levator scapula connects the top of the shoulder blade and the base of the skull and, as its name implies, elevates the scapula. Though they are not designed to stabilize the neck, FHP causes levator scapulae to overcompensate in this way which can cause trigger points to form.

Many people describe "little rocks" that "just live in their neck and shoulders." Generally, those "rocks" or "knots" are trigger points formed because of excessive strain caused by posture. The tangled muscle fibers of these trigger points cause pain in the neck, head, and jaw, as well as triggering cervicogenic headaches (headaches that begin with neck dysfunction). See Trigger point diagram #20 on page 294 for referral patterns.

The straps of a binder or sports bra add consistent pressure into both muscles and require the muscle to strain against the compression in order to contract. The straps can also apply pressure directly on a trigger point(s), causing flares of intense pain and triggering headaches. Wearing binders with straps made of high-compression fabric (or any undergarment with tight elastic straps) forces them to overexert against the resistance of the compression. Shoulder straps, especially those in racerback styles, are also perfectly located to apply pressure to trigger points and intensify pain referred to the head and face. Non-compressive straps in tank-style binders are recommended for people with chronic head, neck, jaw, and face pain.

- Related exercises: #17, 18, 20, 21

Thoracic Spine

When hunched posture strains the thoracic spine, the body responds by reinforcing the muscle tissue along that section of the spine with dense fascia to provide much-needed strength so we are able to stand upright. Unfortunately, the trade-off is that we lose spinal flexibility where the muscles have become so fortified.

The fortified position of the tissue locks down the upper section of the thoracic spine, preventing fluid motion of the vertebra and causing stiffness and pain in the upper back. Mobility of the spine is integral to the scapula's ability to move freely, which enables full range of motion in the shoulders. Therefore, constriction in the thoracic spine can cause or worsen shoulder pain and can make you more vulnerable to shoulder injury.

Binding adds a layer of compression which can further restrict mobility in the thoracic section of the spine. Binders with full-compression back panels create the most force on the spine, and wrap binders apply dangerous levels of immobilization. When the thoracic spine lacks flexibility, pain and dysfunction can develop in the shoulders and the neck, breathing can become more constricted, and headaches can increase. Ribs attach at each vertebra in the thoracic section of the spine so if rib displacement from unsafe binding occurs, it will force the constricted spinal support muscles to tighten in an effort to prevent movement of the injured rib. Restriction in the muscles that support the spine must be relaxed in order to restore the easeful flexion and extension of the spine and proper rib position.

- Related exercises: # 3, 14, 15, 21, 22, 23

Oblique Muscles

The obliques are sheets of muscle which are stretched between the lower ribs and the crest of the pelvis and wrap around the body at the waist. They form a strong muscular wall to protect the abdominal organs, support posture, twist the torso, and bend side to side at the waist.

Binding applies an inward pressure on the rib cage, exerting more resistance and discouraging torso movement, since the obliques must then overexert against that pressure. Many people wearing binders twist and bend the torso less in daily living. Inactivity in the muscle causes fascia to thicken which reduces flexibility in the abdominal muscles, adversely impacts posture, causes low- and mid-back pain from core weakness, and reduces mid-body flexibility.

Full-length binders with low-compression fabric on the back are no greater risk to this muscle group than half-length binders. However, if they roll up, the compression exerted on the vulnerable lower ribs is multiplied. This can result in bruising or, in rare cases, displacement of the lower ribs. For tips on preventing rolling of a full-length binder, see Chapter 3 in Part 1.

Full-length binders with 360-degree compression exert the greatest immobilizing force on these muscles. However, regular care of the side-body muscles can allow for proper functioning and generally avoid injury, provided they are not too small.

- Related exercises: #2, 12, 22, 23

Anterior Torso

When a position becomes chronic, the body fortifies the affected muscles with fascia. Dysphoria hunching collapses the abdomen, shortening the muscles on the front of the body from the collarbones to the pelvis. A large sheet of muscle stretching from the rib cage to the pelvis, called rectus abdominis and known as "the six-pack muscle," gets heavily fortified with fascia when it is shortened.

Wearing a binder discourages torso movement, decreasing mobility of this sheet of tissue. When the tissue on the front of the torso is chronically short, it forces the muscles on the back of the torso, especially along the spine, to become overstretched. Overstretched muscles cause pain, discomfort, and fatigue in thoracic and cervical sections of the spine. Releasing the fascia on the front of the torso and allowing the abdominal muscles to lengthen can reduce this tension on the back and improve neck and back pain.

The shortening of the muscles on the front of the torso pulls the rib cage forward and down which decreases the size of the abdominal cavity, compressing the abdominal organs. This especially impacts the upper gastrointestinal tract and can irritate GERD, IBS, IBD, or other upper digestive discomfort. Releasing the fascia to allow the sheet of abdominal muscle to lengthen allows the rib cage to lift into a more upright position, alleviating these symptoms. In addition to the visceral benefits, lifting the rib cage by releasing anterior torso fascia increases space for the lungs to expand.

- Related exercises: #6, 21, 23

EXERCISES
BREATHING

#1 DIAPHRAGMATIC BREATHING

Objective

Increase breath capacity by relearning the body's natural way to breathe and strengthen the diaphragm muscle to increase fullness of breath in a binder.

See Chapter 8 to learn more about the impact of binding and dysphoria on breathing (page 193).

Symptoms

- Fatigue or low energy
- Brain fog or trouble concentrating
- Heightened anxiety
- Strain and discomfort when taking a full breath when the binder is off

Indications

- Shoulders rise and fall when breathing
- Not participating in activities because of shortness of breath

Technique

- Integrated expansive breathing

Tools Needed

- None

Landmarks

- Lower sternum: the lower section of flat bone in the center of your chest, generally at the cleavage in your chest tissue.
- Clavicles (aka collarbones): the horizontal bones across the top of your chest, starting at your shoulder and ending just below your throat.

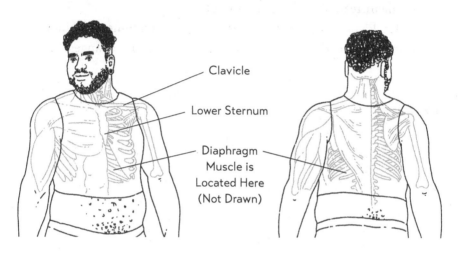

Clavicle

Lower Sternum

Diaphragm Muscle is Located Here (Not Drawn)

HOW DO I KNOW IF I'M CHEST BREATHING?

In diaphragmatic breathing, the belly fills with air, the rib cage expands outwards, and the shoulders and back will remain relaxed when you take a deep breath. In chest breathing, the diaphragm is minimally activated and the upper chest does the work to inhale and exhale.

Take a video of yourself:

1. Breathe normally for 3 breaths and relax your body.
2. Take 3 deep breaths and try to fill your lungs to capacity.

Watch yourself breathe.

Do your shoulders rise towards your ears when you inhale?

Do you arch back as your breath gets deeper? If so, you are chest breathing.

Does your belly draw inward when you *inhale*? If so, you are relying more on your chest muscles than your diaphragm.

Does your belly push outward as you *exhale*? If so, you are engaging your diaphragm on the exhalation instead of the inhalation. Instead, allow the air to deflate from your lungs gently when you exhale instead of pushing the air out.

Track your progress as you practice new breathing techniques by making breathing videos periodically and notice changes.

Exercise

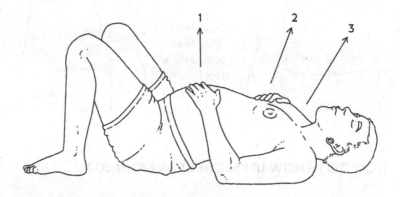

(This exercise should be done while not wearing any binding garment.)

STEP 1: ENGAGE THE DIAPHRAGM

1. Lie down comfortably on your back with your knees bent or sit upright in a chair with your feet flat on the floor. Use pillows to support you wherever you need them.
2. Place one palm on your lower sternum and one on your belly.
3. Inhale through your nose, directing the breath past your chest to your belly.

The hand on your belly should rise and the hand on your sternum should remain still.

4. Gently exhale through your mouth, feeling your belly deflate with ease.

You should feel your belly fall and your sternum remain still.

STEP 2: DIAPHRAGM + LOWER RIB CAGE

1. Keep your hands on your belly and lower sternum.
2. Breathe into your belly as shown in step 1.
3. After your belly-hand starts to rise, keep filling your lungs and direct air into your chest cavity.

You should feel the hand on your lower sternum rise (maybe only slightly—that's OK!).

4. Gently exhale through your mouth and allow everything to deflate with ease.

STEP 3: DIAPHRAGM + LOWER RIB CAGE + UPPER CHEST

1. Keep your hands on your belly and lower sternum.
2. Breathe into your belly and lower rib cage as shown in step 2.
3. After your sternum-hand starts to rise, keep filling your lungs and direct air into your upper chest cavity.

You should feel your clavicles rise (a slight rise is OK!).

4. Gently exhale through your mouth and allow everything to deflate with ease.

STEP 4: PUT IT TOGETHER

1. Set a timer and then put your phone where it won't interrupt you.
2. Breathe this way for 3 or more minutes and notice any change in the ease or rhythm of expanding your abdomen.
3. Say "I am inhaling" and "I am exhaling" slowly in your mind to quiet your brain and increase relaxation.

 Practice this exercise first without a binder so that your body can learn the action and build strength in the muscles. Then breathe diaphragmatically frequently while binding to encourage fuller breathing and reduce discomfort through the day.

 If you have any chronic respiratory conditions (asthma, chronic obstructive pulmonary disease (COPD), etc.), be cautious with any new breathing pattern and build up gradually. If you have any signs of breathing distress, **stop** and consult a doctor before any further breathing exercises.

Frequency

- Practice multiple times daily until breathing with the diaphragm comes naturally.
- On days that you bind:
    - Before binding: Do 3–5 minutes of integrated expansive breathing exercises (exercises #1–4) before putting on your binder to "wake up" all the muscles.
    - Practice diaphragmatic breathing with your binder on.
    - After binding: Do 3–5 minutes of the integrated expansive breathing exercises (exercises #1–4) after taking off your binder to "remind" your body of deep breathing.

#2 LATERAL BREATHING

Objective

Increase breath capacity by activating and stretching the muscles between the ribs on the sides of the rib cage.

See Chapter 8 to learn more about the impact of binding and dysphoria on breathing (page 193) and the lateral torso (page 199).

Symptoms

- Fatigue or low energy
- Brain fog or trouble concentrating
- Heightened anxiety
- Strain and discomfort between the shoulder blades when taking a full breath

Indications

- Not participating in activities because of shortness of breath

Technique

- Integrated expansive breathing

Tools Needed

- Ribbon, fabric strip, belt or resistance band (optional)

Landmarks

- Lateral rib cage: surface of the ribs on the sides of the body from the armpit to the waist.

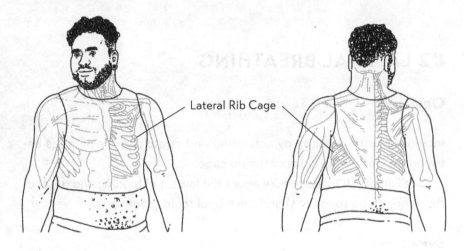

Lateral Rib Cage

Exercise

(This exercise should be done while not wearing any binding garment.)

 Breathing into your side may be hard at first it but gets easier as you do it because you teach your brain to "talk" to these muscles.

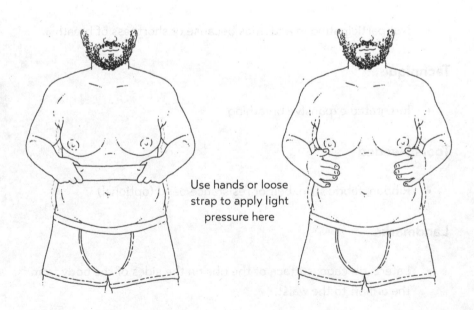

Use hands or loose strap to apply light pressure here

1. Begin with the torso tall and upright either standing or sitting with your feet hip-width apart.
2. Rest your hands on your ribs above the waist.

Variation: Instead of your hands, wrap a band *loosely* around the section of your ribs above your waist. Use only enough tension to feel the band in contact with the surface of your body.

Once you learn to feel the expansion and direct air to the sides of your rib cage, you will not need the band or hands to do this exercise.

3. Keep your shoulders down and inhale through your nose into your belly.
4. After air starts to expand your belly, continue inhaling and push the air into the sides of your ribs against the pressure of your hands or the band.

Concentrating on engaging muscles under your armpits can be helpful.

5. Feel a slight expansion in your ribs.

Try doing this exercise in front of a mirror so you can also watch for your ribs to expand outward.

6. Exhale completely through your mouth, allowing the body to deflate with ease.
7. Repeat 5 times.
8. Return to normal breathing.

If you feel dizzy or lightheaded, sit down and **stop** doing this exercise immediately.

If you have any chronic respiratory conditions (asthma, COPD, etc.), be cautious with any new breathing pattern and gradually build up. If you have any signs of breathing distress, **stop** and consult a doctor before any further breathing exercises.

Frequency

- Practice multiple times daily until lateral breathing comes naturally.
- On days that you bind:
    - Before binding: Do 3–5 minutes of integrated expansive breathing exercises (exercises #1–4) before putting on your binder to "wake up" all the muscles.
    - Practice lateral breathing with your binder on.
    - After binding: Do 3–5 minutes of the integrated expansive breathing exercises (exercises #1–4) after taking off your binder to "remind" your body of deep breathing.

#3 QUADRUPED BREATHING

Objective

Increase breath capacity by activating and stretching the muscles between the ribs on the backside of the body.

See Chapter 8 to learn more about the impact of binding and dysphoria on breathing (page 193) and the thoracic spine (page 205)

Symptoms

- Fatigue or low energy
- Brain fog or trouble concentrating
- Heightened anxiety
- Strain and discomfort between the shoulder blades when taking a full breath

Indications

- Not participating in activities because of shortness of breath

Technique

- Integrated expansive breathing

Tools Needed

- None

Landmarks

- Upper thoracic spine: the section of the spine from the bottom of the shoulder blades to the base of the neck.

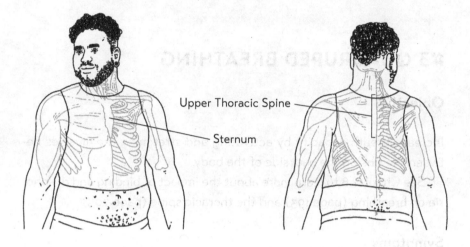

Upper Thoracic Spine

Sternum

Exercise

(This exercise should be done while not wearing any binding garment.)

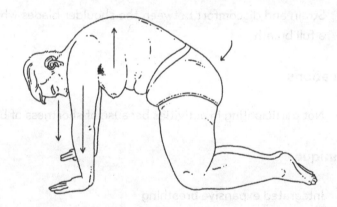

1. Get into a table-top position on your hands and knees.

Variation: Sit upright in a chair with your knees touching the wall. Place your hands on the wall with your arms parallel to the floor.

2. Reach long through the arms, pushing into your hands as you round the upper back.

Imagine that there is a candle flame under your sternum and you are raising your upper chest away from it.

3. Allow your head to drop towards the floor.
4. Tuck your tailbone.
5. Hold the rounded position and take a deep breath through your nose.
6. Direct the air towards the back of your body as though you are inflating the rounded portion of your spine.
7. Blow the air out of your mouth as you return to a neutral table-top position.
8. Repeat for a total of 5 breaths.

 We have to teach our brains to "talk" to these muscles and once we do, it gets easier. So, this might feel difficult (or even impossible!) but keep at it.

 If you feel dizzy or lightheaded, **stop** doing this exercise immediately.

 If you have any chronic respiratory conditions (asthma, COPD, etc.), be cautious with any new breathing pattern and build up gradually. If you have any signs of breathing distress, **stop** and consult a doctor before doing any further breathing exercises.

Frequency

- Daily when feeling strain or discomfort in the upper back, especially when taking a deep breath or maintaining upright posture.
- On days that you bind:
  - Before binding: Do 3–5 minutes of integrated expansive breathing exercises (exercises #1–4) before putting on your binder to "wake up" all the muscles.
  - Practice lateral breathing with your binder on.

- After binding: Do 3–5 minutes of the integrated expansive breathing exercises (exercises #1–4) after taking off your binder to "remind" your body of deep breathing.
- 1–2 times per week for regular maintenance.

EXERCISE

#4 DIAPHRAGM MASSAGE

Objective

Enable smoother and more complete breathing by softening the diaphragm muscle and related fascia at the lower edge of the rib cage.

See the Chapter 8 to learn more about the impact of binding and dysphoria on breathing (page 193).

Symptoms

- Fatigue or low energy
- Brain fog or trouble concentrating
- Heightened anxiety
- Achy feeling when trying to take a full breath
- Tender/bruised feeling along the border between the rib cage and the abdomen

Indications

- Shoulders and collarbones rise when breathing at rest
- Difficulty expanding the belly in diaphragmatic breathing (exercise #1)
- Collapse or hunch of the torso/chest
- Difficulty getting a full breath even when the binder is off

Technique

- Muscle softening

Tools Needed

- Pads of fingers

Landmarks

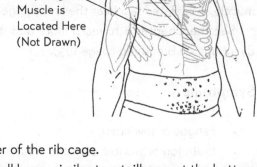

Xiphoid Process

Border of Rib Cage

Diaphragm Muscle is Located Here (Not Drawn)

- Border of the rib cage: the edge where hard bone meets squishy abdomen starting from the sternum and sloping down-ward and outward.
- Diaphragm muscle: dome-shaped breathing muscle inside the rib cage attached to the border of the rib cage.
- Xiphoid process: a small bone, similar to a tailbone, at the bottom of the sternum which hangs down into the abdomen and is usually tender to the touch.

Exercise

(This exercise is best done while not wear-ing any binding garment, but can be done while binding if needed.)

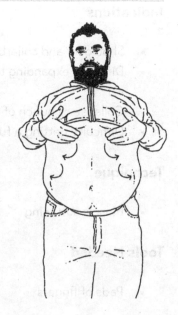

 This is the precursor to the Dia-phragm Release. You will be ready to try the release once the tissue has softened enough to allow you to press your fingers inward and slightly upwards under the edge of the ribs. Though this will be uncomfortable for most people, do not proceed to the Diaphragm Release until it is not painful.

1. Relax your abdominal muscles and let your belly be loose.

2. Stand or lie flat on your back with your knees bent.

3. Find the tender xiphoid process and position your index fingers about 1 inch to either side of it.

4. Lay the other 3 fingers along the rib cage like you are placing them on the next three piano keys.

5. Allow your fingers to rest there while you take a few easeful belly breaths. Notice how the belly rises and falls under your fingers.

6. Apply light pressure with the pads of your fingers into the soft tissue just off the edge of the ribs.

7. Walk your fingers slowly up and down the slope of the edge of the ribs as if you are moving along a curved keyboard.

8. Continue for a full minute (more is great!).

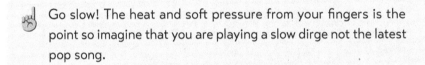 Go slow! The heat and soft pressure from your fingers is the point so imagine that you are playing a slow dirge not the latest pop song.

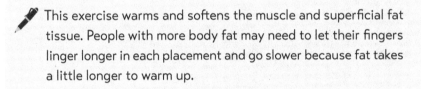 This exercise warms and softens the muscle and superficial fat tissue. People with more body fat may need to let their fingers linger longer in each placement and go slower because fat takes a little longer to warm up.

Do this while lying in bed before sleep, it's gentle and relaxing and it will allow you to breathe more deeply while you sleep and your body is repairing itself.

If you do not feel any resistance and your fingertips curl all of the way under the edge of your rib cage, then you are potentially hypermobile. If this is the case, do not curl your fingers under while you are massaging this area. Keep your focus on massaging the border of the rib cage. See the information about binding and hypermobility in Chapter 5, Section 2.

Frequency

- Daily.

#5 DIAPHRAGM RELEASE

 Diaphragm Massage should always be done before doing a Diaphragm Release to warm the tissue. Until you are able to curve your fingers slightly up and under the edge of the ribs without pain, do not proceed to doing a Diaphragm Release.

Objective

Enable smoother and more complete breathing by releasing constriction in the diaphragm muscle.

See Chapter 8 to learn more about the impact of binding and dysphoria on breathing (page 193).

Symptoms

- Fatigue or low energy
- Brain fog or trouble concentrating
- Heightened anxiety
- Achy feeling when trying to take a full breath
- Tender/bruised feeling along the sloping edge of the rib cage

Indications

- Shoulders and collarbones rise with normal breathing
- Difficulty expanding the belly in deep breathing (see exercise #1)
- Collapse or hunch of the torso/chest
- Difficulty getting a full breath even when the binder is off

Technique

- Active self myofascial stretch

Tools Needed

- Fingers

Landmarks

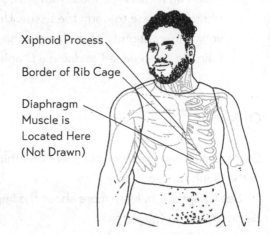

Xiphoid Process

Border of Rib Cage

Diaphragm Muscle is Located Here (Not Drawn)

- Border of the rib cage: the edge where hard bone meets squishy abdomen starting from the sternum and sloping downward and outward.
- Diaphragm muscle: dome-shaped breathing muscle inside the rib cage attached to the border of the rib cage.
- Xiphoid process: a small bone, similar to a tailbone, at the bottom of the sternum which hangs down into the abdomen and is usually tender to the touch.

Exercise

(This exercise should be done while not wearing any binding garment.)

1. Lie down on your back with your knees bent.
2. Do a Diaphragm Massage to warm the tissue and prepare it for release.
3. Find the xiphoid process and position your index fingers about 1 inch to either side.
4. Lay the other 3 fingers close together along the border of the rib cage.
5. Gently apply pressure into the abdominal muscles and slightly

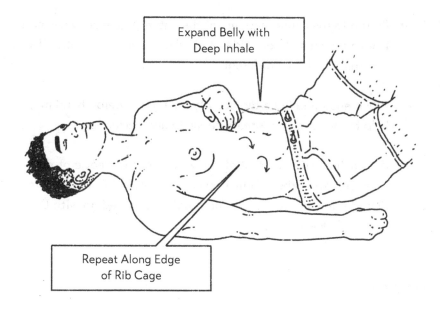

Expand Belly with
Deep Inhale

Repeat Along Edge
of Rib Cage

curl under the edge of the ribs until you feel resistance and mild discomfort but no pain.

 At first, your fingers may barely curl under the ribs. Don't rush it. If it's painful, reduce your pressure.

6. Keep your fingers pressed into the abdomen while you take a deep belly breath that fills your lungs to approximately two-thirds capacity.
7. Exhale as though you are deflating with ease (don't push the air out).
8. As you exhale, *slightly* increase the pressure and curl your fingers *slightly* more.
9. Move your fingers down the border of your rib cage and repeat until you reach the bottom of the ribs.

 Your ribs will be much more mobile near the bottom and you may be able to curl your fingers further. Take care not to pull outward but instead apply pressure in and under.

10. Return to the center and repeat the entire sequence twice more.
11. Lay your hands at your sides and take full breaths. Notice if your breathing feels any different.

 When engaging in cardio activity, doing this beforehand may help to increase your breath capacity and performance.

 If your fingertips curl all of the way under the edge of your rib cage, review the information about hypermobility spectrum disorder in Chapter 5, Section 2 before proceeding with Diaphragm Release.

Frequency

- Daily when breathing feels shallow or restricted.
- Weekly for regular maintenance.
- Before cardio activity.

QUICK BREATH RESET

You can reset your breathing literally anywhere when you realize that you are breathing rapidly and/or shallowly.

When you get used to the steps of this breath, they will flow and the air will seem to roll through your torso, awakening all of the muscles and pushing air into all of the lobes of your lungs.

1. Sit or stand upright.
2. Inhale *slowly* through your nose.
3. Direct the first half of the air to your belly.
4. Direct air to your sternum, keeping your shoulders down.
5. Direct air to the sides of your rib cage, keeping your shoulders down.

---

6. Direct air to your upper thoracic back, allowing your shoulders to roll forward as your spine rounds.
7. When you feel full of air, push a little more air to raise your collarbones and allow your shoulders to raise and roll back.
8. Hold the air for 2 seconds.
9. Exhale through your mouth, deflating with ease and relaxing the entire torso.
10. Shrug your shoulders and shake out your torso.

 Do not do more than 5 breaths in a row without taking a 2-minute break to breathe normally.

 If you cannot catch your breath after exercise, excitement, or panic, find a safe place to remove your binder right away.

 If you feel dizzy or lightheaded, return to regular breathing at a slow and normal pace. Remove your binder if the dizziness does not *immediately* improve.

EXERCISES
RIB CAGE

#6 CHEST OPENER

Objective

Release constriction in the fascia of the upper chest muscles, resulting in greater ease in rolling the shoulders back and deep breathing.

See Chapter 8 to learn more about the impact of binding and dysphoria on the pectoralis muscles (page 196), sternum (page 197), and anterior torso (page 207).

BONUS BENEFITS FROM CHEST OPENING

- More masculine posture: keeping pec muscles pliable and free of adhesions increases your ability to build chest muscle strength and bulk. Regularly doing this release can improve your ability to hold your shoulders in a broader position, support an upright upper chest, and increase the appearance of a strong jawline.
- Decreased anxiety: anxiety often manifests physically as a tight feeling in the upper chest behind the sternum. The body can get into a feedback loop when we are anxious: when we feel the chest tightness from the binder, our body is fooled into thinking we must need to be anxious which, in turn, increases chest tightness. Relaxing the chest muscles can decrease the signal from the body to the brain that triggers anxiety.

Symptoms

- Tight chest or pressure in the center of the chest
- Pain on the front aspect of the shoulder joint

- Tight, hard, or knotty trapezius ("traps") muscle
- Tension headaches or migraines
- Heightened anxiety

Indications

- Forward Head Posture (FHP) or Upper Crossed Syndrome
- Shoulders rolled down and inward (i.e., hunched or rounded)
- Difficulty maintaining an upright posture with the shoulders back and down
- Difficulty taking a full deep breath
- Limited range of motion in the shoulder joints, especially with the arms stretching behind the body

Technique

- Self myofascial release (SMR) with gravity

Tools Needed

- Foam roller or rolled prop
- Yoga blocks or a stack of books
- Music or a timer

Landmarks

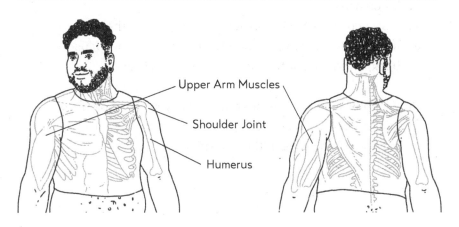

Upper Arm Muscles

Shoulder Joint

Humerus

- Head of the humerus: the bony knob on the front of the shoulder joint which is the top of the upper arm bone.
- Shoulder joint: ball and socket joint where the arm meets the torso.

Exercise

(This exercise is best done while not wearing any binding garment but can be done while binding if needed.)

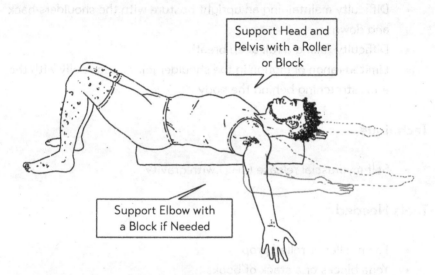

Support Head and Pelvis with a Roller or Block

Support Elbow with a Block if Needed

To position your body on the rolled prop:

1. Place the roll on the floor lengthwise and place the blocks nearby.
2. Sit on one end of the roll.
3. Walk your arms back until you are lying flat on the roll.
4. If your roll isn't long enough to support your head, use a block, book, or firm pillow for support under your head.

Variation: Instead of used a rolled prop, you can lie on the edge of a firm bed, sofa, or massage table and allow one arm at a time to hang off the edge in the 3 positions.

These positions can be uncomfortable but should not ever be painful. Utilize blocks, books, or pillows to support the arms enough to prevent pain and maintain stretch.

POSITION #1

1. Spread your arms in a T shape.
2. Straighten your elbows and reach away from your body and hold for 3 seconds.
3. Relax and allow gravity to gently and slowly lengthen the muscles. You should feel the stretch in your shoulder joint and upper arm muscles.

 Imagine that your elbow is heavier than any other part of your arm and it's pulling the humerus (upper arm bone) away from the shoulder joint and towards the floor.

4. If this stretch is painful, place the blocks under your elbows to reduce the stretch.
5. Set a timer for 3 minutes (or more!).
6. Take slow deep breaths.
    - When you inhale: direct your breath to your sternum and feel it rise.
    - When you exhale: imagine weights in your elbows pulling them towards the floor.

POSITION #2

1. Bend your elbows to 90-degree angles. You should feel the stretch intensify at the front of the shoulder joints or front of the armpits.

 If the stretch causes pain, place blocks under your elbows to reduce the amount of stretch.

It's normal for your elbows and/or forearms not to reach the floor. The goal is to allow the muscle to lengthen; just allow them to stretch as far as you can.

2. Set a timer for 3 minutes (or more!).
3. Take slow deep breaths.
   - When you inhale: direct your breath to your sternum and feel it rise.
   - When you exhale: imagine weights in your elbows pulling them towards the floor.

POSITION #3

1. Slide your arms overhead. You should feel the stretch intensify on the back of the upper arms and/or along the back edge of the armpits.

 If the stretch causes pain, bend the elbows more to reduce the amount of overhead stretch until there is a stretch without pain.

2. Set a timer for 3 minutes (or more!).
3. Take slow deep breaths.
   - When you inhale: direct your breath to your sternum and feel it rise.
   - When you exhale: imagine your shoulder joint expanding as it is being pulled away from your body.
4. Slowly sit up and get up off the roller and shake out your upper body.
5. Take a moment to notice any changes that you feel.

Frequency

- Daily for full-time binders.
- Once per week for occasional binders.
- Daily when experiencing high anxiety.

Musical time keeping: the more relaxed you can be, the more effective this exercise will be. Repeatedly looking at your phone to keep tabs on the time will impede your ability to fully relax the upper chest. A great way to keep time is to create a playlist of chill songs that are each approximately the same length (3–5 minutes). Switch to the next position after each song.

FOCUS ON YOUR BREATH

Beyond the physical benefits, 15 minutes of integrative expansive breathing will create stillness in your mind and body. Maximize this impact by saying silent affirmations with each breath.

Here are some ideas to get you started; then you can create affirmations that feel authentic to you.

With Inhalation	With Exhalation
Breathing in more space for me to exist	Breathing out tension that keeps me in pain
Breathing in resilience	Breathing out trauma
Squaring off my shoulders and standing proud	Releasing my desire to hunch and hide my body
Breathing in wholeness	Breathing out brokenness
Making room for my breath	Getting rid of restriction
Opening my heart	Feeling my feelings
Letting in light	Pushing out darkness

#7 STERNUM MASSAGE

Objective

Loosen restrictive tissue on the surface of the sternum.

See Chapter 8 to learn more about the impact of binding and dysphoria on the sternum (page 197).

Symptoms

- Pain or restriction with deep breaths
- The sternum is tender to the touch
- Jaw pain
- Tension headaches, especially the forehead and behind the ears
- Restricted range of motion of the shoulders

Indications

- Concave upper chest
- Hunched posture
- Large-chested people
- TMJD
- Costochondritis

Technique

- Muscle softening

Tools Needed

- Pads of fingers

Landmarks

- Clavicular heads (aka heads of collarbones): two knobby bones just under your throat.
- Bottom of the sternum: the lower edge of the flat bone in the center of the chest just before the softer tissue of your abdomen.

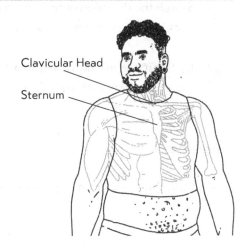

Clavicular Head

Sternum

Exercise

(This exercise should be done while not wearing any binding garment.)

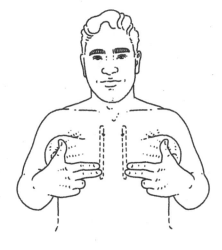

1. Place the pads of 2 or 3 fingers on the heads of your clavicles.
2. Move your fingers slowly in 3 small circles, gently moving the tissue side to side.

You want a small amount of friction under your fingers so that you can see the skin moving in the direction of your circles.

3. Move your fingers down 1 inch and do 3 more slow circles.

If you find a spot that is more tender, lighten your pressure enough so that it's massaging without being painful (it's OK if the pressure has to be *very light*).

4. Repeat until you reach the bottom of the sternum.
5. Switch the direction of the circles and repeat the process, traveling back up the sternum to the clavicles.

 Try this in the mirror the first few times so that you can see when the skin moves with your fingers.

Frequency

• Daily (this is a great exercise to do before falling asleep).

#8 PECTORALIS MUSCLES MASSAGE

Objective

Soothe and soften chest muscles to relieve soreness and tightness from binding.

See Chapter 8 to learn more about the impact of binding and dysphoria on the pectoralis muscles (page 196).

Symptoms

- Dull ache across the upper chest muscles
- Pain or tightness on the front of the shoulder above the armpit
- Pressure or tightness in the center of the chest
- Stiffness with large movements of the arms

Technique

- Muscle softening

Tools Needed

- Heat pack (to make your own, see page 191) (recommended but not required)
- Lotion or oil for your skin (optional)

Landmarks

- Lateral edge of pectoralis major: strong ropey muscle tissue that forms the front border of the armpit.
- Sternum: flat bone in the center of your chest.
- Clavicles (aka collarbone): horizontal bones across the top of your chest, starting at your shoulder and ending just below your throat.

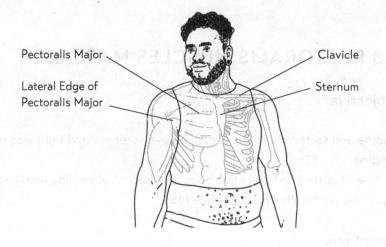

Pectoralis Major

Lateral Edge of
Pectoralis Major

Clavicle

Sternum

Exercise

(This exercise should be done while not wearing any binding garment.)

> ✎ Applying heat to your chest and the front of the shoulders for 10–15 minutes can make the muscles softer and more receptive to massage.

1. Reach across your body to your armpit and locate the ropey lateral edge of pectoralis major.
2. Gently curl your fingertips around the muscle tissue and gently squeeze it between your fingers and palm. This should not cause pain or discomfort.
3. Gently knead the tissue for 1 minute.
4. Hook the pads of your fingers loosely under the ropey edge.

This will be tender so don't curl too deep.

5. Keep your arm relaxed.
6. Slowly slide your fingers in a straight line towards the sternum, gently but firmly pulling the "rope" with you.
7. Repeat this pulling motion 3 times.
8. Repeat on the opposite side.

 If you feel bruised after this exercise, lighten the pressure the next time. This should be soothing and not result in increased tenderness.

Frequency

- Multiple times daily when symptoms are present.
- Every 1–3 days for regular maintenance.

CHECK YOUR ARMHOLES

This exercise is especially important if the armholes of your binder cut into this ropey muscle tissue or you see bruises, calluses, or a hyperpigmented line. If this is the case for you, in addition to massaging it regularly, revisit Chapter 2 and make sure that you are wearing the right size and the binder best suited to your body. If possible, try a different cut to see if it applies less pressure to the area.

#9 PECTORALIS MUSCLES TRIGGER POINT RELEASE

Objective

Relax trigger points in the pectoralis muscles that cause restriction and pain.

See Chapter 8 to learn more about the impact of binding and dysphoria on the pectoralis muscles (page 196).

Symptoms

- Tender "knots" in the pec muscles
- Tenderness along the border of the clavicle
- Diffuse pain across the chest, armpit, shoulder, and inner (pinky-side) arm (see Trigger point diagram #9)
- Stabbing pain deep under the chest tissue
- Pressure or tightness in the center of the chest
- Stiffness with large movements of the arms

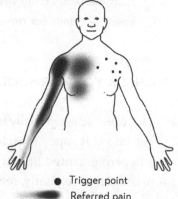

Trigger point diagram #9

● Trigger point

Referred pain (increasing intensity)

Indications

- Limited range of motion in the arms
- Chronically hunched/slumped shoulders
- Chest breathing

Technique

- Self myofascial release (SMR) with pressure aka trigger point release

Tools Needed

- Tennis ball, racquetball, or similarly sized foam or rubber ball

Landmarks

- Head of the humerus: the bony knob on the front of the shoulder joint which is the top of the upper arm bone.
- Heads of the clavicles (aka collarbones): two knobby bones just under your throat.

Pectoralis Major

Head of the Clavicle

Head of the Humerus

Pectoralis Minor

- Lateral edge of pectoralis major: strong ropey muscle tissue that forms the front border of the armpit.
- Pectoralis major: large upper chest muscle that stretches from the center of the chest to the armpit and attaches to the humerus (upper arm bone), clavicle, and sternum.
- Pectoralis minor: small triangular muscle that lays flat on the surface of ribs 3 and 4, and beginning between the head of the humerus and the clavicle and attaching to the ribs approximately halfway between the armpit and the sternum. It is covered entirely by the pectoralis major muscle.

Exercise

(This exercise should be done while not wearing any binding garment.)

1. Stand, sit, or lie on your back with your knees up.

>  Variation: People with a lot of chest tissue may find that elevating the head by sitting, standing, or propping up on a wedge pillow helps create better access to the upper chest.

2. Position the ball against your body just inside and below the head of the humerus.
3. Using your open palm apply firm pressure on the ball.
4. Roll the ball slowly and firmly across the chest, covering each trigger point marked in Trigger point diagram #9.
5. Locate spots that are more tender than the surrounding tissue; these are likely trigger points.
6. Place the ball over the trigger point and use your palm to increase the pressure until it is uncomfortable but not painful.

> When pressure is applied to a trigger point, it can cause the referred pain to intensify so you *may* feel an increase in pain elsewhere in the chest. That's OK.

7. Take deep breaths while maintaining pressure for 30 seconds.
   - *If the tenderness has gone,* move on to other parts of the muscle.
   - *If the tenderness has reduced but not gone,* slightly increase

the pressure until it is uncomfortable but just shy of painful. Hold for another 30 seconds.

- *If the tenderness has not changed,* hold at the same pressure for another 30 seconds.
- *If the tenderness has decreased but is still not gone,* let the tissue rest and do another round the following day.

8. Repeat for each tender trigger point.
9. Move your arms in big circles to allow the muscle fibers to adjust to the untangling.

 Keep your ball by the TV to remind you to do this regularly when you are relaxing at home.

 Some (but not all) people with fibromyalgia, Ehlers-Danlos syndrome (EDS), or similar pain conditions may be highly sensitive to trigger point pain and should avoid this if it causes lingering pain or if deep tissue massage has caused inflammation to flare up in the past.

Frequency

- Daily if symptoms are present.
- 1–2 times per week as maintenance for full time binders.
- Biweekly for occasional binders.

#10 RIB CAGE TRIGGER POINT RELEASE

Objective

Relieve local and referred pain by releasing painful trigger points that form in the muscles between and on the surface of each rib.

See the "Impact on Anatomy" section to learn more about the impact of binding and dysphoria on the intercostal muscles and serratus anterior muscle (page 198).

Symptoms

- Pain with coughing or sneezing
- Pain taking a deep breath
- Stabbing rib pain
- Pain radiating down the pinky-side of the arm
- Sharp pain deep under the chest tissue
- Persistent tension or pain between the lower shoulder blade and the spine
- See Trigger point diagram #10 for areas affected by referred pain

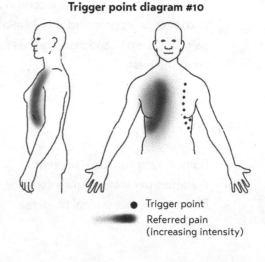

Trigger point diagram #10

● Trigger point

Referred pain (increasing intensity)

Indications

- Pain developing concurrently with or following respiratory infection, episode of vomiting, panic attack, or asthma attack

Technique

- Self myofascial release (SMR) using pressure aka trigger point release

Tools Needed

- Fingers

Landmarks

- Ribs: curved bones wrapping from the sternum on the front of the torso to the spine on the back of the torso.
- Intercostal muscles: muscles between ribs.
- Serratus anterior: a muscle with a series of "fingers" along the ribs on the side of the rib cage.
- Sternum: flat bone in the center of your chest.

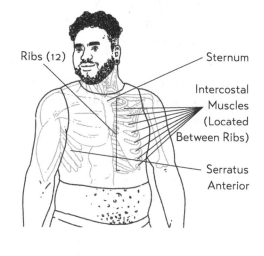

Ribs (12)

Sternum

Intercostal Muscles (Located Between Ribs)

Serratus Anterior

Exercise

(This exercise should be done while not wearing any binding garment.)

1. Use the pad of your finger or thumb to gently feel along the muscle tissue *between* the ribs. Start at the sternum and follow each rib around the side of the body until the ribs become too covered by muscle or fat for you to feel them.

2. Locate any spots that feel more tender than the surrounding tissue.

You may feel a dense area that feels like chewing gum.

3. Using the pad of your finger or thumb gently press into that spot.

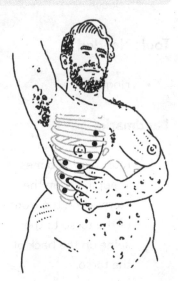

If this is hard on your fingers, overlap 2 or 3 fingers to reduce fatigue or use a small ball under the pressure of your palm.

4. Apply enough gentle pressure to be uncomfortable but just shy of painful.

When pressure is applied to a trigger point, it can cause the referred pain to intensify so you *may* feel an increase in pain in elsewhere in the chest. That's OK.

5. Hold this pressure for 30 seconds while taking deep breaths.
   - *If the tenderness has gone,* move on to other parts of the muscle.
   - *If the tenderness has reduced but not gone,* slightly increase the pressure until it is uncomfortable but just shy of painful. Hold for another 30 seconds.
   - *If the tenderness has not changed,* hold at the same pressure for another 30 seconds.
   - *If the tenderness has decreased but is still not gone,* let the tissue rest and do another round the following day.
6. Repeat for all tender trigger points.
7. Take deep breaths and shake out your torso to allow the muscle fibers to adjust to the untangling.

Cracked ribs are extremely rare but do occur as a result of binding, so if the stabbing pain occurs with a shallow breath and has not changed after trying this exercise, it's important to get that checked by a physician (see Chapter 6 for suggestions for talking to medical providers).

 Some (but not all) people with fibromyalgia, EDS, or similar pain conditions may be highly sensitive to trigger point pain and should avoid this if pressure causes lingering pain or if deep tissue massage has caused inflammation to flare up in the past.

Frequency

- Daily when experiencing symptoms.

#11 SERRATUS ANTERIOR MASSAGE

Objective

Soften the serratus anterior muscle to improve breathing and reduce shoulder pain.

See Chapter 8 to learn more about the impact of binding and dysphoria on the serratus anterior muscle (page 198).

Symptoms

- Difficulty getting a full breath
- Restricted range of motion when reaching toward the ceiling
- Weakness lifting weight above the head or doing a pushup
- Difficulty holding weight in your outstretched arm
- Persistent knot between the bottom of the shoulder blade and the spine or under the shoulder blade
- Tender spots on the ribs below the armpit, see Trigger point diagram #11
- Aching pain on the pinky-finger side of the arm, see Trigger point diagram #11

Trigger point diagram #11

● Trigger point

Referred pain (increasing intensity)

Indications

- Air hunger: gasping for air randomly while at rest

- Limited range of motion in the shoulder joint

Technique

- Muscle softening

Tools Needed

- Hands

Landmarks

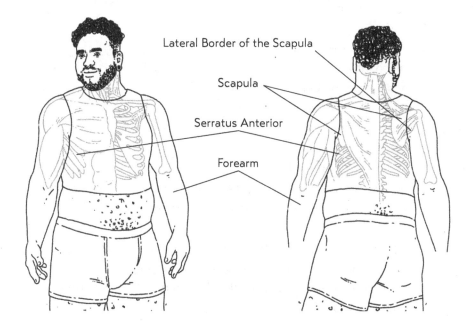

Lateral Border of the Scapula

Scapula

Serratus Anterior

Forearm

- Scapula: flat triangular bone on the surface of the upper back that moves to enable arm movement.
- Lateral border of the scapula: the bony edge of the scapula that you can feel along the back of the armpit (covered by muscle).
- Serratus anterior: muscle that originates under the scapula and wraps around the rib cage under the armpit in finger-like sections.
- Forearm: section of the arm between the elbow and the wrist.

Exercise

(This exercise is best done while not wearing any binding garment but can be done while binding.)

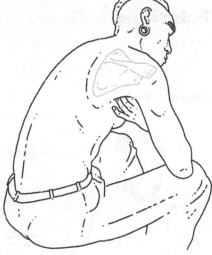

1. Sit in a supportive chair with your feet flat on the floor.
2. Bend your elbow to 90 degrees.
3. Lean forward and place your forearm on your knee.
4. With the other arm, reach into your armpit and locate the bony edge of the scapula.
5. Use your fingers to gently press into the muscle under the edge on the bone, starting with very gentle pressure and only increasing when you feel the muscle tissue warm and soften.

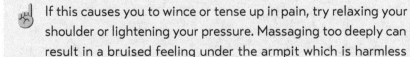

If this causes you to wince or tense up in pain, try relaxing your shoulder or lightening your pressure. Massaging too deeply can result in a bruised feeling under the armpit which is harmless but uncomfortable.

6. Move along the border of the bone from the armpit down for at least 30 seconds on each side.

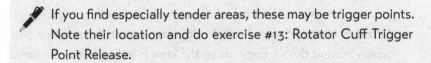

If you find especially tender areas, these may be trigger points. Note their location and do exercise #13: Rotator Cuff Trigger Point Release.

Frequency

- Every 2–3 days when symptoms are present.
- Weekly for regular binders if you use your arms intensively in work or play.
- Biweekly for general maintenance.

#12 LATERAL TORSO RELEASE

Objective

Improve torso flexibility to increase breath capacity and reduce rib cage restriction by releasing the fascia bonding muscles together along the side of the upper body.

See Chapter 8 to learn more about the impact of binding and dysphoria on the lateral torso (page 199) and oblique muscles (page 206).

BEWARE OF THE ROLL-UP

Full-length binders can pose an increased risk to this muscle group when they roll up and exert pressure multiplied by the force of the rolled elastic fabric. This can cause bruising or painful shifting of the lower ribs. Preventing the rolling up of the fabric is essential— see page 90 for tips on how to do this.

Symptoms

- Mid-back stiffness or pain, especially in an upright posture
- Difficulty with getting breath deep in the belly
- Reduced flexibility in twisting at the waist without moving the hips

Indications

- Limited range of motion in thoracic rotation
- Mid-back pain or stiffness

Technique

- Active self myofascial release (SMR)

Tools Needed

- Firm seat

Landmarks

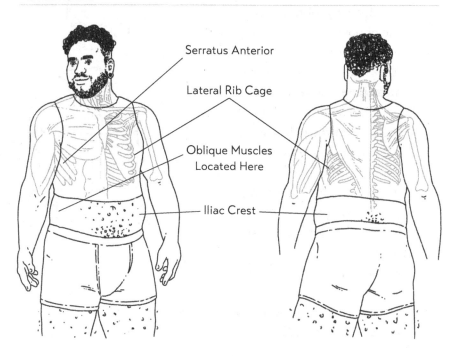

Serratus Anterior

Lateral Rib Cage

Oblique Muscles
Located Here

Iliac Crest

- Lateral rib cage: surface of the ribs on the sides of the body from the armpit to the waist.
- Pelvis: the large bowl-shaped bone that forms your seat when sitting.
- Iliac crest (of the pelvis): curved bony edge of the pelvis on the side of the body just below the waist.

Exercise

(This exercise is best done while not wearing any binding garment but can be done while binding.)

1. Sit tall with your feet flat on the floor and knees at a 90-degree angle. Keep your spine upright and chin tucked.
2. Reach over your head toward the opposite wall, keeping your elbow aligned with your ear.
3. Allow the butt cheek of the stretching side to lift slightly until you feel a stretch from the crest of the pelvis along the rib cage and into the armpit.
4. Breathe deeply to expand your whole rib cage.
5. Hold the stretch for 20 seconds.
6. Repeat 3 times on each side.

 Stretch both sides even if you only feel tightness or pain on one side of the body.

 If you have a history of low back spasms, **stop** this stretch immediately if you feel any twinges in the low back muscles.

 If you have severe scoliosis, conditions affecting discs in your lower spine or other spinal conditions, check with a doctor or physical therapist before doing this exercise.

If you have a hypermobility joint disorder, check with your doctor or physical therapist before doing any stretches. See the information about binding and hypermobility in Chapter 5, Section 2.

Frequency

- 1–3 times daily, especially if you spend the majority of your time sitting.

EXERCISES
SHOULDER

#13 ROTATOR CUFF TRIGGER POINT RELEASE

Objective

Relieve pain and/or weakness and increase range of motion in the shoulder and arm.

See Chapter 8 to learn more about the impact of binding and dysphoria on the rotator cuff (page 199) and scapular mobility (page 201).

Symptoms

Trigger point diagram #13

● Trigger point   Referred pain (increasing intensity)

- Pain and/or reduced range of motion with overhead arm movement or reaching behind the back
- Achy, referred pain in any of the following (see Trigger point diagram #13):
  - Shoulder joint
  - Elbow
  - Wrists
  - On or under the shoulder blade
  - Thumb-side of the arm

- Underside of upper arm

Indications

- Rotator cuff injuries (current or former)
- Supraspinatus tendonitis
- Winged scapula (shoulder blades)
- Weakness in stabilizing the shoulder in weight-bearing activities

Technique

- Self myofascial release (SMR) with pressure aka trigger point release

Tools Needed

- Foam or rubber ball (tennis or racquetball)
- Long sock
- Wall

Landmarks

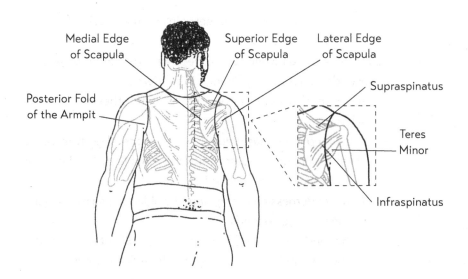

- Scapula (shoulder blade): flat triangular bone on the surface of the upper back that moves to enable arm movement.
- Medial edge of scapula: the bony edge closest to the spine which becomes visible when squeezing the shoulder blades together.
- Superior edge of scapula: bony edge of the scapula located between the neck and shoulder joint.
- Lateral edge of the scapula: bony edge of the scapula that runs vertically from the back of your armpit.
- Posterior fold of the armpit: the fold that forms the back of your armpit.

Exercise

(*This exercise can be done while wearing any binding garment.*)

For each position in this exercise, you will use the following protocol for treating trigger points:

TRIGGER POINT RELEASE TECHNIQUE

This exercise consists of 4 positions in which a ball is used to apply pressure to trigger points.

1. Slowly apply enough pressure to feel pain and then back off slightly until what you feel is tender but not quite painful.
2. Hold for 30 seconds while taking deep breaths. then release for 5–10 seconds to assess any change in tenderness.
   - *If the tenderness has gone,* move on to other parts of the muscle.
   - *If the tenderness has reduced but not gone,* slightly increase the pressure until it is uncomfortable but just shy of painful. Hold for another 30 seconds.
   - *If the tenderness has not changed,* hold at the same pressure for another 30 seconds.
   - *If the tenderness has decreased but is still not gone,* let the tissue rest and do another round the following day.

Before you begin, drop the ball in the toe of the sock in order to dangle it behind your back.

POSITION #1: MEDIAL EDGE OF THE SHOULDER BLADE

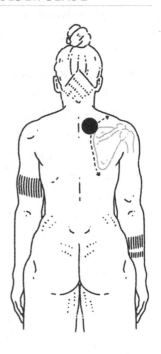

1. Dangle the ball over your shoulder.
2. Stand with your shoulder blades against the wall and your feet 2–3 feet from the wall with your knees comfortably bent.
3. Position the ball at the top of the medial edge of the scapula.
4. Bend your knees and press your body onto the ball against the wall with the pressure of the ball pushing into the edge of the scapula.
5. Slowly straighten your knees to move the ball down the edge of the scapula.
6. As you roll, locate trigger points, which will be more tender than the surrounding tissue.

 This is an area of many potential trigger points so don't worry if you find many tender spots.

7. Position the ball on the trigger point.
8. Use the trigger point release technique described at the beginning of this exercise.
9. Squeeze your shoulder blades together and release a few times to allow the muscle fibers to adjust to the untangling.

POSITION #2: FLAT SURFACE OF THE SCAPULA

1. Reposition the ball in the middle of your scapula.

2. Stand with one shoulder blade pressed flat against the wall and turn the other shoulder slightly away from the wall.

 The goal is for the pressure to be going directly into the surface of the bone.

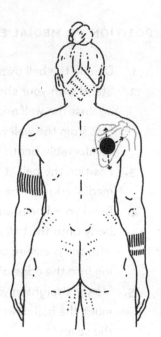

3. Move side to side and up and down to roll the ball over the entire surface of the scapula.

4. As you roll, locate trigger points, which will be more tender than the surrounding tissue (there might be many!). See Trigger point diagram #13 for suggestions on where these points might be located.

5. Use the trigger point release technique described at the beginning of this exercise.

6. Shrug and roll your shoulders to allow the muscle fibers to adjust to the untangling.

POSITION #3: LATERAL EDGE OF THE SCAPULA

1. Reposition the ball in the posterior fold of your armpit.

2. Stand with one shoulder against the wall and turn the other shoulder away from the wall until you are at approximately a 45-degree angle with the wall.

3. Bend your knees and lean your body into the wall to apply pressure into the back of the shoulder joint.

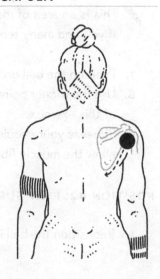

4. Slowly straighten your knees to move the ball down the scapula. Turn your body as needed to keep the pressure along the edge of the bone.

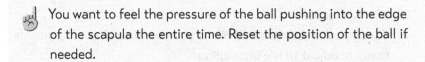 You want to feel the pressure of the ball pushing into the edge of the scapula the entire time. Reset the position of the ball if needed.

5. As you roll down this bony edge, locate trigger points that are particularly painful or tender (there might be many!). See Trigger point diagram #13 for suggestions on where these points might be located.
6. Use the trigger point release technique described at the beginning of this exercise.
7. Do several large arm circles to allow the muscle fibers to adjust to the untangling.

POSITION #4: SUPERIOR EDGE OF THE SCAPULA

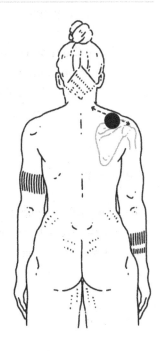

1. Reposition the ball along the superior edge of the scapula.
2. Keep your upper back against the wall and walk your feet away from the wall so that the top edge of your scapula is pressed against the wall.

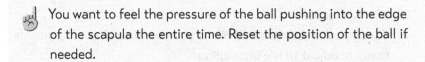 It may take a few tries to get the ball to stay in place. Keep at it, you'll get it!

3. Shift your body side to side in order to move the ball in the direction shown in the diagram.
4. Locate trigger points, which will be

more tender than the surrounding tissue (there might be many!). See Trigger point diagram #13 for suggestions on where these points might be located.

5. Use the trigger point release technique described at the beginning of this exercise.

6. Shrug your shoulders and move your head to allow the muscle fibers to adjust to the untangling.

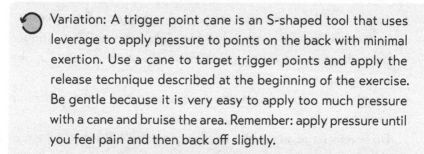

Variation: A trigger point cane is an S-shaped tool that uses leverage to apply pressure to points on the back with minimal exertion. Use a cane to target trigger points and apply the release technique described at the beginning of the exercise. Be gentle because it is very easy to apply too much pressure with a cane and bruise the area. Remember: apply pressure until you feel pain and then back off slightly.

Applying heat to the area for 10 minutes before doing this exercise will soften the muscle tissue and relax your whole nervous system.

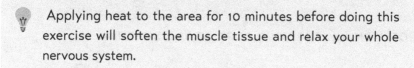

Some (but not all) people with fibromyalgia, EDS, or similar pain conditions may be highly sensitive to trigger point pain and should avoid this if pressure causes lingering pain or if deep tissue massage has caused inflammation to flare up in the past.

Frequency

- Daily when symptoms are present.
- Once a week to maintain a healthy rotator cuff with regular binding.
- 3 times per week if you use your arms intensively in work or play.

#14 SHOULDER ROTATION

Objective

Increase movement and reduce stiffness in shoulders and arms by engaging the muscles that are responsible for forward and backward rotation at the joint.

See Chapter 8 to learn more about the impact of binding and dysphoria on shoulder rotation (page 200), the rotator cuff muscles (page 199), and scapular mobility (page 201).

Symptoms

- Pain or fatigue with upright/shoulders-back posture
- Tightness in the chest just below the shoulder joint
- Aching pain in the shoulder joint

Indications

- Decreased range of motion in the shoulders
- Frozen shoulder

Technique

- Mobilization

Tools Needed

- Wall
- Small towel (optional)

Landmarks

- Scapula: flat tri-angular bone on the surface of the upper back that moves to enable arm movement.
- Forearm: section of the arm between the elbow and the wrist.

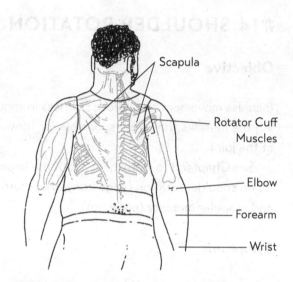

Exercise

(This exercise is best done while not wearing any binding garment but can be done while binding if needed.)

Stand with your back against the wall and your feet far enough away from the wall to feel stable and maintain full contact between your upper body and the wall.

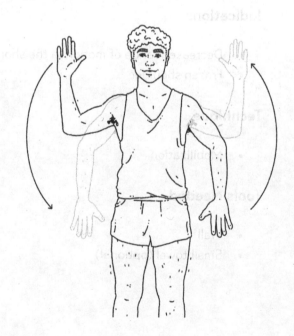

Keep your butt, shoulder blades, and head in contact with the wall at all times. If you're not able to press your head into the wall completely, fold a small towel and place it between your head and the wall.

 This can also be done lying flat on the floor with your knees bent and butt, shoulder blades, and head in contact with the floor.

1. Place your elbows against the wall as pictured with one hand pointing up and the other pointing down.
2. Inhale deeply.
3. As you exhale, slowly reverse the positions of your forearms.
4. Keep your elbows and your shoulder blades stationary and against the wall while you rotate the arm, getting the forearm as close to the wall as possible.

 Your forearm may not make contact with the wall/floor, especially in the downward position. That's OK!

5. Inhale and hold your arms close to the wall without moving the elbow or shoulder blade.
6. As you exhale, slowly reverse the positions of your forearms.
7. Do a set of 10.
8. Drop your arms to your sides and shake out your arms.

 You should not feel sharp pain in the shoulder joint with this exercise. Try easing up the force with which you are pressing your forearms into the wall/floor. If this does not alleviate the pain, **stop** the exercise.

 If you have history of rotator cuff injury, labrum tear, or shoulder dislocation, check with a doctor or physical therapist before doing this exercise.

If you do not feel any resistance and your arms easily lie flat in both positions, then you are potentially hypermobile. Check with your doctor or physical therapist before doing any stretches. See the information about binding and hypermobility in Chapter 5, Section 2.

 Establish a habit of doing this exercise and scapular mobilization (exercise #15) in the shower every day. Let the hot water heat the muscles and then do one set of each—it takes less than a minute and will make a big difference to your upper body posture and comfort.

Frequency

- 2–3 times daily when symptoms are present.
- Daily for regular maintenance.

#15 SCAPULAR MOBILIZATION

Objective

Increase movement and reduce stiffness in the shoulder, neck, and upper back by engaging the muscles attached to the scapula.

See Chapter 8 section to learn more about the impact of binding and dysphoria on scapular mobility (page 201) and the rotator cuff muscles (page 199).

Symptoms

- Pain on the backside of the shoulder/shoulder blade
- Pain on the front of the shoulder
- Stiffness in the shoulder joint
- Stiffness in the upper back, especially when pulling the shoulders back and down

Indications

- Limited range of shoulder motion, especially overhead and reaching back
- Fatigue in the shoulders or chest muscles in activities where the arms are raised for prolonged periods

Technique

- Mobilization

Tools Needed

- A wall
- A small towel

Landmarks

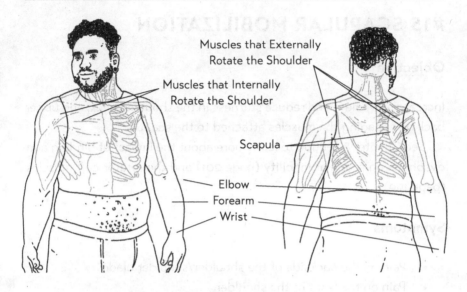

- Scapula: flat triangular bone on the surface of the upper back that moves to enable arm movement.
- Forearm: section of the arm between the elbow and the wrist.

Exercise

(This exercise is best done while not wearing any binding garment but can be done while binding.)

1. Stand with your butt, shoulder blades, and head against a wall with your feet as far from the wall as needed or lie flat on the floor with your knees bent and low back flat.

> If you're not able to get your head against the wall completely, fold a small towel and place it between your head and the wall/floor.

> It is easy to accidentally arch your low back when doing this lying down so be mindful of keeping your spine flat on the floor.

2. Squeeze your shoulder blades together and use your bodyweight against the wall/floor to keep your shoulders back and your shoulder blades flat against the wall/floor for the whole exercise.

3. Keep your chin level and don't arch your back.

4. Bring your arms level with your shoulders and bend the elbows to 90 degrees, with the palms facing out.

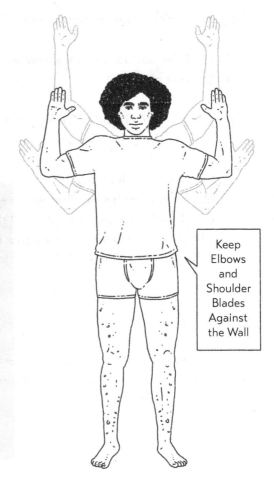

Keep Elbows and Shoulder Blades Against the Wall

🖊 The goal is to keep your shoulders, elbows, and wrists flat against the wall during the entire movement. You may not be able to move your arms very far at first—that's OK! Over time, the muscles will loosen and the range of motion will increase.

5. *Slowly* slide your elbows down as far as you can without your arms coming further away from the wall.

☝ This exercise is called W to Y. This position should be making a "W" shape.

6. Hold this position and take a diaphragmatic breath (exercise #1).

7. *Slowly* raise your arms and straighten your elbows, reaching as high as possible without allowing your shoulder blades or head to come away from the wall/floor.

 This position should be making a "Y" shape.

8. Hold this position and take a diaphragmatic breath (exercise #1).
9. Do a set of 10.

 This exercise should be challenging but not painful. **Stop** the exercise if you feel sharp pain.

If you do not feel any resistance and your arms easily lie flat in both positions, then you are potentially hypermobile. Check with your doctor or physical therapist before doing any stretches. See the information about binding and hypermobility in Chapter 5, Section 2.

Frequency

- 3 times daily if symptoms are present.
- 2–3 times per week for regular maintenance.

EXERCISES
NECK

#16 CHIN TUCK

Objective

Reduce neck pain and stiffness and improve head/neck posture.

See Chapter 8 to learn more about the impact of binding and dysphoria on the neck muscles (page 203) and headache pain (page 201).

DO I HAVE FORWARD HEAD POSTURE (FHP)?

Stand in your normal posture with your back against the wall. If the back of your head is not against the wall, you probably have some degree of FHP. The further away from the wall the head is, the greater the strain on the neck flexor and extensor muscles.

Symptoms

- Pain on the back of the neck
- Tension headaches
- Pain turning the head to look over the shoulder
- Jaw pain

Indications

- FHP or Upper Crossed Syndrome
- Thoracic kyphosis (rounded upper back)
- TMJD
- Cervicogenic headaches and migraines

Technique

- Mobilization

Tools Needed

- None

Landmarks

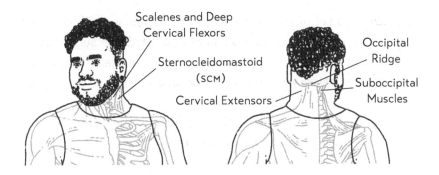

Scalenes and Deep Cervical Flexors

Sternocleidomastoid (SCM)

Cervical Extensors

Occipital Ridge

Suboccipital Muscles

- Occipital ridge: the bottom edge of the skull extending earlobe to earlobe.

Exercise

(This exercise can be done in any form of binding.)

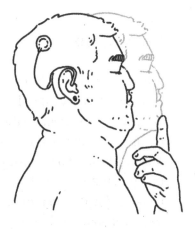

1. Sit or stand upright and look straight ahead with your head level.

 Check in the mirror to be sure that you are not tipping your head back at all.

2. Place a finger on your chin.
3. Without moving your finger, pull the chin straight back like you are making a double chin.
4. Retract the chin until you feel a sensation at the occipital ridge.
5. Hold for 5 seconds.

6. Slowly return your chin back to the finger.

7. Repeat 10 times, rest in between tucks if needed.

 Increase the intensity: place your hand under your chin and press your chin down into your hand while tucking.

 Doing a set of 10 chin tucks only takes 1 minute. Think about daily activities when you can fit in a set. Some suggestions: at red lights, on public transit, while you make coffee, in the shower, before you get into bed, or set a reminder on your phone.

 Consult a doctor or physical therapist before doing this exercise if you have any disorders of the cervical spine.

Frequency

- 8 sets per day if symptoms are present or you have significant FHP.
- 5 or more sets per day for maintenance.

HEAVY HEAD

When the head sits in front of proper alignment with the spine and looks downward to look at a phone, for example, the weight effectively increases and the spine and muscles are forced to strain to support it. In a neutral position, the head weighs 10–12 pounds. Moving the head only 15 degrees forward (you wouldn't even notice this much FHP in daily life) increases the weight to 27 pounds. Looking down at your phone in your lap can increase the effective weight of your head to 60 pounds. That's the average weight of an 8-year-old! No wonder our necks and backs hurt.

EXERCISE

#17 OCCIPUT MASSAGE

Objective

Reduce pain level and frequency of tension headaches, migraines, and stiff neck.

See Chapter 8 to learn more about the impact of binding and dysphoria on the neck muscles (page 203) and headache pain (page 201).

Symptoms

- Headaches with these patterns: band above the ears, forehead/hairline, center line from forehead to neck, eye sockets
- Neck fatigue, especially after working at the computer or looking down at the phone
- Tight, tender muscles on the sides of the neck behind the ears
- Tenderness to the touch at the occipital ridge

Headache referral pain patterns

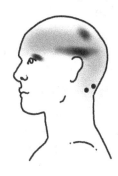

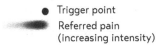

● Trigger point

Referred pain (increasing intensity)

Indications

- Forward Head Posture (FHP)
- Cervicogenic headaches or migraines

Technique

- Muscle softening

Tools Needed

- Thumbs

Landmarks

- Mastoid process: small bony protrusion under the earlobes and behind the jaw.
- Occipital ridge: the bottom edge of the skull extending ear to ear.

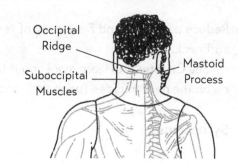

Exercise

(This exercise can be done in any form of binding.)

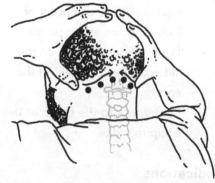

1. Place each thumb on the mastoid process on each side your head.

 The mastoid process will likely be tender.

2. Rest your palms on the sides of the head for stability.
3. Move your thumbs in 5 small, gentle circles over the bony ridge without causing pain.

 Tenderness and minor discomfort are OK but this is intended to relax the muscle not cause pain.

4. Move your thumb 1 inch along the ridge towards the spine.

5. Repeat until your thumbs meet in the middle of your occipital ridge.

If you find an area that is particularly tender, do extra circles in that area to relieve tension.

6. Reverse the process until your thumbs are back to the mastoid processes.

Try doing this in conjunction with the chin tuck (exercise #16) to relax and strengthen these muscles.

Headaches can be signs of other more serious conditions. Seek the advice of a doctor if you have chronic or debilitating headaches.

Frequency

- At the onset of a headache.
- 5–10 times per day if you suffer from regular tension headaches or migraines.
- Daily for regular maintenance.

#18 NECK MOBILIZATION

Objective

Reduce a stiff and painful neck by stretching and engaging muscles that are overtaxed by dysphoria hunching and chronic chest breathing.

See Chapter 8 to learn more about the impact of binding and dysphoria on the neck muscles (page 203) and headache pain (page 201).

Symptoms

- Sharp pain moving or turning the head
- Stiff neck or difficulty looking over the shoulder
- Jaw pain
- Headaches or migraines
- Aching pain in the shoulder or upper arm

Indications

- Forward Head Posture (FHP) or Upper Crossed Syndrome
- Chronic chest breathing
- TMJD

Technique

- Mobilization

Tools Needed

- None

Landmarks

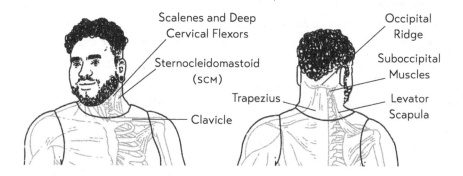

- Clavicles (aka collarbones): the horizontal bones across the top of your chest, starting at your shoulder and ending just below your throat.

Exercise

(This exercise can be done in any form of binding.)

1. Sit or stand tall with your shoulder back and your chin level.
2. Place a hand on your chest just below the throat with the thumb and fingers on the collarbones.
3. Keep your chin level and rotate your head to the right, moving your chin towards your shoulder as far as it can go without turning your torso or causing pain.

 Use the hands on your chest to notice if your torso moves.

4. Hold this position for 3 seconds and slowly return to neutral.
5. Repeat 5 times on each side.
6. Return your head to neutral position.
7. Tip your left ear toward your left shoulder without lifting either shoulder.

Use the hand on your chest to notice if either shoulder lifts up.

8. Raise your right ear toward the ceiling to feel a stretch in the muscles on the right side of the neck.
9. Hold this position for 3 seconds and slowly return to neutral.
10. Repeat 5 times on each side.

Take up the intensity by putting a slight downward pressure on the collarbones with your hand.

You may hear crunchy noises as you do this exercise. That's OK as long as there is no pain. You may notice that there is less of the noise as you do this exercise more frequently.

Challenge yourself to get 10 sets in every day! Attaching a new habit to an existing habit is the best way to make it stick. Doing a set of full series of neck mobilization takes less than 1 minute so get creative. Try doing a set whenever you go to the bathroom, park your car, check social media, or hear a commercial.

If you have any condition of the cervical spine, consult with your doctor or physical therapist before doing this exercise.

If you have a hypermobility joint disorder, check with your doctor or physical therapist before doing this exercise. See the information about binding and hypermobility in Chapter 5, Section 2.

Frequency

- 10 sets daily, especially if you are in class for long hours, work at a computer, drive for work, or spend a lot of time on your phone.

#19 SCM MASSAGE AND TRIGGER POINT RELEASE

Objective

Relax and soften the sternocleidomastoid (SCM) muscle to reduce headache pain and support free, unrestricted range of motion in the head, neck, and jaw.

See Chapter 8 to learn more about the impact of binding and dysphoria on the SCM muscle (page 204), the neck muscles (page 203), and headache pain (page 201)

Symptoms

- Headaches (in/behind the ears, forehead, temples, cheekbone, eye sockets, top of the head)
- Neck pain, especially near the base of the skull
- Difficulty projecting the voice
- Ringing in the ears
- Stiff or limited range of motion in the neck
- Pain in areas of trigger point referral (see Trigger point diagram #19)

Trigger point diagram #19

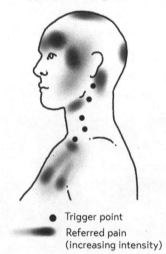

- Trigger point
- Referred pain (increasing intensity)

Indications

- TMJD
- Migraines or chronic headaches
- Tinnitus

Techniques

- Muscle softening
- Trigger point release

Tools Needed

- Hands

Landmarks

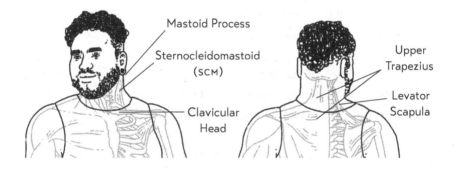

- Mastoid process: small bony protrusion under the earlobes and behind the jaw.
- Heads of the clavicles (aka collarbones): two knobby bones just under your throat.

Exercise

(This exercise can be done while wearing a binding garment.)

MASSAGE THE SCM MUSCLE

1. Locate the SCM muscle by turning your head as if you are looking at the person next to you. Feel for a ropey muscle to pop up. It follows a line from the mastoid process and the head of the clavicle.
2. Let your chin drop slightly to your chest in order to relax the muscle.

3. With your thumb and forefinger, gently pinch the midpoint of the muscle, getting a gentle grip on the ropey muscle.

4. Keeping a light grip, jiggle the muscle side to side while pulling slightly away from the body to lift the muscle.

5. When you feel the muscle get a little easier to move, shift your grip 1 inch up the muscle and repeat until the muscle meets the bone under your earlobe.

 As you move closer to the mastoid process, it will get more difficult to get your fingers around the muscle—that's OK, just keep trying to move the tense muscle side to side.

6. Return to the midpoint of the muscle and gently pinch the SCM again.

7. Move 1 inch downward towards the head of the clavicle and repeat until the muscle meets the bone.

8. Repeat 3 passes of the muscle on each side.

RELEASE TRIGGER POINTS IN THE SCM MUSCLE

1. As you travel the length of the muscle, locate spots that are more tender than the surrounding tissue.

2. Settle your fingertips around that section of the muscle and slowly apply enough pressure to feel pain and then back off slightly until what you feel is tender but not quite painful.

 When pressure is applied to a trigger point, it can cause the referred pain to intensify so you *may* feel an increase in pain in the head or face. That's OK.

3. Hold for 30 seconds while taking deep breaths, then release for 5–10 seconds to assess any change in tenderness.
   - *If the tenderness has gone*, move on to other parts of the muscle.
   - *If the tenderness has reduced but not gone*, slightly increase the pressure until it is uncomfortable but just shy of painful. Hold for another 30 seconds.
   - *If the tenderness has not changed*, hold at the same pressure for another 30 seconds.
   - *If the tenderness has decreased but is still not gone*, let the tissue rest and do another round the following day.

4. Do gentle neck circles to allow the muscle fibers to adjust to the untangling.

5. Apply pressure to each trigger point (indicated by the tender spot) that you find in the muscle. The typical locations are marked on Trigger point diagram #19.

 There can be up to 7 trigger points in just this one muscle!

 Some (but not all) people with fibromyalgia, EDS, or similar pain conditions may be highly sensitive to trigger point pain and should avoid this if pressure causes lingering pain or if deep tissue massage has caused inflammation to flare up in the past.

Frequency

- At the onset of a headache, jaw pain, or tinnitus.
- 5 times daily when symptoms are present or if you clench/grind your teeth or have chronic headaches/migraines
- Daily for regular maintenance.

#20 TRAPEZIUS AND LEVATOR SCAPULA TRIGGER POINT RELEASE

Objective

Relax shoulder and neck tension and release trigger points that frequently cause headaches.

See Chapter 8 to learn more about the impact of binding and dysphoria on the trapezius and levator scapula (page 204) and headache pain (page 201).

Symptoms

- Headache pain at the base of the skull, behind the ear, or at the temple
- Jaw pain or fatigue when chewing
- Neck pain, stiffness, or fatigue/weakness
- Palpable knots on the top and inside of the shoulder blades
- Pain in areas of trigger point referral shown in Trigger point diagram #20

Trigger point diagram #20

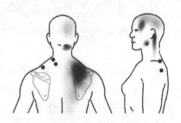

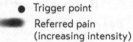
● Trigger point
　Referred pain
　(increasing intensity)

Indications

- Cervicogenic headaches or migraines
- TMJD

Technique

- Active self myofascial release (SMR)

Tools Needed

- Tennis ball or similarly sized rubber or foam ball
- The corner of a wall or doorway

Landmarks

- Intersection of trapezius (aka traps) and levator scapula: the bend where the neck and shoulder meet.

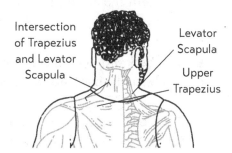

Intersection of Trapezius and Levator Scapula

Levator Scapula

Upper Trapezius

Exercise

(This exercise is best done while not wearing any binding garment but can be done while binding if needed.)

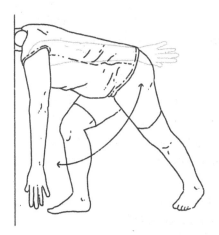 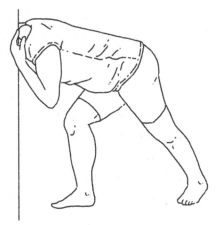

1. Stand torso-length away from a doorway or corner wall with legs hip-width apart.
2. Position the ball at the intersection of your traps and levator scapula.

3. Align the ball with the edge of the wall and hold it on the intersection of trapezius and levator scapula (see Trigger point diagram #20 for the location of the trigger points).
4. Bend at the waist and get as close to a "table-top" as you can.

Bend your knees a little or a lot (but don't lock them) and adjust the width and distance of your feet into the position that best suits your body.

5. Step back with the leg on the same side as the ball.
6. Sandwich the ball between your shoulder and the wall.

If the ball is slipping out from you and the wall, try getting further from the wall and/or deeper into table-top position.

7. Allow the neck muscles to relax some and let the head hang.
8. Push with your back foot and use the wall to apply pressure through the ball and into your body.

This should be a challenging sensation but if it is painful or you are unable to allow the muscles to relax into the pressure, reduce the force with which you are pushing.

9. Let your arm hang, allowing gravity to pull it to the ground.
10. Take 3 diaphragmatic breaths (exercise #1).
11. Inhale and slowly retract your arm towards your hip.
12. Exhale and slowly lower it back down.
13. Repeat 5 times.
14. Move the ball 1–3 inches toward the shoulder and locate another area that is more tender than the surrounding area.
15. Repeat steps 9–13.
16. Stand up and roll your shoulders in forward and backward directions.
17. Reposition and repeat for the other side of the body.

Your legs control the position and the force of the pressure. Your back leg is your way to increase and decrease the pressure. Putting the weight in the ball of your back foot can make it easier to find exactly the right pressure for you.

 Applying pressure to trigger points can increase referral pain. Doing this exercise might cause a headache sensation during the exercise. If it triggers a lasting headache or migraine, either try again later with lighter pressure or discontinue this exercise.

Frequency

- Daily when symptoms are present.
- Weekly for regular maintenance.

EXERCISES
SPINE

#21 THORACIC MOBILIZATION

Objective

Loosen muscles along the spine to increase movement of the thoracic spine and scapula, increasing mobility and reducing shoulder, upper back, neck, and chest pain.

See Chapter 8 to learn more about the impact of binding and dysphoria on the thoracic spine (page 205) and scapular mobility (page 201).

Symptoms

- Upper back pain and tightness
- Pain between shoulder blades
- Pain at the spine below the shoulder blade
- Neck pain and stiffness
- Shoulder pain

Indications

- Reduced range of motion in shoulder joint
- Forward Head Posture (FHP) or Upper Crossed Syndrome
- Thoracic kyphosis

Technique

- Active self myofascial release (SMR)

Tools Needed

- "Peanut" tool (see page 189 for further information)

Landmarks

- Top of the thoracic spine: the base of the neck, generally a knobby, protruding vertebrae.
- Bottom of the thoracic spine (T12 vertebra): point on the spine level with the bottom of your ribs.

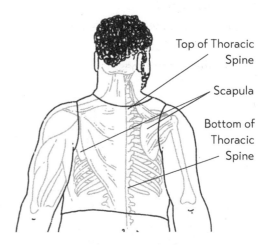

Top of Thoracic Spine

Scapula

Bottom of Thoracic Spine

Exercise

(This exercise should be done while not wearing any binding garment.)

1. Lie on your back with your knees bent. If needed, fold a towel under your neck.
2. Place the "peanut" at the bottom of your thoracic spine as shown.
3. Position it so that the balls are on either side of the spine.
4. Relax your weight onto the peanut and breathe to allow your muscles to soften and become less resistant to the pressure.

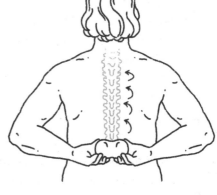

 If after 15 seconds you are not feeling the muscles soften, move to a softer surface (carpet, a yoga mat, mattress, etc.).

5. Place one arm straight at your side and the other arm straight overhead.
6. Keeping your arms straight, switch positions as if you are doing the backstroke.
7. Repeat 10 times.

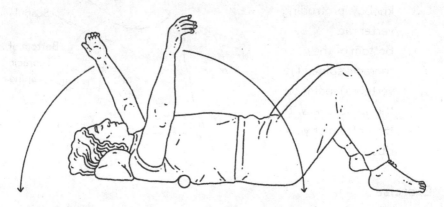

8. Move the "peanut" up 1–2 inches and repeat. Continue all the way to the top of the thoracic spine.

 If you have a hypermobility joint disorder, check with your doctor or physical therapist before doing this exercise. See the information about binding and hypermobility in Chapter 5, Section 2.

Frequency

- 1–2 times daily when symptoms are present.
- 1–2 times per week for maintenance.

#22 THORACIC OPENER

Objective

Improve flexibility in the lower half of the rib cage by lengthening abdominal muscles and loosening muscles along the spine.

See Chapter 8 to learn more about the impact of binding and dysphoria on the thoracic spine (page 205), oblique muscles (page 206), and lateral torso (page 199).

Symptoms

- Mid-back stiffness or pain, especially when maintaining an upright posture
- Difficulty with getting breath deep into the belly
- Rib pain, especially ribs 7 through 10

Indications

- Slipping rib syndrome

Technique

- Active self myofascial release (SMR)

Tools Needed

- Yoga mat or other cushioned surface under the knees

Landmarks

- None

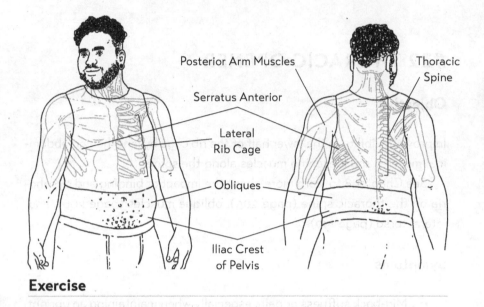

Posterior Arm Muscles

Thoracic Spine

Serratus Anterior

Lateral Rib Cage

Obliques

Iliac Crest of Pelvis

Exercise

(This exercise should be done while not wearing any binding garment.)

1. Get onto the floor in a table-top position. Place your hands and knees far enough apart to be comfortable for your body.

   Variation: Sit upright in a chair facing the wall with your feet flat on the floor. Place your hands on the wall shoulder-width apart.

   Engage your core muscles to maintain a flat back with no arch or bowing.

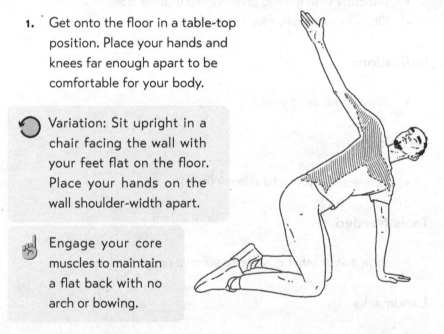

2. Inhale deeply.

3. As you exhale, press into the floor/wall with one arm and raise

and reach wide with
the other.

4. Twist at your waist to
   open your torso.

Keep your hips par-
allel to the floor/wall
as you twist.

5. Turn your head and
   shoulders and follow
   your hand with your
   eyes as you twist.

6. When you reach your
   natural endpoint,
   hold the position.

7. Inhale and exhale
   deeply; notice the places on the front and back of your body
   where you feel the stretch.

8. Inhale deeply and as you exhale, come back to table-top in a slow,
   controlled untwisting motion.

9. Repeat this 5 times on each side.

To increase the intensity, begin in a lunge rather than table-top
position. Proper lunge form: the front knee should not go over
the toes, hips pointing forward, back heel can be on or off the
floor. If this causes joint pain (knee, hip, ankle, spine), stick to
the table-top version of this stretch.

If you feel muscle pain or cramping, try reducing the amount of
stretch. If it doesn't improve, **stop** the exercise.

If this causes joint or spine pain (not just tightness and discomfort), **stop** the exercise immediately.

If you have a hypermobility joint disorder, check with your doctor or physical therapist before doing any stretches. See the information about binding and hypermobility in Chapter 5, Section 2.

Frequency

- Daily when symptoms are present.
- 2–3 times per week for regular maintenance and to increase flexibility.

#23 ANTERIOR TORSO RELEASE

Objective

Release the constriction on the front of the torso to improve upright posture, decrease neck and back pain, and improve breath capacity.

See Chapter 8 to learn more about the impact of binding and dysphoria on the anterior torso (page 207) and thoracic spine (page 205).

Symptoms

- GERD and other gastrointestinal symptoms
- Mid-back and neck pain, stiffness, or weakness
- Difficulty with getting breath deep into the belly

Indications

- Forward Head Posture (FHP) or Upper Crossed Syndrome
- Thoracic kyphosis
- Bruised xiphoid process

Technique

- Active self myofascial release (SMR)

Tools Needed

- Blanket or towel (optional)

Landmarks

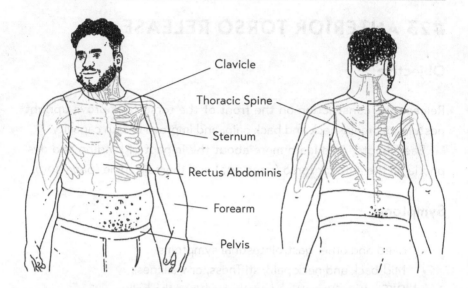

- Forearm: section of the arm between the elbow and the wrist.
- Pelvis: the large bowl-shaped bone that forms your seat when sitting.

Exercise

(This exercise is best done while not wearing any binding garment but can be done while binding if needed.)

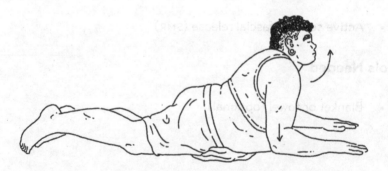

1. Lie face down on the floor with your arms bent and forearms resting flat on the floor beside your shoulders.

Place a folded towel or blanket under your hips to reduce the pressure on your low back.

2. Press down into the floor with your entire forearm.
3. Lift your chest off the floor and keep your pelvis firmly on the floor.

Imagine that you are pulling your sternum away from your pelvis rather than arching your back.

4. Adjust the pressure of your hips and forearms and the lift of your head and sternum until you feel a stretch along the front of the torso.
5. Hold this position and take 3 diaphragmatic breaths (see exercise #1).

If you experience pain in your back, reduce the amount that you are arching your back.

6. Slowly bring your face back to the floor and rest for 1 normal breath.
7. Repeat 5 times.

SEATED VARIATION

1. Sit upright in a chair.
2. Place a firm pillow or other prop across your lap so that when you rest your forearms on it, your elbows are at roughly a 90-degree angle.
3. Lean forward slightly and press down firmly into your lap.
4. Lift your upper chest upward.

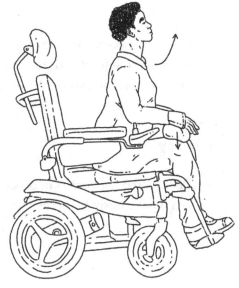

Imagine that you are pulling your sternum away from your pelvis rather than arching your back.

5. Adjust your position until you feel a stretch on the front of your torso.

 If you experience pain in your back, reduce the amount that you are arching your back.

6. Hold this position and take 3 diaphragmatic breaths (see exercise #1).
7. Slowly relax until you are sitting easefully and rest for 1 normal breath.
8. Repeat 5 times.

 If you experience sharp neck or back pain, decrease the amount of arch in your head and neck. If that does not relieve the pain, **stop** the exercise.

 If you have a hypermobility joint disorder, check with your doctor or physical therapist before doing any stretches. See the information about binding and hypermobility in Chapter 5, Section 2.

Combine this exercise with Thoracic Mobilization (exercise #21) to release the front and the back of the torso at the same time and maximize the impact of both.

Frequency

- Daily for regular binders or people with significant dysphoria hunch.
- 2–3 times weekly for occasional binders.

Symptom Index

Symptom	Exercises to Address Symptom
Fatigue or low energy	1, 2, 3, 4, 5
Brain fog or trouble concentrating	1, 2, 3, 4, 5
Heightened anxiety	1, 2, 3, 4, 5, 6
Difficulty taking a full breath	1, 2, 3, 4, 5, 6, 7, 10, 11, 12, 22, 23
Shortness of breath	1, 2, 3, 4, 5
Discomfort between the shoulder blades	1, 3, 10, 11, 12, 22, 23
Rib pain	4, 5, 9, 10, 11, 22, 23
Hunched shoulders/FHP/thoracic kyphosis	4, 5, 6, 7, 9, 16, 17, 18, 21, 23
Aching or pressure in the chest	6, 7, 8, 9
Shoulder pain	6, 8, 9, 13, 14, 15, 18, 21
Stiffness or restricted shoulder range of motion	6, 7, 8, 9, 11, 13, 14, 15, 21
Headaches/migraines	6, 7, 16, 17, 18, 19, 20
Difficulty maintaining an upright posture	6, 12, 14, 15, 21, 22
Jaw pain	7, 16, 18, 19, 20
Arm pain	9, 10, 11, 13, 18
Arm or shoulder weakness	11, 15
Mid-back pain	12, 21, 23
Neck pain	6, 16, 17, 19, 20, 21, 23
Restricted range of motion in the neck	16, 18, 19, 20, 21, 23
Chest or rib pain with coughing, sneezing	10
Difficulty projecting voice	1, 2, 3, 4, 5, 6, 19
Chronic shallow breathing	1, 2, 3, 4, 5, 6, 9, 18
Shoulder blade pain	13, 15
GERD	23
Sharp pain under chest tissue	9, 10

Index